PRAISE FOR
THE EDGE

"*The Edge* is an important reminder that life in nature can only survive if we accept our responsibility to be good stewards."
—**Leon Panetta**, former congressman and chair of the Pew Oceans Commission

"I loved this book. A paean to the California coast, weaving together science, history, and politics, from two of the most eminent, and personally invested, scholars on the subject. If you want to pull together the myriad impressions and questions of a drive or hike down the coast, if you want to understand it on all its many facets—read this book."
—**Andreas Merkl**, President, Ocean Conservancy

"This book captures the magic of the coast. It has an intimate blend of nature, science, politics, policy, culture, history, and adventure, and there is a well-informed urgency that gives readers more than just the information and heightened awareness they need to bring about real change to our ocean policies and practices: It is a personal call to action. Dive in!"
—**Sam Farr**, former congressman and ocean advocate

"*The Edge* is an extremely readable and personal exploration of the history of California's coast and the issues that face this extensive and diverse boundary with the ocean. Steinhardt and Griggs are true to the science of the coast while making it accessible to the casual reader."
—**Margaret Leinen**, Director, Scripps Institution of Oceanography

"Kim Steinhardt and Gary Griggs each have had a long love affair with the California coast. You can see it in their personal stories, and how they worry about the long-term effects of human interaction between land and water. This is a must read for anyone who shares their love for the coast and concern for its future."
—**John Laird**, California Secretary for Natural Resources, and Chair of the California Ocean Protection Council

"Kim Steinhardt and Gary Griggs skillfully weave together environmental science, history, politics and law with their personal experiences in a wonderful presentation of the incredible diversity, vitality and social significance of the California coast. A must-read for anyone concerned about protecting this incredible coastal experience for future generations."
—**Charles Lester,** former executive director, California Coastal Commission

"*The Edge* melds natural history and personal memories to reveal the shifting baselines of the California coast . . . and our role in maintaining its beauty."
—**Meg Caldwell**, Packard Foundation Deputy Director for Oceans and former chair of the California Coastal Commission

"Steinhardt and Griggs have created a delightful and insightful tour of California's coastal edge, past, present, and future. They do a masterful job of weaving together the interconnections of the changing natural world over different time scales with the changing societal landscape and human interventions to modify the coastal edge as population grew and societal priorities changed. Their discussions of how those interventions were shaped by clashes between conservationists and those with strong economic motivations are infused with some of their own values. Their stories of the boom and bust cycles of many of our fisheries and of populations of marine mammals have many lessons for us today, not only for resource managers, but for everyone concerned with human rights. I recommend this book to all who are interested in one of the most beautiful coasts in the world."
—**Jerry R. Schubel**, Ph.D., President and CEO, Aquarium of the Pacific

THE EDGE

THE PRESSURED PAST AND PRECARIOUS FUTURE OF CALIFORNIA'S COAST

KIM STEINHARDT
& GARY GRIGGS

CRAVEN STREET BOOKS

FRESNO, CALIFORNIA

THE EDGE

The Pressured Past and
Precarious Future of California's Coast

All rights reserved.
Published by Craven Street Books,
an imprint of Linden Publishing.
2006 South Mary, Fresno, California 93721
559-233-6633 / 800-345-4447
CravenStreetBooks.com

Craven Street Books and Colophon are trademarks
of Linden Publishing, Inc.

ISBN 978-1-61035-309-0

35798642

Printed in the United States of America
on acid-free paper.

Library of Congress Cataloging-in-Publication Data
Names: Steinhardt, Kim, author. | Griggs, Gary B., author.
Title: The edge : the pressured past and precarious future of California's
    coast / Kim Steinhardt & Gary Griggs.
Description: Fresno, Calif. : Craven Street Books, 2017. | Includes index.
Identifiers: LCCN 2017038402 | ISBN 9781610353090 (pbk. : alk. paper)
Subjects: LCSH: Coastal ecology--California. | Coastal ecosystem
    health--California. | Shore protection--California. | Pacific Coast
    (Calif.)--Environmental conditions.
Classification: LCC QH104.5.P32 S74 2017 | DDC 577.5/109794--dc23
LC record available at https://lccn.loc.gov/2017038402

CONTENTS

We gratefully dedicate this book to the many individuals and groups who have made California's shoreline the people's coast, protecting it in the past, treasuring it now, and preserving it for the future.

FOREWORD

The Edge: A Reminder of Why We Must Be Good Stewards

John Kennedy once reminded us that our oceans are the "salt in our veins." Having been born and raised on the central coast of California, the "salt" in my veins comes from the unique beauty of the Pacific coast.

The Edge is a dramatic portrait of the California coast and the challenge of protecting that coastline in the future.

The oceans are not only where life began, but where life itself is sustained. They are critical to our coastal communities—to their economies, to tourism and recreation, to the livelihood of fishing families, to weather patterns and ocean currents, to our health, to the natural beauty of coastlines and beaches, to our very spirit.

And yet, as confirmed by ocean commissions and scientists, our oceans and our coastlines are threatened. Increasing pollution and deadzones, the loss of critical wetlands, depleted fisheries, the impact of climate change on rising oceans, changing currents and toxicity, and the continuing threat of offshore drilling all threaten the life of our coastal communities, the beauty of our oceans, and life itself.

The Edge is an important reminder that life in nature can only survive if we the living accept our responsibility to be good stewards. The legacy of the beauty of our coastline that was passed on to us must be protected for future generations. *The Edge* is a comprehensive portrait of the Pacific coast and why we are responsible for its future.

Leon E. Panetta
Former Congressman and Chair of the PEW Oceans Commission
Author of legislation establishing Monterey Bay National Marine Sanctuary.

INTRODUCTION

The People's Coast

The California coast is an edge. It is a place where the largest ocean on the planet meets 1,100 miles of shoreline, creating a grand hub of several still-evolving worlds. It is geologically alive, zippered to North America by 800 miles of the San Andreas Fault. But it is also a social, political, cultural, spiritual, economic, and technological edge. It is an edge of history, where east has always met west, and where past meets future. It carries a legacy of threats and uncertainty along with new ideas and hopes.

It has always been a human edge, both for historic peoples finding their way around and across the Pacific Rim, and for the modern mix of people in the most populous of the United States, supporting the sixth-largest economy in the world. It is a vulnerable edge because it's the edge of a continent. It is ground zero for the looming changes in climate and sea level that promise to impact us in ways that we haven't ever experienced and perhaps never imagined.

The coast is iconic, the image of California to much of the rest of the world. It is a place millions of people call home, and a place that millions of others apparently would like to call home. It is also familiar and exotic, rugged and dangerous, dynamic and vital, ancient and new.

It is tempting to say that this unique coastal edge is what you make of it. But that would be a gauzy Hollywood fiction. The truth is likely the other way around—it is what it makes of you.

The forces of the Pacific Ocean and the California coast have shaped us in little ways and big ones, just as surely as the forces of nature have shaped the coastline itself. Tectonic plates slowly, inexorably crushing against each other, the level of the ocean continuously rising and falling over long spans of time, and the everyday forces of wind, waves, and water all come together to create not only where we live but who we are.

These natural forces are not the sole influences. The intangible spirit of the coast can also be seen by looking into our history, the way we interact with nature and our relationships to each other. We are the blended result of these natural and cultural forces. Perhaps it has taken the better part of a lifetime for the two of us to begin to truly appreciate this truth and the degree to which it has affected us.

It is easier to see this now, in relief against a lifetime, and for us to make some of the broad connections. Perhaps like the majestic redwood trees along the western edge of California, the coastal fog has nourished us and provided some tantalizing hint at the wisdom of age and experience. Or like a smooth, shifting, sandy beach, the ocean's endless motion has sculpted our senses and taught each of us how to change through the seasons of our lives. Or like a sharp rocky cliff, perhaps the attack of surf from below, erosion from above, and movement from within have given us strength and resilience and shown us how to cope with change—older, and yet newer, at the same time.

The cultural history teaches us about courage, selflessness, and generosity. Unfortunately, it also reveals exploitation, greed, and shortsightedness. We haven't always been good to each other or to the environment in which we live, especially our oceans and the creatures around us. Nor have we always been good to the people who were here before us, or to those arriving at the edge today. And even though the coast has been a unique place for wildlife, we have sometimes pushed it to the edge of extinction, only infrequently providing cutting-edge protection before it was too late.

We have often made a mess of the coast—poorly planned development, unfairly restricted access along social and economic lines, reckless oil drilling, unbridled pollution, and a litany of other misguided policies and actions over the decades. We face daunting challenges. Yet little by little, through changes in perception and protection, in science and stewardship, in research and policy, in legal and political action, we have made progress. Current threats to that progress serve as a wake-up call. The words of longtime California Coastal Commission executive director Peter Douglas have never rung more true: "The coast is never saved, it is always being saved."

It would be a mistake to tackle writing a book that pretended to capture all these larger connections between the California coast and the people who are intertwined with its forces and future. This is just a beginning, one piece of an immense puzzle.

Our purpose is to make some of the smaller, personal connections that begin to clear the mist and expose the bigger picture we all share, as well as to tell stories and paint specific scenes of a whole that makes up not only our coast, but the coast that belongs to everyone.

In that spirit, we have jumped into uncharted waters, the ocean geologist and the lawyer in the boat together. We hope we've made a good start. The tales and essays in each chapter ahead are some of Kim's, some of Gary's, most blended beyond recognition. So if you read "me" or "I," it could be either of us, or both of us, and we'll leave it at that.

One thing is clear to us: The California coast is always on the edge of disaster. One earthquake, one tsunami, one extinction away from a different story with a different ending.

In the end, this is no small matter. The forces of the coast influence all life within its wide reach. For some of the millions of people who actually live on or close to the California coastline, it is more than merely a backdrop. Many experience it as central, indeed essential, to their daily lives. Others share a less active sensibility about the impact of the coast. Yet its force still influences their lives. There are still others, too: people searching for the coast or lost from different journeys; people protecting the coast; people studying the coast; people extracting resources and wealth from the shoreline; and people for whom access to the coast is but a distant or foggy dream.

We have jumped into uncharted waters, the ocean geologist and the lawyer in the boat together.

Those visiting here from elsewhere experience the California coast in yet another way, as outsiders entering a zone influenced by powerful forces of nature and culture. Some have come to savor the coastal experience with countless pictures and endless dreams. Others are merely travelers, passing through with different business, not ensnared by the mystique and little aware of the beauty and power.

But no matter what the relationship, this coast belongs to everyone. We, the people, have inherited the coast and we have inherited the challenges that come with it. We are the chosen stewards of this edge for this moment, and we can no longer simply take advantage of it, pretending there is no tomorrow—lest there be no tomorrow.

It is the People's Coast.

Coastal Kid

Steinhardt

Icy water and stinging spray flooded the slippery decks, making my attempt to maneuver forward to the bow so I could free a jammed jib sail an experience in understanding what lifelines are really all about—something to hold on to for dear life.

Mayday, Mayday, Mayday!" Even as a 10-year-old boy, I was well aware that my dad's calling out those words of last resort into the mic of a ship-to-shore radio meant we were losing our struggle with the raucous Pacific Ocean. This was rapidly turning into one of those classic life-defining moments, and my relationship with nature would never really be quite the same afterward.

Growing up on the water's edge in Northern California had given me a youthful fascination with the ocean, a love of the broad sweep of its beauty and power. To that sense would now be added genuine fear and a different kind of respect, a more mature awe.

In what seemed like the blink of an eye, the situation deteriorated from what had started as a much-anticipated family sailing adventure in a borrowed boat. We were on the gentle swells of the great blue ocean not far off the Southern California coast near Oceanside.

It changed quickly into an uncomfortably wet and cold, increasingly tough sailing experience brought on by an unforeseen squall that threw gusts of wind upward of 50 miles per hour. That wind whipped up 15-, 20-, and even spectacular 30-foot waves,

Fig. 1.1. Sailing on San Francisco Bay always offered an abundance of adventures to a family growing up at the shoreline.

transforming the water. A bright, friendly blue turned into furiously spraying deep green, with gray and white crests, in the sudden shadows of dark overcast.

Unusual, to be sure, but still nothing to dampen the spirit of a family used to the wind-driven roughness of many sailing days, mostly on San Francisco Bay or the ocean just outside the Golden Gate (Figure 1.1). It wasn't the first time my fingers were numb from the cold and wetness of handling icy, salt-soaked lines and frozen gear alongside my older sister Barbara and my younger brother Jeff. We made a pretty tight crew, especially for our ages. And especially when conditions became demanding, which for us they seemed to do with unusual regularity in what passed as a "recreational" activity. We had been taught to sail at a very young age, spending a lot of time on the water.

But on this day, the weather and darkening, angry sky weren't our only concerns. The bow was rising 15 or 20 feet in the howling wind, only to crash back down in slow motion into the giant swells. Icy water and stinging spray flooded the slippery decks, making my attempt to maneuver forward to the bow so I could free a jammed jib sail an experience in understanding what lifelines are really all about—something to hold on to for dear life.

While I was awkwardly reaching out to free the jib with one hand while clinging to the lifeline with the other, an unfamiliar thunderclap interrupted the shattering of the waves. The boat jolted. We suddenly lost our steering.

We didn't know it at that instant, but the sound came from beneath the water's surface, where a large section of an unseen, stray, downed U.S. Navy target plane had collided with our sailboat's rudder, completely destroying that vital piece of the boat. This small aircraft—a 30-foot drone replica of a fighter jet—had apparently been blasted out of the sky during target practice hours earlier. The storm had blown the wreckage outside the U.S. Navy's restricted hazard zone.

The ocean is like that; it doesn't adhere well to human efforts to compartmentalize or control it. Everything moves around. For better or for worse, what happens in one place always has an impact beyond the immediate area.

Losing control over the rudder changed things dramatically. Now, rather than merely being inconvenienced and challenged by bad weather, we were disabled, without any way to steer. The winds were forcing us toward shore.

That rocky shore. Those dramatic California rocky cliffs. Those beautiful testimonials to the power of millions of years of colliding tectonic plates, earthquakes, uplift, and erosion. Of new earth emerging from the ocean floor. The results of eons of repeated sea-level rise and retreat, and the legacy of distant glaciers and rivers, all sculpting a spectacular coast.

That noisy shore. When you can hear wind at sea, even howling wind, you are not necessarily in peril. But when you can hear wind and the telltale crashing of surf against rocks, you know you are in trouble. And when you hear the crashing of surf in powerful wind that is driving you toward those rocks, plus you have no means to steer, you are in big trouble. Even trying to drop an anchor in our circumstances would not have done any good.

So the Mayday call for help seemed very rational, even if terrifying. My brother and sister and I had each been taught how and when to use those words if the need ever arose. But I don't think I ever really expected to hear them used in earnest. It probably hit us all that much harder to hear my dad use them, for him to yield to the power of the ocean and acknowledge our helplessness. After all, he was the one who was supposed to have all the answers.

Despite the storm and the accident, we got a lucky break. Our repeated distress calls were eventually answered. By chance, a U.S. Coast Guard cutter was several miles away but, based on the rate at which we were drifting helplessly in the waves, still likely close enough to reach us before we crashed onto the rocks.

Reach us, that is, if it could actually find us in the dimming light, the huge waves, and the chaotic winds. It would also need to manage to hook up and make the tow without the 45-foot steel-hulled cutter slamming into us, bringing both boats down in the storm. Unlike road service, for a rescue at sea there is no convenient side of the road onto which you can pull off to attach tow truck to car.

With mountainous waves and heavy winds at sea, such a rescue must be accomplished by firing a thick towline from a cannon aboard the Coast Guard cutter while it holds off at a safe distance. With any luck, you can receive that shot by grabbing the line once it has flown across your boat's deck. You then secure sailboat to cutter, get towed safely to shore, and you all live happily ever after—under ideal circumstances.

But from a young boy's viewpoint, that rescue looked a little more like this: You are terrified, soaked, freezing, on board a boat that is violently pitching and out of control, and inexorably being driven toward deadly rocks of the shoreline with the sound of crashing surf loud in your ears. A U.S. Coast Guard ship appears in the distance. It takes aim and fires a cannon at you. You take cover as you see the muzzle's flash and almost instantly the rope shoots past you. In our case, the first shot missed the boat and they had to retrieve the line, reload, and fire a second shot. Time is ticking. Rocks are getting closer. Surf is getting louder. The second shot missed again—it's not ideal circumstances today. Far from—

The third shot worked, and we finally hooked up. Happily, from that point on the adventure wound down safely, although not without the additional navigational difficulty of having to enter the treacherous, narrow entrance to a sheltered harbor while under tow, in the dark, unable to steer, between the two rows of rocks protecting the harbor entrance.

This nerve-racking experience became a lesson in the balance of power between humans and nature. That balance generally tips in favor of nature, by the way. As has been said, nature always bats last.

The next day, when we were safely moored in port, a U.S. Navy helicopter noisily landed on a nearby jetty and a team of Navy divers emerged, dove beneath the boat, and removed all traces of the drone's pieces that were still engaged in our now-ruined rudder. To say they were tight lipped would be an understatement: there were no greetings, no explanations, and they said almost nothing during the entire cleanup operation. For our young minds it fueled a bit of Roswell/Area 51 mystique about the whole experience, especially given the large area of ocean marked off-limits by the Navy on the nautical charts. Apparently for target practice and *other* activities.

When I look back at this and some other adventures that fall into the unsettling category of that newly found fear and mature awe, I sometimes wonder how I continued to embrace the sea. But it never felt like the coast was a dangerous place to be, just a place to be always vigilant. "Never turn your back on the waves." Good advice.

A coastal kid

For years both before and after that experience, I spent nearly every day I could after school walking the San Francisco Bay shoreline, where I grew up. My elementary school was on the water's edge. My walk to and from school was along the water. Our home was at the edge of a forest on the bay. So I was a shoreline explorer learning about fishing, the sand, the mud, the tides, the

Fig. 1.2. Learning to fish was just one of many explorations, but fish were not always safe to eat because of high levels of toxicity in polluted bay waters during the 1950s.

rocks, the sounds of the birds and the waves, even the unmistakable smell of the bay. Instead of being a latchkey kid, I was a coastal kid (Figure 1.2).

And when I was 11, two memorable things washed up on the shore. Each is as clear to me today as on the day I discovered them. One was the carcass of an 18-foot long, 600-pound thresher shark. While I had seen and caught many fish, including lots of striped bass and rockfish, and even accidentally caught and released a small shark or two, I never before had this close a look at such a huge shark. This was long before the campy movie *Jaws*, and this shark was real, dramatic, and the news spread across the nearby schoolyard and throughout the neighborhood.

My younger brother and I carefully approached and inspected those rows of razor-sharp teeth revealed in the giant jaws. It didn't escape our notice that this shark had been inhabiting the waters around which we spent so much of our time.

> **During the 1950s and into the 1960s, industrial chemicals made San Francisco Bay one of the most polluted waterways in the country.**

I say *around* which we spent so much time because even though we spent time near and *on* the bay waters, we rarely swam *in* them. In those years, San Francisco Bay was so polluted that swimming was decidedly not among favored or recommended bay activities—although we still spent some time in the water, unintentionally. I have to admit to my share of capsized canoes, sunken rowboats, crashed kayaks, collapsed docks, swimming ashore from stranded vessels, even sibling rivalry pranks and shoreline scuffles ending in splashdown or a mud bath in some cases . . . but no one would ever, deliberately, spend more time than was necessary in that water.

During the 1950s and into the 1960s, the accumulation of industrial chemicals and waste products from the rapid post–World War II growth of the Bay Area community made San Francisco Bay one of the most polluted waterways in the country. Toxic chemicals like mercury reached dangerous levels, and health warnings limiting fish intake were routine, as were warnings regarding shellfish consumption. "No more than one striped bass a month." "No seafood for children under the age of five." "Warning: mussel quarantine."

Only in the 1960s did citizen activism and the imposition of strict environmental regulations begin to reverse the impending ecological disaster and restore some measure of health to the bay. Gradually over more than five decades, the bay waters have returned to a significantly healthier state, even allowing the return of various kinds of plants and creatures that had become scarce, although many serious water-quality concerns remain. Regulation, close monitoring, research, and cooperation remain vital to effectively combat new threats as increased commerce, population growth, and the wastes from evolving technologies keep the health of the bay a work in progress.

That shark left a big impression. Even though I later saw and closely examined a giant whale carcass washed up on an ocean beach along the north coast, and saw other fascinating fish and marine mammals as well, for me at that young age the shark triggered big questions about the nature of our relationship with the ocean.

Today, humans are still sorting that one out with sharks among others, emerging from a preconceived, sharks-as-evil perspective to one that recognizes their important role in the ocean ecosystem. Efforts to end the ill-advised slaughter of an estimated 100 million sharks each year have begun to gain traction throughout much of the world, hopefully with enough time left to avoid the complete loss of these animals. Because sharks are apex predators, their role in balancing and maintaining the ocean food chain is unique and critical.

The other item that washed ashore was a small, half-swamped, gray wooden rowboat. It was clearly abandoned as a wreck by whoever once owned it, leaking and sad. A perfect fixer-upper, as might be said in the real estate business. Fortunately, these finds were months apart, and I don't think there was any evidence that the shark and the loose skiff were related.

Once my brother and I convinced our parents to let us keep the boat (like bringing home a stray puppy), we set to work fixing it up. When it was repaired—although it never completely stopped leaking—I was free to roam the nearshore waters from a different vantage point and reach new destinations. There were several islands made of fill that had been dredged out of the bay floor to make artificial boat channels. Although I didn't know it at the time, the fill was also intended to be the modest beginning of a much more ambitious plan, creating a dry land base for a proposed commercial housing development of 2,000 homes to be built on the bay.

For me, it was fertile new territory for exploration. I used to beach the rowboat on these islands and wander the shoreline for hours, looking at the seashells and the birds, studying the strange plants that grew in the intertidal zone, and analyzing the fascinating debris that had washed up . . . and discovering arrowheads.

I was thrilled to find these remnants of a prior coastal civilization that had inhabited what was now my home territory. But the small bits of stone were not easy to come by.

Magical discoveries

There are several ways to walk a beach. People can be destination oriented, playful, or contemplative. But there is another way. It is to walk searching for arrowheads, the way I walked for many, many hours. You have never really walked a beach until you have inched your way along right at the edge of the tide line, slowly as a snail, head tilted down, fixated on the sand immediately ahead of you, lulled into a hypnotic state by the melodic sounds of the nearby birds, the waves lapping at the shoreline, and the smell of the wet mud and salt. Searching for the tiniest variation in the random sand patterns, a tip-off to a treasure. Yearning for that slightest outline of the ragged edge of an arrowhead, the mother lode of a beachcomber's find.

I was literally looking for buried treasure given up by the earth and the ocean's ceaseless exercise of moving, removing, and replacing sand. I learned that if I was very quiet, very patient, and very lucky, once in a while I would be rewarded.

Today, a cottage industry in (metal) detecting devices has been developed for use on the beach. They offer the allure of the big find, buried treasures, lost watches, rings, coins, castaway fortunes supposedly ripe for the plucking. But for an 11-year-old boy in the 1950s or '60s, the arrowhead was pretty much the be-all and end-all. Now, these stone products wouldn't even register on the detectors, much less the wish list of most beachcombers.

I don't know what drove me to spend so many hours searching, except that I was driven by the excitement I felt upon my first magical discovery. To me, there was always the chance that the magician's hand would conjure up the next treasure before sunset.

On one of those many walks along the beach, slow, steady, silent, eyes focused down on the shoreline in front of me, I became carried away and lost in my search. After an hour or more, something caused me to look up. Maybe it was a sudden silence of gulls.

My eyes locked on another's eyes and we both froze.

Less than 3 feet in front of me stood a giant buck. He was quite a bit larger than I, with a rack of twisted antlers that seemed to stretch to the sky far above me. We had almost collided, and stood eyeball to eyeball. Both silent. I could feel his breath.

I'm not sure which one of us was more surprised at this interruption of our respective silent wanderings. It took a few seconds for each of us to register what was going on, to assess and make a decision about what to do next. Neither he nor I turned around, or retreated, although I'm pretty sure we both would have liked to have done so.

During that brief instant, I felt nothing more than surprise and perhaps a brief flash of camaraderie. It was a chance encounter between two species wandering the bay's shoreline, something that brings together so many connected by the coastal habitat, on the edge. We each had our bond with the water and sand.

I recall it as a peaceful instant, not a fearful one, even though by all rights I should have been scared to death by the possibility of a single, swift snap of his deadly antlers in my direction. And by all rights he should have been deathly afraid of a human being, even a small one, with all the harm we are capable of inflicting on such creatures.

We quietly started to back away from each other, to begin to put a greater distance between us slowly, then quickly. Restoring order. Until he finally turned completely and trotted off down the beach, silently disappearing into the brush leading into the nearby forest without disturbing so much as a leaf.

As I recovered my rhythm and resumed my beachcombing I spied the biggest object I had ever discovered, half hidden in the sand. Without any clue as to what it was, I carefully removed a 3-inch, unusually shaped gray-green stone. Only later did I learn it was an ancient weight, used long ago by the Native American residents of the region to hold fishing nets under water. It had been carved in an ice cream cone shape, rounded on one end and coming nearly to

Fig. 1.3. This Pomo fishing weight is a several-thousand-year-old reminder of the cultures that previously occupied the coast of California.

a point on the other. A hole was bored through the thickest part to accommodate the rawhide cord that would have suspended it into the water from the edge of the net. A tough hole to carve through stone; what did they use without electric drills to make it easy?

Given the history of the Pomo, the Native Americans who inhabited the north side of San Francisco Bay, it would likely have been several thousand years old, perhaps even older. Perfectly preserved in the ancient layers of mud, just waiting for some little boy to rediscover it on the shoreline. Ironically, it would never have been found if it had not been taken from the floor of the bay in a huge scoop of mud by the tall crane of a developer's dredge, then dumped ashore on that island, and later slowly exposed by the action of waves lapping away at the shoreline.

I keep that fishing weight to this day (Figure 1.3). It is a reminder for me of how the coast connects us to the past and how continuity to the future rests on our stewardship of the coast today.

These buried treasures, remnants of our collective past, going back as many as 10,000 years, were my earliest exposure to the artifacts of geology, history, and oceanography. I knew that the mud and the ancient fishing weight had been sitting on the floor of the bay for an awfully long time. It raised all kinds of questions in my mind about how the bay got there, where the water was coming from, how deep the mud and sand were and, especially, who had been there before us? I also wondered what changes the future held.

Trying to answer those questions has taken a lifetime, and new questions about the coast always replace the old ones.

Sailing against the current

By the time I was 16, apart from delivering newspapers, my first "real" job was working on small sailboats in a marina in the little town of Sausalito on the shore of San Francisco Bay. Mostly it was a quite unglamorous job—cleaning out rented sailboats, and sanding, painting, varnishing, and repairing them. But sometimes people would rent sailboats and need a "skipper." There were times when the boss was too busy, and I jumped up to volunteer for the task. Today, I suspect liability concerns would make such an arrangement with a 16-year-old very unlikely. As an attorney, I would never recommend it.

But I was eager, the owner was shorthanded, and the customer always gets what he or she wants, so there I was taking people out on the bay that I knew and loved and relishing every minute of it.

Fig. 1.4. Nearly 400 billion gallons of water move beneath the Golden Gate Bridge each day, filling and draining the bay.

Sailing on the bay can be spectacular, but it can also be a challenging adventure when the weather turns sour. The people I took out on the water placed their trust in me and put their lives in my hands. Although I didn't think about it at the time, I now wonder if they actually realized how young I was.

Few realize that the Golden Gate is often a wild cauldron of powerful currents.

The most common request from visitors, the biggest draw, was to sail from Sausalito and go underneath the Golden Gate Bridge (Figure 1.4). They were eager to see that grand structure and towering expanse from a thrilling new point of view. Few realize that the gateway it bridges between bay and ocean is often a wild cauldron of powerful currents and whirlpools that can hang up a boat for hours if the tide is actively flowing the direction opposite from where you want to go. You can be under full sail in a strong breeze and still not make any forward progress whatsoever. The current easily reaches velocities that are several knots faster than most of us can swim.

An easy way to visualize the power of these currents is to imagine the bay as a gigantic bathtub, and the very narrow entrance to the bay over which that spectacular bridge presides as the drain. The tide partially drains and refills the tub, moving about 390 billion gallons over the course of two incoming and two outgoing tides each and every day of the year. To achieve this incredible volume of filling and flushing, currents move that water in and out at between 3½ to 7½ knots or, in English, about 6 to 12 feet per second. Whenever the tide is shifting, changing from outgoing to incoming or vice versa, the colliding currents cause powerful foaming whirlpools, bigger than small boats.

The tsunami of 1964

That is under normal conditions. But things changed on a mild, sunny day in 1964 when I was in junior high school. On March 27 of that year, a Good Friday that wasn't all that good, the West Coast was rocked by the Northern Hemisphere's largest earthquake ever recorded in the twentieth century. The Great Alaskan Earthquake, as it is often known, registered at 9.2 on the Richter scale and killed nearly 140 people. For comparison, the great 1906 San Francisco earthquake that killed some 3,000 people and destroyed much of the city registered "merely" at 7.8 on that scale. To further understand that comparison, each number on the Richter magnitude scale is equivalent to about thirty times more energy. So the 1964 Alaskan quake released several hundred times more energy than the more "modest" 1906 event that destroyed San Francisco. However, the San Francisco earthquake had greater impact because it hit a major population center and caused a furious fire that engulfed the city. By contrast, the Alaskan quake hit a sparsely populated area, causing less—but still quite serious—damage.

The sudden explosion of movement between two tectonic plates, the North American Plate and the Pacific Plate, which had been colliding for millions of years at the Aleutian Trench, released energy that gave rise to a large tsunami. This tsunami emanated from Alaska and worked its way across the Pacific Ocean and down the West Coast of the United States, along the edge of the continent.

By the next day, although the waves of the tsunami had been somewhat reduced by thousands of miles of travel along the West Coast, it still generated waves 7 to 21 feet in elevation along the Northern California coast. By the time it reached the central California coast, these waves still had enough power to enter the Golden Gate and make their way throughout the bay like the tentacles of a giant octopus.

I recall anxiously awaiting the arrival of this unfamiliar beast. School was canceled along the shoreline, and I followed the tsunami's progress down the coast, listening to radio news moment by moment. The tracking of such phenomena is much more sophisticated now, with the advent of satellites, seismograph arrays, buoys that track the transit of tsunamis across the Pacific, robust computer modeling, and instantaneous communications. In 1964, tsunami monitoring relied on human observers, telephones, and clumsy radio reports.

When the tsunami finally entered the bay through the Golden Gate, I recall watching the bay waters rise 6 or 7 feet over a 15-minute period. Then the water dropped just as quickly, only to repeat that cycle a half a dozen times.

Although this stressed some docks and boats, there was thankfully little serious damage where I witnessed the tsunami's arrival. But this was not the case throughout the coast. At the far northern reaches of California, along the rugged coastal edge at Crescent City, 11 people died as a result of the devastating reach of the waves that ravaged 21 blocks of the downtown area.

The respect, fear, and love I felt for the ocean was jolted just like the tectonic plates in Alaska, taking a quantum leap in the wake of this earthquake and the tsunami it spawned.

The vulnerability that comes as a given with life along the California coast only occasionally reveals itself in such large and dramatic actions, such as the 1989 Loma Prieta earthquake, known to many around the United States and even elsewhere due to its widespread media attention. After all, it had the temerity to interrupt Game 3 of baseball's World Series, which was being held in San Francisco that year. With the epicenter less than 5 miles from my home near the Monterey Bay, this 6.9 magnitude earthquake caused less harm, generally, than either the 1906 San Francisco earthquake or the 1964 Alaskan shock. But it was still a tragedy, killing 63 people in the Bay Area and causing billions of dollars in damage, generating what was, by comparison, only a very small local tsunami.

That coastal vulnerability also plays out in the constant change that sculpts the coast in less immediately dramatic ways. Forces such as the wind, the waves, and the tides are more silent and steady. The subterranean tectonic forces are more like that octopus lurking in the crevices of the rocks, waiting for an unpredictable moment to strike.

Fig. 1.5. Surfing the waters of Southern California, where the water is much warmer than in Northern California, in the 1960s.

Big Sur

My family moved away from the shoreline of the bay in the year following the Alaskan earthquake, ultimately coming to live along the rocky coastline near Big Sur. So once again I was the explorer, spending as much time as I could observing the ocean and nature, taking endless pictures, clambering over rocks, studying tide pools, learning

what was in them and why
they exist, and reading about
Doc Ricketts, Cannery Row,
and the once-thriving sardine
fishery of Monterey Bay. With
my brother Jeff, sister Barbara,
and high school friends Roy,
Tom, and Bruce, I hiked
and slept out on the nearby
beaches overnight, usually
in the foggy cold, sometimes
with a fire, often not. I surfed
(Figure 1.5) and learned
to scuba dive. Of course,
Northern California waters
are so chilly that I quickly
discovered a good wetsuit was

Fig. 1.6. Sailboat-sitting.

necessary and my hastily-purchased, used $10 wetsuit was ill fitting,
leaky, and chafing. I'm sure this subpar equipment fully explains why
I failed to become a champion surfer.

It was during those excursions that I discovered sea otters and
began a lifelong attachment to the troubled species, which was facing
its against-all-odds struggle to come back from near extinction. More
on that later.

But I remained attached to the Golden Gate's rocky shores and bay,
and returned to work on the sailboats in Sausalito during summers
through high school. I was lucky enough to live as a boat-sitter on
a friend's sailboat in a marina in San Francisco during what is now
ancient history, the Summer of Love, when George Harrison in his
rose-colored glasses thought it right to visit Golden Gate Park on a
sunny summer's day, and the Fillmore auditorium saw the birth of a
new generation's music (Figure 1.6).

Antiwar and pro-environment

During my college years, my attachment to the coast was stretched
a bit as I immersed myself in the anti–Vietnam War movement. I left
California to go to college on the East Coast, but in hindsight I see how
even on that edge I brought a California coastal culture to my East

Coast antiwar organizing work. A little cross-coastal pollination. Soon enough, I found the Pacific attachment tugging at me and I returned to the California coast to continue my life and organizing efforts there.

I got back to the San Francisco Bay Area just in time to lend a hand to a hastily created rescue center for birds to try as-yet untested techniques of washing crude oil off seabirds in the wake of an oil spill disaster of unprecedented magnitude inside the bay. The January 19, 1971, collision of two oil tankers operated by Standard Oil dumped 800,000 gallons of oil into the bay waters. In the following days, a group of several hundred volunteers traversed the beaches at the edge of the bay and for 10 miles north and south, up and down the coast, to capture some of the more than 3,000 oil-soaked birds hit hard by the toxic crude oil. In the days, weeks, and months that followed, we used various techniques for trying to clean, rehabilitate, and release the birds into the wild but, sadly, with very limited success. Only about 300 or so of the thousands of injured birds were successfully released.

Probably the most important outcome of this incident was the honing of a new approach to intervening in these mass wildlife disasters by harnessing the power of hundreds or even thousands of volunteers. The approach coincided with and was part of the

Fig. 1.7. KGO-TV spot opposing the Devil's Slide Bypass proposal, which was scrapped and then renewed more than 40 years later with a much-modified approach.

advancement of newer environmental groups, joining older ones, focusing on a more widespread campaign for habitat preservation along the shorelines in many communities.

With the momentum of these events, I took the first steps toward a more public activism on the environment. It always starts small . . . I appeared on a San Francisco Bay Area network television station urging people to resist the state highway department's plans to blast off a mountaintop to construct an eight-lane freeway leading from San Francisco to the coast-side town of Half Moon Bay (Figure 1.7). This massive project over Montara Mountain was intended to bypass the difficult and narrow Devil's Slide stretch of Highway 1, which had been carved into the rocky cliffs. The plans for such a bypass had been on the books for years. It was not widely known that the bypass had been first justified as an evacuation route from San Francisco in the event of a nuclear attack. However, the real reason for this high-capacity freeway was to turn Half Moon Bay into an easily accessible bedroom community for San Francisco, thus vastly increasing the value of real estate in the coastal area. The ostensible purpose, making Highway 1 safer and less costly to maintain, was really secondary.

Looking back at my early efforts joining with others to urge a more restrained approach to developing that stretch of shoreline, I see the long, slow hand of economic and demographic pressure on the coast. The plan for a wide freeway over the mountain was finally abandoned because of community opposition. But the plan was later replaced by a proposal to build a pair of two-lane tunnels through the mountain that would have the advantage of not destroying the forests and meadows at the surface. It took more than 40 years after that television appearance, but in 2005 the state broke ground on the twin-bore tunnels and they were opened to traffic in 2013. Delayed by decades, the easier (to drive and to maintain) commuting access to the coast had finally been completed, although with fewer lanes facilitating incrementally smaller growth and less destructive environmental impact in the design. Success or failure? Or business as usual in fighting to preserve our coast?

I remember those days as a mélange of working with oil-soaked birds by day, going to hear music of the Grateful Dead and other counterculture groups by night, and continuing full-steam-ahead efforts to end the war even as a fledgling but growing environmental

Fig. 1.8. A California condor with tag and radio transmitter. The endangered species is making a slow comeback from near extinction.

awareness and revolution in thinking about human impacts on our ecosystems was taking shape. I took one of the earliest college "ecology" classes and can recall one class session devoted entirely to DDT, the toxic chemical still in wide use at the time even though by then it had been found to have severe adverse impacts.

Among other creatures, DDT drove the great California condor, a truly spectacular bird with a wingspan of some 10 feet, to within two dozen birds of extinction (Figure 1.8). DDT residue accumulated in the eggshells and made the eggs too thin to support healthy chicks. In 1987, the U.S. Fish and Wildlife Service captured the remaining 22 birds to focus on a last-ditch effort to save the species in a captive breeding program. Five years later, some birds were released into the wild. Today, a careful and dedicated release program, along with a continuing captive breeding program, has led to a partial recovery of this species, which still is highly at risk. The condor still faces threats from lead poisoning, among others, that comes from ingesting lead from spent ammunition that hunters have used to kill the condor's prey, such as wild boar and deer. California has enacted legislation banning the use of lead ammunition, but recovery is a slow process, and the birds still remain listed under the Endangered Species Act.

At my ecology class a spokesperson for Monsanto, the chemical company that had been manufacturing DDT for decades, appeared as a guest speaker. During his presentation, he pulled out what he claimed was a handful of DDT powder. With a great flourish, he made a show of eating it. I guess he thought that somehow this would impress upon a very skeptical student audience that there was nothing dangerous about DDT. I have no idea how his health is today, but DDT was banned nationwide within a few years, in large part owing to the clear scientific evidence of its effect on reproduction and egg survival in condors, pelicans, peregrine falcons, and other birds. The controversy over the balancing of benefits against harms in the use of DDT had been boiling for many years, especially after pioneering environmentalist Rachel Carson's 1962 publication of *Silent Spring*, which brought the issue to a national audience in dramatic fashion.

The Bay Area grew in its central role as a vibrant coastal community, though its continuing rapid expansion contributed to environmental problems. But at the same time it also proved to be fertile ground for developing cutting-edge solutions to some of those problems, such as the continuing improvement in bay water quality. This is in part due to the vigilance of the Bay Area community and its commitment to assuring that coastal occupation by humans and coastal health remain in something of a sustainable balance.

By the mid-1970s, having finally reached an age when coastal "kid" could no longer fairly be applied to me, I moved down the coast to the Monterey Bay area. I have remained on that coast ever since, deepening my engagement with the ocean and the shoreline, even proposing to my wife on the Golden Gate Bridge, getting married in a blazing winter's sunset on a beach near Monterey, and generally staying firmly within the embrace of the People's Coast.

I saw the Pacific Ocean for the first time ever in my life last year, on a visit with my sister and my parents from my home in Dallas. I had never seen any ocean except in movies and pictures, and I expected it to be perfectly blue, with sand of a certain texture and color. But it surprised me. The water wasn't perfectly blue, but a little more greenish, and the sand was not the color I expected. And it smelled like, well, the sea and beach, I guess. Like no place else in the world I've ever been to. And there were sounds you never hear anywhere else. There was kelp everywhere, and the smell of kelp.

I was a little scared, at first, of the waves. But I ran into the water and it was cool, and the water seemed like it kept coming at me. One wave was calm and the next was stronger and then stronger. But it was OK, now I like the waves.

Being in the ocean and on the beach I felt so very calm. Really a state of mind. If you're anywhere and get stressed and you go to the ocean, you just immediately feel very calm.

It has changed my life. I live in the city, and I always thought there was one way to live. Lots of buildings. I've not really been a fan of nature, I never had a love for the ocean. But the ocean is nature at its best, it is pure nature. So I think of the world differently now. I think maybe I might rent a boat and sail the oceans. I think that I'd like to live right next to the ocean so I can be close to the calmness, whenever I'm stressed.

Now I'm more aware of the ocean's problems, and seeing it has made me want to be sure people take care of it. There might not be beaches anymore if people don't take care of the ocean.

—11-year-old girl, Moss Landing State Beach

Coastal Kid II

Griggs

There was one memorably bad winter day when I thought I was going to die surfing.

The Pacific Ocean is almost unimaginably large, covering one-third of the entire surface of the planet. We could stick all of the continents of the world into the Pacific Basin and still have some water left over; all of 'em, North and South America, Europe and Asia, Australia and Antarctica, and Africa. Over the years, I've crossed the Pacific three times by ship, each time teaching on a floating university full of hundreds of hormone-crazed college students. What made the hugeness of this huge body of saltwater so memorable was that it took 18 days and nights to get from one side to the other! There was ample time on each trip to think about the "what if" of falling overboard somewhere very far from land. All I can say is that it wasn't a particularly comforting thought (Figure 2.1).

Not satisfied with being the largest body of water, it's also the deepest. The bottom of the Mariana Trench is nearly 7 miles down, and only three people on Earth have ever visited this very deep depression in the seafloor. Jacques Piccard, a Swiss oceanographer and engineer, and Don Walsh, a U.S. Navy officer, descended to the bottom with some anxiety in the bathyscaphe *Trieste* in 1960. After all, no one had ever gone 7 miles into the ocean where pressures reach almost 8 tons per square inch, over a thousand times greater than at sea level.

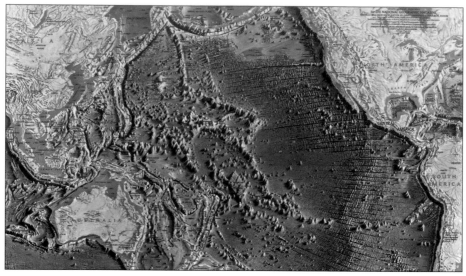

Fig. 2.1. Topography of the Pacific Ocean seafloor.
courtesy **National Geographic**

Were something to have failed in the *Trieste,* things would have gone very bad very quickly.

Fifty-two years later, probably with some trepidation as well, James Cameron reached the bottom of the Mariana Trench in his own submersible. He is probably best known as the popular film director of such ocean-themed movies as *Titanic* and *The Abyss,* although he also directed other hits such as *Terminator* and *Avatar.*

I've always believed that living on the edge of this vast and deep expanse of ocean gives us a unique perspective, particularly when compared with living in landlocked states such as Kansas or Nebraska. I've felt great comfort and security in knowing the Pacific Ocean is right there, covering my back, and providing perspective, inspiration at times, but also capable of both calm and great violence and destruction. As I gaze out the window from my second-floor home office and lookout tower and glimpse that vast expanse of ocean just two blocks away, I realize that even on the clearest of days I'm able to see only about 5 miles offshore. Australia is another 8,200 miles away across an empty and very deep body of saltwater, way beyond the distant horizon.

A family journey from Atlantic to Pacific

Although life began for me not far from the Pacific Ocean, in Pasadena during World War II, it wasn't so for my predecessors. One of my ancestors, a young girl of 13 named Mary Chilton, arrived at the other coastal edge on the *Mayflower* nearly 400 years ago and was reported to have been the first woman to step off the ship at Plymouth. There wasn't any knowledge in 1620 of what lay to the west. I think they were just happy they had arrived safely after 66 miserable days in the North Atlantic in a leaky and overcrowded boat. But her descendants gradually worked their way across what was then the frontier, through Vermont, New York, Ohio, Indiana, Illinois, Iowa, and Nebraska.

They must have been somewhat bold and adventurous as each successive generation pushed a little farther west, heading gradually toward the other edge of North America, the distant Pacific shoreline. My mother's parents first reached the West Coast in the Puget Sound area in the 1890s, which evidently appealed to them more than the uniform wheat fields of South Dakota because they never went back. My mother and her three sisters and parents left Port Angeles for California in the 1920s when oil was discovered at Signal Hill near Long Beach. Economic opportunities looked good, it rained much less than the Pacific Northwest, and they decided to stay.

Things were a bit less crowded then, and the cloudless skies of Southern California became a magnet for lots of people from many other places. Los Angeles County had fewer than a million people in 1920, although they had run out of local water several decades earlier and had already started looking north for more. Today the greater Los Angeles area has a population approaching 19 million, and it looks and feels like it. Angelinos have continued their search for water, and have sometimes been accused of stealing it from every other place within 500 miles where they could wrangle or finagle a deal. The Water Wars of California are another story. They are long standing, very nasty at times, and still very much alive today.

My dad's father, who had spent his early years in the flatlands of Iowa, bought a train ticket from St. Joseph, Missouri, to San Francisco in 1901 for $25 and, at the age of 21, headed west. This was his first exposure to the continent's western edge, and after a few months, working odd jobs, he headed back to Iowa. I think he was just homesick or lonely, but the allure of the West Coast must have already been embedded in his mind. One day on the street of Rudd, Iowa (the name itself, maybe sounding a bit like rut, would have driven me west), Fred Griggs ran into the old family doctor. My grandfather, then 23, was in his own words "about 6 ft. 3 in., rather skinny and somewhat stooped." The doctor suggested "that he get a bedroll and go traveling again, sleeping out in the open whenever possible."

He took the doctor's advice and soon heard of a local farmer shipping his stock and farm implements to Everett, Washington. The farmer gave my grandfather permission to ride in one of the cars with the livestock. A week later, probably smelling a bit like the farm animals he was riding with, he stepped off in Everett, which is on Puget Sound about 35 miles north of Seattle. He picked up his bedroll and started off. He walked the rails north about 70 miles to the coastal town of Bellingham. Although he had a job offer from an old friend, he decided to continue his wandering but started walking south this time, up to 30 miles a day. An early Forrest Gump? He worked briefly in a sawmill but quit that job and started walking south again, heading to Portland, Oregon.

Traveling at this point must have been in his blood, as he climbed on top of a passenger train heading east along the Columbia River, lying with his feet toward the locomotive in order to stay warm. He pulled his coat around his neck to keep from being burned by the hot cinders, writing later, "I would not do this again." He was a man of few words. Although my grandfather was moving away from the coast, an adventurous spirit continued to drive his travels.

He had seen the West Coast and it was irresistible.

His next stop was Umatilla, Oregon, which had a population at the time of fewer than 200 people. He got a job on the Pendleton Indian Reservation, working in the wheat fields from dawn to dark. One week of that was enough, so he walked 12 miles across the desert to Echo, where he jumped on another train heading east again. He boarded a car loaded with ore, although a railroad employee unfortunately closed the door and locked him in. After pounding on the door for two days and 600 miles, it opened and he found himself in Pocatello, Idaho. From there he went on to Glenn's Ferry, on the Snake River, where he went to work pitching alfalfa. Within a few months he was back in Iowa again; but he had seen the West Coast and it was irresistible. In 1914, at age 34, he returned to Southern California with a wife and two young sons.

I dug my grandfather's history out of a short hand-typed autobiography that I discovered in an old trunk, 40 years after he had died. The first two sentences on the opening page intrigued me enough to keep reading: "Maybe sometime someone may wonder what Fred Ward Griggs did all his life. The following is far from being complete but does give a concise report of how I spent 77 years of my life." He died just three years later, with this history buried in a trunk.

I was fascinated by his history because I had never heard about any of his cross-country adventures getting to the coast from my own dad, and I'm not even sure he knew much about his father's early life. I knew him only as a

Fig. 2.2. Gary's father, Dean Griggs, looking out over the Pacific at age 3 in 1916.

grandfather, in later years. He was still very tall and thin, and no matter what the occasion or temperature, he wore a double-breasted suit, a starched white shirt, and a tie. He looked to me like the Grant Wood *American Gothic* farmer, except with a suit instead of coveralls. Formal, quiet, and very serious. He rarely smiled, and in fact, I don't think I ever heard him laugh. So as I read about his treks across the west as a young man, walking halfway across the state of Washington, working in wheat fields and lumber mills, and ultimately being called by the California coast, I got an entirely different sense of who this quiet man was, or at least who he was when he was 50 years younger.

I have several old very memorable photographs of my father, one when he was about 3 years old in 1916, looking seaward to the Pacific (Figure 2.2); and another a few years later in 1920, on a Southern California beach with his father, now nearly a century ago (Figure 2.3). These old photographs got me thinking that perhaps my own attachment to the Pacific Coast had deep roots.

Fig. 2.3. Gary's grandfather and father (Fred Griggs, left rear, and Dean Griggs, right front) on the beach in Southern California in 1920.

Coastal childhood

Although I was born in Pasadena, which is about an hour-long drive from the coast when the freeways are completely empty, I can recall the occasional summer weekend trip to the beach to cool down from the inland heat. Summers in Los Angeles were actually hot, well before the planet started seriously heating up.

Being a high school teacher gave my dad summers off, and my parents seemed to live for the time each year when they could stuff my two brothers and me into the family station wagon, along with a tent, sleeping bags, and an old Coleman two-burner stove and lantern, and get out of LA (Figure 2.4). We worked our way up the California coast, three brothers trying our best to get along in the backseat for hours on end. Our first night's stop was always in Berkeley, in the San Francisco Bay Area, after what seemed to us a long, monotonous drive from the freeways and crowds of Southern California. But it was always worth the boredom when we finally arrived.

In the 1930s, my dad had gone to the University of California at Berkeley, along the edge of San Francisco Bay. One of his college roommates and a good friend, Jim Parsons, had gone on to get a PhD in geography and was a professor on the Berkeley campus. He had

Fig. 2.4. Packed for a month of camping, Big Sur, 1956 (Gary in middle, with brother, Jeff, on left and mother, Barbara, on right).

traveled and worked throughout much of Central and South America, taken sabbaticals in Spain, and explored what seemed to me like a lot of strange and exotic places. The old two-story family house in the Berkeley hills was, to me, something between a museum and a library. Being a university professor, he had shelves of books that seemed like they reached to the ceiling. In our own house, in contrast, we never had a bookshelf, and we had very few books.

As a 12-year-old, I found Jim's house a fascinating place to explore and always looked forward to our overnights. Jim had collected so much interesting stuff from his travels and always told us such great bedtime stories that I wanted to become a university professor. I didn't fully appreciate at the time what the difference was between an MD and a PhD but was impressed that he was a "doctor."

With a very naive fantasy in my adolescent mind about being a professor when I eventually grew up, I asked my dad during one of our visits what you needed to do to get a "doctor's degree." My dad replied, "You have to write a book." Well, I suppose he was technically correct but, unfortunately, to my immature mind with its 12-year-old level of self-confidence, I pretty much crossed that career off my dream list.

After leaving Berkeley, we took the Richmond–San Rafael ferry across to Marin, which was another one of those unforgettable boyhood adventures I recall all these years later. Driving the family car across a rickety ramp onto the ferry, smelling the diesel and salt air, hearing the sounds of the engine, and then standing by the rail as we crossed the bay—it was a short trip but one that I always wanted to last much longer.

Eventually, sometime late in the day, we arrived at a state park, in the redwoods or on the coast, where we paid $1 a night to camp. We had our chores, unpacking the car or the small trailer we sometimes pulled, getting the tent set up and air mattresses inflated, and scrounging for firewood for the evening campfire. Life couldn't get much better. The 1950s summers were easy times for a kid—no computers or Internet, no cell phones or iPods, no weed or drugs, just having fun, and not wanting it to end and have to return to school in September. I realize now how much those summer trips and adventures on the coast have influenced me throughout my life.

Paradise in the pines

In 1950, when I was 7, my parents decided to escape the crowds of Southern California. They took a chance, left all the relatives and friends behind, and bought a 50-acre ranch in southern Oregon, south of Grants Pass, for the outrageous price of $10,000. For my brothers and me, this was a dream we could have never imagined, paradise in the pines. The part of that year I best remember consisted of summer months exploring the woods, fishing, picking wild blackberries, swimming in creeks, and having our own farm animals (Figure 2.5). These adventures and the memories of living in a log cabin in the woods forever left images deep in my head of what life could be. It clarified one thing: I knew I didn't want a desk job when I grew up. I wanted to be outside doing something, and it didn't seem to matter at the time what that something was going to be, but that's where I was headed.

Family economics conspired to put an end to our Oregon paradise after two years on the ranch, however. So, sadly, my parents made the difficult decision to return to Southern California where my dad could get a teaching job. We weren't happy with the move, but we were just kids going along for the ride at that point.

Fig. 2.5. Gary (second from left), brothers, and cousin in front of
the log house on the ranch near Wilderville, Oregon, 1952.

Valley boy

We settled in what was soon to become known as The Valley,
Woodland Hills in the San Fernando Valley. It wasn't on the coast,
but it wasn't far off. We could get to the beach in an hour, driving
the curvy roads over the Santa Monica Mountains, either Topanga or
Malibu canyons. Until my older brother started driving, it was family
trips to Zuma Beach. That area wasn't yet called Malibu and there
weren't the Hollywood star mega-mansions of today. My folks didn't
have much spare change in those days; in fact, they never had much
spare change but somehow managed to buy two lots in the 1950s, one
right on the coast near Trancas Beach and another higher in the hills.
When they had an opportunity to sell at $4,500, almost twice what
they paid, they thought they had made a fortune and were quite happy
with their investment.

It was at Zuma Beach, where we spent many weekends
bodysurfing and where we got our share of sunburns, that I first
discovered rip currents. I think I had a vague idea about them,
although I don't recall any warning signs on the beach or any
cautionary words from my dad. But on a summer day, a small group
of us playing in larger-than-usual waves just a few feet from the shore
suddenly found ourselves about a quarter-mile offshore, wondering

what just happened. I don't remember any panic; concern but not panic. Fortunately, the water was warm and we were all reasonably capable swimmers. I recall treading water for a while and then working our way to the beach, none the worse for our unexpected seaward journey.

As the number of visitors to our coastal beaches has exploded, and the number of visitors with little or no experience in ocean swimming has grown, warning signs advising of the possibility of rip currents and other ocean hazards are now commonplace up and down the coastline.

Surfing and woodies

My older brother, Dean, graduated from high school in 1959 and had a friend who had started surfing. These were the early days when only a handful of surfers, mostly from places like Santa Monica and the South Bay cities, hung out at places like Malibu, San Clemente, Manhattan Beach, Huntington Beach, and San Onofre. Surfers at the time were typically thought of as barely above outlaws and somewhere below delinquents. The Valley was more or less off the surfing grid, however, and news traveled slowly. But my brother began surfing at Malibu, and before long he and his friend both had 1948 Ford woodies, which remain the iconic symbol of Southern California surfing almost 60 years later (Figure 2.6).

Every summer in Santa Cruz, which I've called home for nearly 50 years, there is a weekend celebration in July showcasing dozens of these old cars, Woodies on the Wharf. Some of the old surfers, as well as some modern wannabes, drive or trailer their vintage wagons from all over the west and sit proudly in their beach chairs by their often professionally restored woodies for a day of tourist admiration and photographs. It's the Santa Cruz equivalent of the Concours d'Elegance of Pebble Beach, some 40 miles away.

My older brother often looked after me in high school, helping me through the challenges of adolescence. He would drag me away from my homework to accompany him and his friends on their adventures and pranks. None that I want to repeat here, but it was a rite of passage that I grew to appreciate. There was a coastal turning point for me in the summer of 1960 that I owe to Dean. He had enrolled in what was then known as Valley State, now elevated to California

Fig. 2.6. Gary (left) and older brother, Dean, and 1948 Ford Woody in Woodland Hills, 1961.

State University, Northridge, but was transferring in the fall to the Santa Barbara campus of the University of California. He had his own surfboard by then and took me with his surfing buddy, Mike Rarity, one weekend. We went to Malibu Colony, where some of the old Hollywood celebrities had homes.

The Colony was just west of the main break at Malibu. Instead of a hoped-for point break, where waves peeled off perfectly for a right-hand ride, it was essentially a shore break on that humiliating day. Not even good conditions for surfers who knew what they were doing. Most people at the Colony just hung out on the beach rather than surf. But Dean asked me if I wanted to take his board out. I hesitated for about half a second, grabbed his board, and headed for the water. He gave me absolutely no advice or tutoring. It was just me, the board, my first time surfing, and at Malibu, the most legendary of Southern California surfing spots. Things could have gone worse, I suppose. All of my friends could have been sitting on the beach watching.

I didn't have to paddle out far as the waves were breaking almost on the sand, which should have given me some warning about what possible problems lay ahead. Although this incident, my first day on a real surfboard, took place 56 years ago, it is still indelibly etched in my brain. It all looked pretty easy. I saw a good-size wave approaching, managed to turn the board around, and, lying face down, started paddling quickly to get into the wave. It steepened quickly, and my brother's board, with me on it, started down the face of that wave. For an instant, I felt a rush of adrenaline. But that sensation lasted about a second. I was still lying on the board, nowhere near being able to stand up yet, and saw the sand coming up fast. The wave was too steep, I was too far forward on the board, and the water was too shallow. I recall my face grinding into the sand rather abruptly.

Fortunately I didn't break my neck and went on to better days. Dean's board was fine, I hadn't wrecked it, but a lot of skin was gone from my nose and forehead.

I quickly realized that surfing was going to be more difficult than it looked. Staggering up the beach, still in shock and carrying the board, I could feel warm blood trickling down my face. As I walked somewhat sheepishly toward my brother, who was sitting with Mike, a seasoned surfer, Dean said only one thing: "Did some pearl diving, huh?" *Pearling* is common among beginning surfers when they are too far forward on the board and there is too much weight on the nose. As the wave steepens, the nose of the board dives beneath the surface. I had indeed been pearl diving and didn't have the courage or desire to go back out again that day. My face and my ego also took awhile to recover.

> **I quickly realized that surfing was going to be more difficult than it looked.**

During my senior year in high school, Dean would return home on vacations from UC Santa Barbara in his woody with his board hanging out the back. Listening to him describe living the college life on the coast, going to class between episodes of surfing, and hanging out at the beach all sounded pretty inviting to me. Unlike high school seniors of today, who hedge their bets and apply to so many colleges that they often hire a consultant to coordinate the increasingly competitive and complicated process, I applied to one school, UC Santa Barbara, and was excited to be accepted.

Worker, student, surfer

After graduating from high school in June 1961 and needing money for school in the fall, I took a job working in a factory on the other side of Los Angeles, in Gardena, 45 freeway miles away. I was so excited to have landed my first full-time job, recommended to me by the next-door neighbor who I worked for on weekends, that I gave little thought to the daily 90-mile round trip. I can only describe it as a three-month ordeal and important learning experience on what it took to earn a dollar in 1961.

At $1.45 an hour, I was saving money for college, although I have to admit that I spent a lot of my paycheck on gasoline that summer. Gas was only 27.9 cents a gallon, almost free by today's prices. I could fill the tank with about two hours of work, but I had to fill it several times a week. Leaving home in the valley about 7 a.m., five days a week, I drove an hour when traffic was manageable, worked nine hours, and then got back on the freeway to start home. The return drive was mostly miserable. It was rush hour by then and traffic for about 35 of the 45 miles was usually stop and go, bumper to bumper. To make matters worse, the 1949 Chevy I was driving had no radio and so no music. It was a grind and got old real fast. The only salvation was the $60 check I received every Friday and knowing that I had to suffer through this for only three months. Then I would be leaving for UCSB and what I was envisioning as a much more enjoyable time.

I learned a lifelong lesson from that summer job, and another factory job I had the next summer: it takes a lot of hours of monotonous work to make a minimal amount of money. I counted the days until summer was over for the first time, surrounded by those whom I looked at as "lifers" in the factory. From my temporary worker point of view, I didn't envy those who had limited options. But as I finished up my summer labor sentence, many of my temporary coworkers expressed joy in knowing I was escaping life in the factory and was going on to college. They wished me well.

It gave me then and still gives me a lot of pride and self-confidence knowing that I was helping pay my way through college. I was fortunate to receive a partial scholarship, and with the help of my mother and dad, who were able to cover the $45 per semester tuition, I nearly had enough to get through each year. Serving meals in a sorority house helped close the food gap, since I was paid the princely sum of $12 a month, plus dinner, for working six nights a week. Life was good.

Although I frequently boasted of paying my way through college, I made a surprising discovery many years later after my mom died and I was going through her things. She had saved every card and letter that my two brothers and I had sent home, not only from college but also from our various global adventures. My younger brother, Jeff, had served on an aircraft carrier during the Vietnam War. He chronicled his life on a carrier as an aerial photo interpreter during the war and his interesting adventures while on leave. My older brother, Dean, had written home regularly during his two years in the Peace Corps in Liberia, where life was challenging but safer and less threatening than in later years. I had spent the summer of 1964 in East and West Pakistan (before the East became Bangladesh) and sent home those paper-thin air letters, stuffed full of stories and sights from a 20-year-old who had never been farther away from home than Tijuana in Mexico on a surfing trip.

In going through those old postcards I had sent home to my mom and dad during my freshman year at UCSB, I noticed that the short and most common message read something like: "I got an A on my calculus/history midterm, waves have been good, can you please send $5 for food." This reminded me of two things I had forgotten—everything was a lot cheaper in the early 1960s, and I still needed some help from home to keep from starving.

Although I had only surfed a few times before I headed off to UC Santa Barbara, the surfer image in the '60s was bleached-blond hair to go with a year-round tan. On a lark, during the summer after high school graduation, and while my parents were off on vacation, I tried bleaching my own hair. It worked well (Figure 2.7). By the time I arrived at Santa Barbara a month later, I discovered a new image and presence. While I didn't have the money to buy my own board, I spent every fall weekend at the campus beach, borrowing a board from anyone who wasn't using it at the moment. As my skills improved, I gradually began to identify with this newly discovered lifestyle. It fit, it worked, and it was fun. I was hooked, and surfing became a central part of who I was over the next four years.

Through that first year at Santa Barbara and the next summer as well, 1961–62, the earliest surfing movies by Bruce Brown and Bud Browne began to appear. They were typically shown at local high school auditoriums: *Slippery When Wet*, *Barefoot Adventure*, *Cat on a Hot Foam Board*, and *Surfing Hollow Days* were a few of the early films I remember. I found myself looking like every other young surfer walking into the auditorium, wearing cords, white T-shirts and Pendleton shirts, black

Fig. 2.7. Gary starting his freshman year at UCSB, 1961.

low-cut tennis shoes or Mexican sandals, and bleached-blond hair. In retrospect it was a fashion statement that we were all making to feel part of a culture. We belonged to a group, which can be comforting, although looking back it often felt like staring into a giant mirror because almost everyone else looked exactly like you. Nobody stood out at those events, and the only thing that distinguished my college roommates and me—we all surfed—from the 500 other surfers in the auditorium was that we were four or five years older and were college students.

Unlike the lack of tutoring before my first attempt at surfing a year before, Dean did give me one piece of advice as I started UCSB. "Gary, just study all the time and you'll be OK." That was pretty simple: "Study all the time." I had done well enough in high school so I figured if I just studied all the time, things would work out. If I wasn't in class or studying, I was on the beach or in the water, but I spent a lot of time in the library that first year, reading textbooks and going over lecture notes.

"Gary, just study all the time and you'll be OK."

Although I changed my major five times as an undergraduate, I kept coming back to geology. When I wasn't in class listening to lectures about how the earth worked, I could surf or wander the beaches, watching the ocean and picking up interesting rocks and shells. This was the first time in my life that I actually lived right at the edge. From my dorm or, later, my apartment, I was 5 minutes away from the sand and saltwater. I couldn't imagine life being much more idyllic. All the pieces of the puzzle were fitting together as school and the ocean merged into one package. Instead of cramming before midterms and finals, I usually walked on the beach, swam, or took my board out to clear my mind.

Santa Barbara really doesn't have any seasons. It rarely rains, especially now, and it seldom gets very cold. The ocean did cool off in the winter, however, which meant we stopped surfing about December and then started in again about March when we could just barely handle the cold water. This was in the days before wetsuits were in common use, although I couldn't have afforded one even if they had been. Nine months of surfing every year, almost across the street from your apartment, was pleasantly addictive.

There was one memorably bad winter day, however, when I thought I was going to die surfing.

There was one memorably bad winter day, however, when I thought I was going to die surfing. My first class wasn't until late morning so I went out at campus beach, which was a nice right-hand point break. I had the place completely to myself on a cold, foggy morning with 5-foot waves. I took off late on a wave, stood, turned, and then lost it as the wave broke over me. The buoyant board erupted from the water and caught me right between my legs, squarely in my groin, which was intensely painful. Continuing its upward trajectory, the board then caught me right between my eyes. Stunned for a minute, I reached for my forehead and realized there was a lot of blood. Initially I thought it must be my brains oozing out of the wound, but it was just blood and later an ugly bruise. My ego was temporarily shattered, but being a compulsive optimist, I was happy that no one was on the beach to witness the embarrassing event.

Marine geologist

A critical academic turning point took place in my senior year when I enrolled in a class with an appealing name, Marine Geology. I discovered that all that I had been studying on land, during geologic mapping trips to Hollister Ranch, into the mountains behind Santa

Barbara, and out in the desert, was just beginning to be studied underwater as well. I had spent the previous summer in what seemed like a dream job at the time, lifeguarding on East Beach in Santa Barbara. People got paid well, $1.75 an hour, to go out paddle-boarding, to sit in a tower for eight hours on the beach getting a tan, to break out an occasional Band-Aid and, generally, to try appear capable and alert, and to be ready for any emergency. Although I hadn't begun to think about what I was going to do after graduation, being a professional beach lifeguard had briefly entered my mind.

I was fortunate because the Geological Sciences Department at UC Santa Barbara had just started a graduate program during my senior year. I would notice these older guys wandering around who wore long pants, shoes, and shirts with buttons and who seemed to have a plan for their lives, or else they were just putting off the inevitable job search by becoming graduate students. At the same time, a poster on the department bulletin board caught my eye. It showed some scientists hanging over the side of a ship bringing in a long core of sediment from the seafloor. It was announcing a new graduate program in oceanography at Oregon State University.

Nine months later I arrived in Corvallis, Oregon, in a VW van, having just gotten married and ready to start a new life chapter. The move was a good choice, although after the endless summers of Santa Barbara, the endless drizzle in Oregon got old almost immediately. "Real men" didn't carry umbrellas, I thought, but after two weeks of getting soaked every day, I swallowed my pride and bought one.

The new program was rigorous. Weeks at sea in the North Pacific, several hundred miles offshore, usually under less than idyllic conditions, and hours spent collecting sediment cores from the seafloor 12,000 feet below opened my eyes to both the challenges and rigors of working at sea (Figure 2.8). But it also exposed me for the first time to the pleasure and exhilaration of actually *doing* science. The sediments slowly accumulating on the ocean floor provide a record of what the overlying oceans have experienced over time, just as the pages in your journal record your own travels, experiences, emotional pleasures, and personal disasters. Or at least those that you care to write about. The evidence of the last 50,000 or so years of Pacific Northwest geologic history was all there in the mud, and I spent three years trying to figure it out—volcanic eruptions, mega-

Fig. 2.8. The research vessel *Yaquina*, returning from another expedition in the Northeast Pacific, 1967.

earthquakes, changing climate, drifting icebergs, and huge submarine mud flows.

Every sediment core I opened was like plunging into a new novel, only it was real stuff. It all reinforced my decision to immerse myself in the ocean, working on the edge. Even oceanographic cruises 200 miles offshore were at the edge of the continent, and much of what had been recorded in the seafloor sediment involved events along this geologically active edge.

Through a bit of discipline and focus, but mostly either working or "studying all the time" (I was still following my older brother's sage advice), I left Corvallis with a PhD three years later. Despite what my father had unwittingly discouraged me from doing 12 years earlier, needing to write a book to get a "doctor's degree," I had made it through that burning hoop. And my quicker than normal pace for a graduate student netted me an unusual result: in 1968 at 24, I had an offer to go to work for Humble Oil (later to become Exxon) in Houston, Texas, exploring for offshore oil.

As serendipity would have it, the day before I was going to get a plane ticket for Houston and interviews with Humble, I got a call from Aaron Waters, who had been the chairman of the Geological Sciences Department at UC Santa Barbara. He had been hired at the new University of California, Santa Cruz, campus to start an Earth Sciences Department. I had gotten to know Aaron during my last year at UC

Santa Barbara, and he had served as an informal advisor of sorts. At 62, he was a seasoned professor, a veteran of faculty positions at Stanford, Johns Hopkins, and UC Santa Barbara, and had provided invaluable perspective and advice. He remembered I'd been selected as the outstanding graduating senior in geology three years earlier, and we had kept in contact during my graduate school years in Corvallis.

Professor

The Santa Cruz campus was just in its third year. Aaron thought the school should have an oceanographer on the faculty and offered me a position as an assistant professor at $9,300 a year. A lot of waves have washed across the shoreline in the subsequent 48 years, but accepting that offer and coming to Santa Cruz in 1968 was probably the best decision I've ever made. For me, living and working on the edge, with the ocean for a backyard, is about as good as it gets. This is where virtually my entire career has been spent. Every day brings a new mystery to solve, a question to answer, another battle to fight, a lecture to give, or a story to tell.

Not long after I arrived as a young professor at UC Santa Cruz, a strange encounter reminded me of my academic discipline and study habits while a student at Santa Barbara. I was headed for the library and had just boarded a minibus that snaked its way around the hilly and expansive Santa Cruz campus. Sitting right next to me was a guy carrying a wetsuit who looked very familiar. He looked me right in the eyes and said "I know who you are. You're the guy who was always in the library studying at Santa Barbara. What are you doing here?" I told him my name and that I was a new professor of oceanography. He replied, "I knew it! I knew you were going somewhere." At this point I recognized him. Kemp Aaberg, a Gidget-era Malibu icon and at age 18 the costar of Bruce Brown's 1958 surf movie *Slippery When Wet*. Kemp was one of a family of three surfing brothers who were among the earliest and best-known Southern California surfers in the late 1950s at Malibu and Rincon. Kemp, one of the greatest of his era, was photographed at Rincon, doing an amazing back arch. That photograph is probably one of the best-known surf shots ever taken and became the first logo for *Surfing* magazine (Figure 2.9). I had known Kemp while we were both students at UC Santa Barbara, but seeing him in the coastal redwoods at UC Santa Cruz was a surprising

Fig. 2.9. Kemp Aaberg and a soul arch, Rincon, 1959.

reminder for me of the convergence of surfing and studying.

The westward migration for my ancestors came to a halt here on the shores of the Pacific Ocean. The ocean has been both an edge and a border, and also a new frontier for many of us. There has always been something very reassuring and comforting to me about living on the coast, knowing a few hundred feet away there is wide-open ocean that stretches westward for thousands of uninterrupted miles.

Since 1961, when I first began looking at beaches more carefully, I guess I've had a love affair with the California coast. Perhaps like many others, I've walked miles of beaches, taken thousands of pictures, collected hundreds of glass bottles full of different colored sand, and never grown tired of yet another day along the shoreline (Figure 2.10). I've seen the coast from the air, from on and under the water, and from the shoreline. I don't recall ever having a bad day at the beach and have never grown tired of another day on the edge. I think that's just the way it's always going to be for me.

Fig. 2.10. A small portion of Gary's beach sand collection.

I can't walk too far. I used to walk the whole beach, years ago. Now I'm lucky to do it once in a while, but as often as I can—oh, I've been walking here 40 years and longer. I don't know why. But when I was a kid, we would go to the ocean and have a picnic. There's something that draws you. There was just something about the Pacific that I liked. It is almost spiritual.

I was born in Watsonville, so I'm a native of the Pacific coast. I don't mind telling you that was 93 years ago. Being born near here, I enjoy the coast, I had some attraction to the ocean. When I was younger, we would go clamming at Palm Beach (I'm going back a few years; now they call it Pajaro Dunes). We would catch clams, and the limit was five. And we'd go home, and my mother would clean them up and fix them with eggs. Five was plenty, the clams then were really big, you were getting meat the size of your whole hand. One clam was enough meat for two people!

I can remember I was 10 years old when my father took me out on the pier, and on the cement ship here, on a Sunday afternoon. And he bought me an ice cream cone off the ship and I remember him putting 5 cents down and I got a big ice cream cone. Maybe it seemed big because I was a kid.

On the cement ship when we went out there, in those days, on Sunday evenings, we could have dinner and there was a dance. What's going to happen to that ship now? I hope they never dynamite the ship into pieces, and they just let it go naturally.

I've noticed that compared with 10 years ago, the beach seems a lot dirtier. There just seems to be more junk piling up, more of everything.

I sit here and I watch out over the water, and I wonder if you just continued to head out, straight out from the shoreline, whether you would reach the Asian continent? Or Australia? But I think the direction would probably wind you up at the upper edge of Antarctica.

—Visitor to the coast for most of 93 years

A MIGRATING EDGE

Seawalls and other barriers will help for a while in some locations, but inevitably in the future it will be necessary to plan a retreat from the most vulnerable low-lying shoreline areas.

Twenty thousand years ago the Farallon Islands, 30 miles due west of the Golden Gate Bridge, were the coast of California. While this would have been a very long day's hike for anybody, a good mountain biker could have probably gotten out there in time for lunch.

What happened to the Farallons? Why are they just desolate granite pinnacles today, surrounded by great white sharks looking for dinner instead of being a rugged, offshore extension of the Marin Headlands? Why has the edge of California shifted inland?

Well, California isn't alone. Every coastline in the world has migrated landward over the past 20,000 years as sea level rose following the last ice age, inundating the edges of continents across the face of the Earth.

The Bering Strait off Alaska, a 50-mile wide tongue of ocean connecting the Bering Sea in the south with the Chukchi Sea in the north, was also dry land 20,000 years ago. The strait is only 100 to 160 feet deep today and connects Siberia to Alaska (Figure 3.1). With this land bridge between two huge continents exposed by a serious drop in sea level, the first members of *Homo sapiens* were able to venture from Asia into North America. No one knows for sure if they were traveling on land, perhaps following game, or just exploring, or if they were moving along the shoreline in primitive boats. We do know that they entered an entirely new world, uninhabited by any other

The Bering Strait, connecting Siberia to Alaska, was dry land 20,000 years ago. The light blue is the continental shelf, all less than 400 feet deep. *Google Earth—Image IBCAOP, Data SIO, NOAA, U.S. Navy, NGA, GEBCO, Image Landsat/Copernicus*

human beings. The archaeological record indicates that they migrated southward rather quickly. To the amazement of archaeologists and anthropologists, they had reached the tip of South America, nearly 15,000 miles away, by at least 14,600 years ago. Thinking about this migration another way, early humans were advancing south into the Americas at about a mile a day for 15,000 years.

Sea level was nearly 400 feet lower 20,000 years ago, so the shallow continental shelves bordering all landmasses were exposed as dry land. With a lower sea level, California's four northern Channel Islands (San Miguel, Santa Rosa, Santa Cruz, and Anacapa) in the area off what is now Santa Barbara were all joined, although there was still a deep, 5-mile wide channel separating this mega-island from the coastline of the rest of California. Native Americans managed to cross this ocean barrier, however, and inhabit the islands (Figure 3.2).

In 1959, a partial skeleton dated at about 13,000 years old was found on Santa Rosa Island and is still one of the oldest North American human skeletons discovered. The skeleton, named the Arlington Springs Man after the location on Santa Rosa Island where

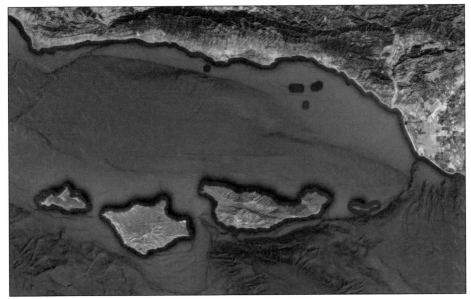

Fig. 3.2. The coast between Point Conception (on the upper left) and Ventura (on the right) and the offshore Channel Islands. The flatter area of seafloor along the coastline is the continental shelf, which was exposed during the low sea level of the last ice age. *Google Earth—Data LDEO-Columbia, NSF, NOAA, SIO, U.S. Navy, NGO, GEBCO, Image Landsat/Copernicus, Data MBARI*

he was found, shared the island with a pygmy or dwarf species of mammoth, which also made the 5-mile transit across the channel. Elsewhere in California in this era of very early occupancy, Native Americans shared the coastal terraces and grasslands with now-extinct camels, horses, dire wolves, and sabertooth cats.

Today, on the other side of the world, the English Channel between the British Isles and France is as shallow as 50 feet in places. With sea level 400 feet lower, this land bridge would have provided an easy connection for early humans to tramp back and forth between what was to become England and the European Union millennia later.

What triggered this large drop and then a subsequent rise in sea level and where did all the water go? If we lower the level of the oceans 400 feet, we have to find somewhere to put about 10 million cubic miles of water. That's a lot of ocean to just stick under the carpet somewhere.

Throughout the history of the oceans, which goes back about 3.5 billion years, give or take a few million, climate has constantly changed. In response, sea level has gone up and down like a yo-yo, except over periods of thousands of years. The location of California's shoreline at any particular time in the past is inextricably tied to the level of the ocean. If we take water out of the oceans, sea level has to drop and the coastline moves offshore, just like the tide going out. If we add more water to the oceans, sea level has to rise, moving the shoreline inland.

> **Throughout the history of the oceans, climate has constantly changed. In response, sea level has gone up and down like a yo-yo.**

To provide some perspective, the oceans are spread out over about 139 million square miles and cover 71 percent of the earth's surface, so it takes one heck of a lot of water to increase the level of the oceans very much. To raise global sea level just 1 inch requires about 2,075 cubic miles of water.

When the climate warms, two processes take place that conspire to raise the level of the oceans. One is the expansion of seawater as the ocean temperature rises. Warm water takes up more space than cold water, so as the oceans heat up they expand, raising the water level. Your home water heater was designed with this thermal expansion in mind. You fill the water heater initially with cold water up to a certain level, but directions instruct you to leave some extra room at the top so when the water is heated, it has room to expand and doesn't blow up your house. Actually, there is also a high-pressure release valve or overflow to keep that from happening. The ocean also has space for that extra water to go; it's called the continental shelf.

Glaciation and ice ages

The other 800-pound gorilla in the climate room is ice, and there is quite a lot of it scattered around the planet, most of it in the Arctic and Antarctic. And there was a whole lot more during past ice ages. The warmer the earth's climate, the more of that ice melts.

There are two huge reservoirs of ice on the planet, Antarctica and Greenland, and then a bit more spread around in all of the small mountain glaciers in places like the Himalayas, Patagonia, Alaska, the

Fig. 3.3. A glacier in Patagonia. All of the continental glaciers on earth contain enough ice to raise sea level about 2 feet if they were all to melt.

Alps, the Andes, and a few others (Figure 3.3). As the earth warms, the ice sheets in Antarctica and Greenland and the mountain glaciers gradually melt. The meltwater flows into the oceans, raising their levels. We believe today that about two-thirds of all the sea-level rise we are experiencing at present is due to glacier and ice sheet melt and the rest due to the expansion of a warming ocean.

One hundred and eighty years ago, Louis Agassiz, a Swiss naturalist who was described as well-educated, outgoing, articulate, charming, and ambitious—a set of traits not commonly found among scientists—first suggested the odd notion that there had been periods in the past when glaciers and ice covered large areas of the earth's surface. He spent a lot of time wandering around his native Switzerland observing the natural world. He noticed in his hikes the frequent occurrence of large rocks, some the size of cars or school buses, stranded out in the middle of meadows or pastures. These rocks baffled him at first, but he then reasoned from his observations of existing glaciers that as they melted and retreated, they left their sediment loads behind in the form of sand, gravel, and even very large rocks. The most logical explanation to him was that glaciers had

Fig. 3.4. Erratics dropped by the melting glaciers that covered north-central Washington near Okanogan during the last ice age.

covered much more of the earth's surface in the past than today and that there must have been much colder periods or ice ages.

Then, like now, it often took a long time for new and completely outlandish or unheard-of scientific ideas to be accepted by others. We also didn't have email or the Internet, so news traveled very slowly. But over time, others began to recognize evidence for prehistoric glaciation all over the place. Large areas at higher latitudes and higher elevations had preserved these random boulders, known as erratics— bedrock that had been scoured and polished by roving glaciers—and also the debris left behind when the glaciers halted their march and melted (Figure 3.4). Glacial erratics are scattered across New York City's Central Park. Yosemite Valley was scoured out by glaciers, as were the Great Lakes. Those glaciers have all now completely melted. Cape Cod, Martha's Vineyard, and Nantucket are nothing more than the sand, gravel, and other debris carried from hundreds of miles away and left behind as ice age glaciers melted.

The last several million years of earth history were dominated by ice ages. There were a number of ice ages, on roughly 100,000- year cycles, when the climate got cooler and glaciers and ice sheets expanded. Thousands of feet of ice covered much of North America, from Seattle extending down into the Midwest and back east to Cape Cod.

The last ice age or glacial epoch ended about 20,000 years ago. Overall, the earth was about 9 degrees Fahrenheit cooler than today. Somewhere in the neighborhood of 10 million cubic miles of seawater were evaporated from the oceans. Much of it precipitated out over the northern continents as well as Greenland and Antarctica as snow, which was compacted into ice, gradually forming extensive ice sheets and glaciers. Taking all of that water out of the ocean dropped sea level about 400 feet.

Over periods of many thousands of years, sea level dropped during ice ages, and then rose again when the climate warmed and the ice sheets and glaciers melted. This wasn't a big deal along the California coast ten or twenty thousand years ago. The few people living along the state's shoreline ten thousand years ago didn't take much notice, even as sea level rose as much as an inch a year. What difference would it make? California's earliest inhabitants were living a pretty simple existence, focused on finding the next meal, not getting eaten by one of those now-extinct dire wolves or saber-toothed cats, and finding some shelter.

The northern Channel Islands were united as a mega-island, then separated from each other every time the level of the oceans rose again. The Farallons were islands and then were reunited with the rest of California each time sea level dropped. During warm or interglacial periods, San Francisco Bay was a saltwater estuary, where the waters of the ancestral Sacramento and San Joaquin rivers merged and met the tidewater of the Pacific. But when it cooled off again, and the ice sheets and glaciers expanded and sucked all that water out of the ocean, the coastline receded out to the Farallons, and the bay became a river valley surrounded by marshes and grasslands.

Twenty thousand years ago, as sea level started to rise again, those animals living along the coast migrated away from the shoreline. Habitats, whether intertidal, estuary, or marsh, gradually responded and reestablished themselves farther inland. It was just the way things had always been. Sea level rose and fell with climate, and climate changed on somewhat regular cycles, ultimately tied to how much solar energy we get.

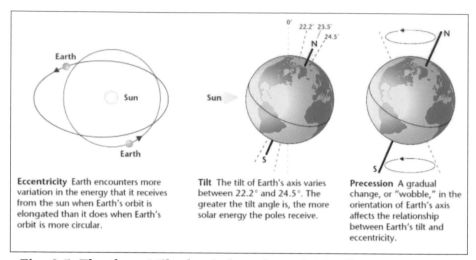

Eccentricity Earth encounters more variation in the energy that it receives from the sun when Earth's orbit is elongated than it does when Earth's orbit is more circular.

Tilt The tilt of Earth's axis varies between 22.2° and 24.5°. The greater the tilt angle is, the more solar energy the poles receive.

Precession A gradual change, or "wobble," in the orientation of Earth's axis affects the relationship between Earth's tilt and eccentricity.

Fig. 3.5. The three Milankovitch cycles, which affect the distance between Earth and the sun and play a major role in Earth's long-term climate changes. *image courtesy http://www.slideshare.net/ syadur/milankovitch-theory*

And that, in turn, is directly related to how far our planet is from the sun. That distance, and therefore how warm or cool Earth gets, is affected by some unique but well-understood irregularities in Earth's orbit around the sun.

Earth actually wobbles like a top, but in a regular and predictable way. Our axis of rotation is not vertical but is tilted at an angle, which changes a little over time and produces the seasons (Figure 3.5). When California and the Northern Hemisphere are tilted toward the sun, it is warmer and we have summer. When we are tilted away from the sun, we are a bit farther away, which makes it cooler and winter sets in. Then there is our orbit around the sun; it's not a perfect circle but an ellipse, and this orbit changes slightly over time.

These cyclical irregularities in Earth's rotation and orbit set in motion the climate changes that bring on or end ice ages. We live on a planet whose surface temperature is very delicately balanced and makes life possible, at least life as we know it. Those planets closer to the sun are way too hot for life; those farther away are way too cold, at least for us.

Human-caused climate change

So without human civilization, climate changes and giant swings of hundreds of feet in sea level were of little consequence. There were no coastal communities, no megacities with condominiums, houses, hotels, and other businesses built on the shoreline. There were no sewage treatment facilities, power plants, ports or harbors, airports, highways or bridges, refineries, or other infrastructure at the ocean's edge. All of our permanent coastal development in California was built during an era when the level of the ocean was relatively stable. Along California's coast, although there are some small local differences, sea level has risen about 7 or 8 inches over the past century.

Looking at the long-term patterns of climate change and the resulting sea-level fluctuations connected to those Earth-sun cycles, we are due for another glacial cycle to begin about now. This would slowly begin to lower sea level again after the last 7,000–8,000 years of little change.

But this isn't happening. Instead, and unfortunately, we are heading in the other direction, and quickly. The year 2014 was the warmest year on earth since we started measuring temperatures in 1880. But this was topped by 2015, and now 2016 has exceeded 2015 as the hottest. Sixteen of the seventeen hottest years since 1880 have all been since 2000. The only exception is 1998, which was an El Niño year.

Sea-level rise in the years ahead isn't going to be pleasant for anyone along the coast of California.

Sea-level rise in the years ahead isn't going to be pleasant for anyone along the coast of California. Towns and cities don't just step back gracefully from the ocean's edge, even after a disaster. Look at New Orleans, New York, and New Jersey— thanks to a lot of federal aid, they are rebuilding right where they were. We could call this stubborn reconstruction in harm's way collective amnesia—or just failing to learn from the long-term history.

The question isn't "Is sea level rising?" We know it's rising and we measure this continuously with water level recorders scattered along the state's coastline from Crescent City to San Diego. The average global rate of rise over the past twenty years has increased to about 13 inches per century. You might think "This isn't something worth losing any sleep over. I've got other things to worry about"—which is partly true. Only those other things are probably pretty short term and not likely to affect the state's coastal communities and their residents (like you and your family) for decades and generations to come.

California has lost a lot of coastal land and homes over the past century. Many older and even some newer developments took place without much long-term planning or history in mind. But the edge keeps moving inland, in fits and starts, usually during large El Niño events, or when very high tides coincide with large storm waves. This occurs when water comes through those sliding-glass doors, whether open or closed, for homes that were built and sold because they were "on the sand." This waterfront proximity is a very compelling enticement for folks from some midwestern state looking for their dream retirement home. While being able to step from their backdoor or deck onto the sand may sound enticing in the middle of July or August, many newcomers don't realize that soft sand was left behind by waves that had been there at their doorstep before. And as sea level continues to rise, the ocean is going to get closer more often.

The edge of early California started moving eastward about 20,000 years ago without any reaction or resistance. Today things are different. Much of the developed central and Southern California shoreline has now been covered over with rocks and concrete in efforts to halt the inland march of the sea. Understandably, people who built or bought oceanfront houses want to protect their investment and save their homes. Communities want to protect their sewage treatment facilities and power plants and their roads, parks, and access to the beauty of the coast. We sometimes forget, however, that the Pacific Ocean is about 8,000 miles wide and isn't too concerned about shifting a few feet on either edge. And we have frequently built to the water's edge, without thinking of the hazards and risks. Our disaster memories tend to be quite short.

We've lost not only individual homes and land but also complete neighborhoods from the state's coastline. Over the past century, from the redwoods of Humboldt County to the palm trees of San Diego, entire blocks of cliff-top homes have been lost to the sea, and more are on the chopping block. The Big Lagoon/Ocean View subdivision in Humboldt County, Gleason Beach in Sonoma County, Bolinas Bluffs in Marin County, the Esplanade and Moss Beach in San Mateo County,

Depot Hill in Santa Cruz County, Carpinteria in Santa Barbara County, and west Newport Beach in Orange County have all been victimized by the retreat of California's edge. The inland march of the coastline isn't a process that started yesterday, and it is going to plague and challenge us for a long time to come.

There's good news and bad news about sea-level rise, though. The good news is that it's still happening somewhat slowly, and the bad news is that it's happening slowly. As a result, people tend to think "Why worry about it now?"

King tides

Living on the edge already has its challenges at very high tides. Water sloshes over the sidewalk from the bay along San Francisco's Embarcadero today at very high tides. The on- and off-ramps from State Highway 101 for Mill Valley and Stinson Beach are also awash at extreme tides. Newport Bay is inches from entering the backdoors of some low-lying and very expensive real estate at extreme high tides.

A few years ago, a new threat was given a name, one that few living along the California coast had previously given much thought to. We imported the term *King tides* from Australia, New Zealand, and other Pacific nations, and this colorful label put these tidal extremes on coastal communities' radar screens.

Tides are really all about gravity, and we owe our understanding of them to Isaac Newton. In 1687, after watching the apocryphal apple fall and figuring out this universal attraction, he became the first to understand and explain that the tides observed along the shoreline were due to the gravitational pull of the sun and the moon on the oceans. Tides are a result of the relative positions of Earth, moon, and sun. They vary around the shorelines of the world depending upon the size and shape of each ocean basin, as well as local coastal configurations or landforms. When there is gravitational attraction between the sun and the moon, we get the highest and lowest tides, usually called spring tides, which recur about every 14 days and correspond to the full and new moons.

Everything is more complicated than it initially seems, however, and the tides are no exception. The moon rotates around Earth in an elliptical orbit with a cycle of about 28 days. Because the moon's path is elliptical, the gravitational pull is greatest when the moon is closest to Earth, called the perigee, to add even greater complexity. Everything else being equal, which it rarely is, this would be the time of the greatest high tides—when water gets closest to your back deck.

But Earth moves around the sun, also in an elliptical orbit. When Earth is at its closest point, it is given another hard-to-pronounce and harder-to-remember name, perihelion. This also is a time of the very highest tides. When these two conditions conspire, that is when the gravitational pull of the moon and the sun is at its maximum, Earth has its highest high tides and its lowest low tides. These are the King tides. They occur only several times a year, usually in January along the California coast.

Once we gave these extremes a name, a website sprang up, and now dozens of tidophiles head to the closest shoreline during King tides to take photographs and share their findings online. This has brought to the attention of everyone who happens to accidentally stumble across the site that the ocean and sea levels aren't as far away as they may have believed, especially for those who are near a shoreline.

Stockton and Sacramento are hot Central Valley cities, a long way from the coast. The state capital is 90 miles, more or less, from the Golden Gate Bridge. Hard to imagine, but the Pacific Ocean comes all the way to Sacramento and Stockton, which both have ports for oceangoing ships. With King tides, or sea-level rise, not only will the coastal cities feel the effects of rising sea water, but so will any place within a few feet of sea level, places as far from the ocean as Stockton and Sacramento. The edge of the state where land meets ocean follows a not-so-obvious route through California.

Where does all this leave us? Well, thanks to Isaac Newton, we at least understand why the tides rise and fall each day, and why we have a few extreme or King tides each year, getting places wet that usually aren't reached by the ocean. Then there was Louis Agassiz, who put forward the bold notion that Earth had been through multiple ice ages, although it took some tedious work by several other scientists later in the nineteenth century, without the benefit of calculators and computers, to figure out what drove the ice ages. It wasn't until the middle of the 1900s, however, that a handful of marine and coastal geologists began to recognize evidence offshore and onshore suggesting that sea level had risen and fallen hundreds of feet and, in the process, had moved the location of the shoreline back and forth repeatedly.

The future of the coastline

So much for the past, how about the future of California's coastal edge? This is a line, a line in the sand in many places, which is advancing landward, slowly but as surely as the sun rises in the east most days. There are some things we know and a lot more that we don't. A famous but unnamed baseball player once said: "Prediction is difficult, especially about the future." Can't disagree with that. An infamous politician, who shall also remain unnamed, once explained a complex Middle East situation with "There are known knowns ... known unknowns ... and unknown unknowns." And so it is with the coastline, which is tethered closely to sea level, which is inextricably in step with climate change.

While we don't know the precise future location of the California coastline, how far inland it will be and how much land will be underwater in, say, 2020, 2050, or 2100, we do know it is totally dependent on our future global climate. And that depends in large part on how much more greenhouse gas we will continue pumping into the atmosphere (carbon dioxide and methane are the big players here). The volume is still increasing every year.

Climate scientists use mathematical models, as well as what we know about the relationships between past climate and sea level, to project or predict how much sea level will rise at various times in the future depending on how much more carbon we put into the atmosphere. The issue really isn't that we are running out of fossil fuels—we're running out of atmosphere. The Stone Age didn't end because we ran out of stones; early humans discovered better ways of doing things. We need to do what our Stone Age ancestors did, that is, find new ways of doing things and then make the plunge into new technologies that are, to use an often misunderstood word, "sustainable."

The state of California, with its myriad agencies that deal with the coast in one form or another, has for now accepted one set of future sea-level estimates. These figures can be used to project where the coastline will be at various future times, up to 2100. Keeping in mind the uncertainties and the unknown unknowns, the average value for 2030 is a sea level about 6 inches higher than in 2000. By 2050, the average value predicted is 12 inches higher, and by 2100, 36 inches or 3 feet higher than 2000. Three feet is not a huge threat if you are living on top of a granite bluff 50 feet above the ocean. But if you live on the sand or along the shoreline of any of the state's bays or estuaries where King tides already reach within a few inches of your floor level, 3 feet is far more than an annoyance and just may not be covered by your homeowner's insurance policy.

Courtesy of the federal government, we now have very precise elevation information for all of California's developed shorelines, which has been determined using an airborne laser system. These elevation figures, combined with today's best estimates of projected future sea levels, are good indicators of when coastal streets and highways, airports and sewage treatment plants, parks and pathways, and low-lying homes and neighborhoods will begin to be submerged.

Seawalls and other barriers will help for a while in some locations, but inevitably in the future it will be necessary to plan a retreat from the most vulnerable low-lying shoreline areas. And we can already identify a number of those by watching how far inland or how high the King tides of today reach.

This is probably a good place to wrap up this unpleasant discussion of unavoidable scenarios of where the edge of California will be in the future, but there is one more future shock extreme to think about—it probably won't affect any of us living today, but its severity depends on how we treat the atmosphere in the next 40 or 50 years and how soon we can turn around the direction of climate change.

A lot of potential sea-level rise remains out there, wrapped up in the ice sheets and mountain glaciers still remaining frozen. They are shrinking as you read this, and we are measuring how quickly. While nobody believes that these are likely to completely melt in the next several centuries, they contain enough water to raise sea level around the world about 216 feet. You don't even want to think about what that means for the edge of California.

But the known unknown is the probability of a tipping point, or a threshold that is crossed with ocean or atmospheric temperatures when ice sheets start to collapse at a more rapid rate. Should this happen in the next 50 or 100 years, and some very credible climate scientists believe it could or even will, we could see a 5- to 10-foot rise in sea level by 2100—a very frightening proposition and most undesirable occurrence. About 150 million people around the planet are already living within 3 feet of high tide, and they are going to need to go somewhere. Our migrating edge is going to continue to move inland for many future generations, but the sooner we get a grip on major reductions in our carbon emissions, the sooner we can slow this down and the more time we will have to adapt.

We live in the Sierra Nevada, and we like it there. But we have always vacationed on the coast. The whole coast of California has been our vacation destination. When our kids were young, we would pick an area and just go out to the shoreline. And now we have an RV.

We like the sound of the ocean. It's very soothing. We open the windows of the RV at night, no matter what the temperature is, so we can hear the waves. In fact, my one-year-old granddaughter visited us here at the beach recently, and her mom uses one of those wave sound machines, and she fell asleep in the middle of the afternoon sitting nearby the ocean because she could hear the real waves, the surf. She just goes right out. It's very soothing.

By comparison to when we were coming here in the early 1970s, the bay seems so much cleaner, and there is so much more wildlife. We sit here, it's just amazing, we watch everything. It's easy, like today we saw the pelicans coming. We had seen no pelicans for a while, and a whole flock of 'em just came in and landed. So they're back. No whales yet this year, but last year was a banner year. At this spot. You didn't have to go out on a boat or anything. We could see them so close you hear them breathe, just right from our camp site at the beach.

But we also see that it is more crowded with people each year, it's getting harder and harder to move around this area, so many people along the coast, and all the vehicles. It's so crowded. So I worry about how the coastal areas can support as many people as come here to visit, or who live here. It looks like many things are strained, looks like the transportation network is strained, along with everything else.

But down at the beach, you don't see or hear any of that, you don't hear sirens or any of the rest of the busy-ness. You're kind of insulated from that world, all the sounds of the world, all the traffic.

—RV visitor to a state park

4

Moss Landing

Small Harbor—Big Business

"Oppose this refinery project with all your strength of mind and heart!" –Ansel Adams

Along the edge of Monterey Bay lies a small harbor known as Moss Landing. It is halfway between the city of Santa Cruz at the northern end of the bay, and Monterey at the southern end. The tiny town that surrounds this port is classic California coast: a stone's throw west of Highway 1, a celebrated seafood restaurant with a right-off-the-boat fish market, two worthy Mexican restaurants, newer California Thai cuisine on the edge of town, and fried artichoke hearts. These fried treats are a specialty derived from the tasty thistle, flourishing in the fields less than a mile away (Figure 4.1).

Artichokes, along with brussels sprouts, might be dubbed delicacies of California's central coast, requiring a climate of just the right balance of daytime ocean breezes, bright sun, damp fog, and cool nights. The eating world seems evenly divided between fans who

Fig. 4.1. Artichokes thrive in the unique microclimate of the farmlands near Moss Landing.

Fig. 4.2. Newer experimental approaches to growing strawberries do not involve methyl bromide, although some still involve a sea of plastic.

can't get enough and those who can't fathom how or why anyone would ever have thought to pick, prepare, or swallow these odd morsels. Like them or not, it is more than a little hard to imagine the first person who was inspired to eat a prickly, bitter artichoke, let alone a brussels sprout.

Strawberries also thrive in this unique coastal microclimate, defined on land by its giant, ancient sand dunes and fine-grained, sandy soils. This earth derives its highly productive and fertile quality from its proximity to the edge, once mud at the bottom of the ocean, then uplifted, broken down, weathered, eroded, and carried back toward the shoreline by rivers and streams and the wind. The now-nutritious soil lies atop the bench-like marine terrace that was formed by the combined processes of fluctuating sea levels and tectonic uplift caused by the motion of the Pacific Plate as it engaged the North American Plate in a never-ending dance.

For a time each year during the early part of the strawberry growing season, all that the eye can see over the vast coastal fields are acres upon acres of continuous plastic sheets stretching out into the distance. The plastic gleams like the surface of another ocean in the midday sun, oddly smooth and without ripples. Newcomers seeing these mysterious fields along the west side of Highway 1 might believe they've reached the water's edge, only to discover they are still a mile or more inland, looking over a faux sea (Figure 4.2).

Hidden beneath this sea of plastic lurk several powerful chemicals. They are used to fumigate the soils, to protect against destructive fungi and other threats to the health of a lusciously red, tasty strawberry. Strawberries are particularly vulnerable to these dangers, and the berries are big business. The stretch of coastal California from Santa Cruz to Oxnard supplies almost nine out of ten of the nation's strawberries, nearly 1.7 billion pounds worth $2.6 billion.

Although the use of deadly chemicals satisfies the need for efficiently grown, bug-proof, and uniformly large strawberries, it leaves a legacy of environmental and human health concerns. These, in turn, have led to increasing pressure by consumers for less dangerous, nonfumigant production methods. Strawberry farming techniques are always evolving, and the strawberry farming industry is constantly researching, in part looking for safer alternatives that can meet consumer concerns. Today, there is even a growing number of organic strawberry producers that do not use any fumigants.

As if the chemicals weren't trouble enough, tens of thousands of square yards of discarded, contaminated plastic sheets and drip tape from the fields have posed a major problem to the environment because they have been difficult to recycle, winding up in landfill. However, since 2014, a facility in Salinas—close to many of the fields—has been able to recycle up to 100 million pounds of this plastic annually.

So it goes along the vulnerable coast, a legacy of tasty strawberries and tricky environmental challenges.

Although the environmental impact of agriculture along the coast is an ongoing concern for nearshore ocean waters, our focus on agriculture sometimes diverts attention from other issues involving runoff water. Urban runoff—from gutters, storm drains, development, and dumping—is not nearly as well regulated as agricultural runoff. Lawn fertilizers, pesticides, oil, chemicals, and toxic household liquids are often washed out through drainage systems and can reach rivers, lakes, and the ocean. Growing awareness of these issues has led to improvements in practices, but new development along the coast and the growing number of people always demand heightened attention.

When it comes to agriculture, the Monterey Bay area serves as home not just to the rare, specialized crops such as artichokes, brussels sprouts, and strawberries, but also a multitude of others—raspberries, blackberries, boysenberries, blueberries, currants, loganberries, and sizable apple orchards. These crops are now distributed across the nation and throughout the world in an increasingly competitive and global food economy. Modern methods of transport—trucks, trains, huge container ships that traverse the ocean, even planes—have replaced the painstaking methods employed during the 1800s and the early 1900s.

From horse wagon to worldwide shipping

During the 1800s, the subsistence farming of the native Ohlone (formerly referred to as the Costanoans) living in the region was overtaken by marketable crops cultivated by early European settlers. The shift away from local use meant a weeklong journey in a horse-drawn wagon to get produce to San Francisco, followed by another week's return trip. This trade was difficult and time consuming.

By 1850, schooners began to make stops along the coastline to pick up produce and transport it to San Francisco and elsewhere. "Coasting," as this came to be known, dramatically altered commercial farming along the coast, including the vast Monterey Bay area fields, by easing and expanding distribution.

But it still wasn't simple or smooth. Now farmers and ranchers had to bring their goods by wagon to piers at the upper end of the Elkhorn Slough, which drains into Moss Landing. Next, the cargo would be loaded onto small, shallow draft steamships that could move down the 5 miles of slough to be transferred yet again to rowboats that could take the crops out to the larger schooners anchored just offshore. Only then could the crops finally head northward along the coast, against the wind, mostly to San Francisco.

Coasting meant schooner captains had the flexibility to stop just offshore at any point up or down the coast to pick up goods. As this type of commerce evolved, for Moss Landing it meant the construction of several long wooden wharves to help transfer goods to waiting boats for transport to the schooners. Moss Landing was named after Captain Charles Moss, who built such a pier in the late 1860s, along with Portuguese whaler Cato Vierra.

The distribution methods—what consultants might now call consumable supply chain logistics—continued to evolve once the earliest bridge was built at the mouth of the slough. This development displaced a horse and cable–drawn ferry that had been the only way to cross the watery gap. With their masts, the steamboats couldn't pass under the new bridge, and they could no longer ply the slough to retrieve the goods at the upper inland end. It became necessary to use "lighters," low, flat-bottomed barge-like boats without masts that could fit under the bridge.

The rapid evolution continued. By 1872, Southern Pacific built a railroad line crossing the upper end of the slough and the shipments by boat, barge, and schooner soon were relegated to historical footnotes. Yet the several wharves and warehouses along the ocean shoreline still survived in different incarnations for many years, even including the nearby whale-processing station, which ceased carving up and cooking whales for oil and other products only in 1926.

The railroad line across the slough still operates today, although a rise in sea level and the frequency of extreme high tides have begun to pose serious new threats to the routine of the rail. Delays of one or two hours are not uncommon during the highest tides while trains, such as the passenger-loaded *Coast Starlight*, stop in their tracks a safe distance from the water to await the retreat of the slough that temporarily covers the tracks. Moving trains and water don't mix well. Even the many tons of gravel that were imported at great trouble and expense during the construction of the rail line to raise it above the slough's 1800s water level are no longer sufficient. Change will be required to avoid the damaging impacts of a rising sea.

These methods of moving goods continued to evolve into the massive processing and shipping operations we see today. Where vegetables, fruit, wheat, and other goods had been shipped through these labor-intensive, expensive, and sluggish processes, today the movement of seaside crops from field to market is dramatically faster, more efficient, and less costly (in strictly dollar terms, setting aside the questions of impacts on labor forces, environment, and food quality). Refrigeration hadn't been invented a century ago; now huge plants that freeze vegetables in vast quantities stand within just a few miles of the fields. Sophisticated harvesting machinery can pack certain crops in boxes on flatbed trucks for shipping before they even leave the field. However, even with advances in technology, some unconscionable, backbreaking human labor is still involved in much of the harvest. Coastside livelihoods can be demanding and also dangerous.

Despite these global and highly industrialized commercial operations and tough social issues, at several busy roadside produce stands in Moss Landing a visitor can still buy fresh vegetables gleaned from the rich agricultural fields visible from the highway. Some of these simple stands sit near the very same sites as the warehouses that Captain Moss and the others built when they set up the wharves to move crops to market by way of the sea in the 1800s.

> **Today's working harbor is an economic engine with global reach, generating more than $20 million annually in fishing activity.**

Today's working harbor is an economic engine with global reach, generating more than $20 million annually in fishing activity. For example, in 2014, Moss Landing, Santa Cruz, and Monterey, the three small ports of the Monterey Bay, produced a combined 36 percent of all commercial catch (in tons) in California, ranking no. 1. Together, these sister harbors ranked no. 2 in total income.

Near the main docks of the harbor, the unmistakable odor of fish being unloaded, along with that of squid and Dungeness crab, mix with the musty smell of antiques from the row of a dozen antique stores lining the single road meandering through town. These shops cater to the tourists passing by on Highway 1. But just 100 feet away you can also buy the freshest of fish from a small cooler on the dock if you are so inclined and are willing to tolerate the occasional chaos of diving gulls, Caspian terns, and other birds calling out in a cacophony of ocean-side avian competition.

A handful of marine supply and repair shops that cater to the more than 500 boats—many of them commercial fishing vessels—call the harbor home. But for those visitors who combine the antique hunter's sharp eye with a fascination for all things marine, nautical oddities are still to be found for sale.

The harbor, the power plant, and the marsh

The harbor wasn't fully developed into the port it is today until reengineered by Army Corps of Engineer dredges in 1947. The corps decided to replumb the harbor to make it more usable and manageable for vessels. They filled the old natural river outlet, which was a mile to the north of where the port sits today, and created a new 20-foot-deep entrance channel controlled by jetties, opposite the mouth of Elkhorn Slough.

Moss Landing itself is hard to miss. There are two 500-foot tall concrete and steel towers directly across Highway 1 from the entrance to town (Figures 4.3 and 4.4). When not hidden by fog, these twin gray towers can be seen from almost anywhere along the 40-mile shoreline of Monterey Bay as well as

Fig. 4.3. The twin towers of the natural gas–fueled power plant at Moss Landing are a landmark that can be seen far out to sea.

25 miles out to sea, where they guide boats back to the harbor. They even provide a reference point at night, watching over the edge of the bay with their rings of reddish lights, like strands of a ruby necklace, blinking near the top. The towers stand out as such a clearly visible landmark they are included on nautical charts and aviation maps.

Along with a nine-story tangle and maze of concrete and steel machinery, pipes, tanks, and electric lines, these towers are the exhaust stacks of the Moss Landing Power Plant, a natural gas–fueled

Fig. 4.4. The Moss Landing Power Plant looms over the harbor.

plant with the largest electric power–generating capacity in California. At the time of its opening in the early 1950s, it was the second-largest fossil fuel thermal electric plant in the world.

This massive facility coexists with Moss Landing harbor and the nearby bay in an uneasy truce. To cool its electricity generating units, the plant can pull in, circulate, and discharge as many as 12 billion gallons of seawater every day, depending on how much electricity is being generated. This staggering volume of seawater is sucked in from two innocuous-looking intake structures within the harbor. The casual passerby would never notice, much less imagine, how much activity was seething under way through these screens and pumps.

In addition to concerns related to the array of marine life that can be stuck on the intake screens or entrained into the intake water, there are concerns about the effects on life in the adjacent ocean from the discharge of these high volumes of water once it has been heated to approximately 20 degrees above intake level. This warmer water is discharged through a pipeline that opens into the bay about 600 feet offshore.

Remarkably, this fragile coexistence has not yet resulted in more issues from impact to the adjacent Elkhorn Slough, a federal estuarine reserve covering California's largest tract of tidal salt marsh outside San Francisco Bay (Figure 4.5). This slough stretches more than 6

Fig. 4.5. Elkhorn Slough.

miles inland from the harbor and is currently home to the largest single population of southern sea otters—now more than 100—anywhere along the California coast. It also attracts sea lions and seals and is home to some of the coast's most visible populations of nesting blue herons and egrets, as well as hundreds of other marine, bird, and plant species (Figures 4.6, 4.7, and 4.8). It is a sensitive and vulnerable habitat that defines bountiful. Yet it is always under the shadow of uncertainty because of the industrial giant that shares its shore.

The refinery proposal

That shadow has a history. Both the large power plant and the small commercial harbor are minor players compared with what might have been. In the 1960s, Moss Landing was targeted for major development. Planning was under way to implement an industrial and commercial vision of the region encompassing Elkhorn Slough that included a nuclear power plant, a 50,000-barrel-a-day oil refinery, a world-class shipping and commercial harbor, hundreds of condos with several marinas along the slough, and a multilane freeway cutting right through the adjacent lands and across the middle of the slough. Among other intrusions, the rerouting and expansion of Highway 1 would have required construction of a massive bridge over the broad

Fig. 4.6. Great blue heron.

center of Elkhorn Slough. The refinery would have required supply by huge tankers coming into and out of Monterey Bay, made possible by the deep nearshore waters of the Monterey Submarine Canyon, with a pipeline to transport the crude oil to shore with all the risks that would bring.

Granite Construction, the very large construction company, Pacific Gas and Electric, the giant utility, as well as Southern Pacific and others, negotiated for large tracts of land to position themselves for implementing this ambitious and dramatic vision. The slogan "Where Water, Power, and Electricity Meet" was posted on signs near Moss Landing as part of the effort to build public awareness and support for this new future.

It was touted as the foundation for a new Salinas–Moss Landing industrial corridor. And by 1965, Humble Oil (related to Standard Oil, later Exxon, and today ExxonMobil) moved forward openly with its proposal to build the refinery and purchased more than 400 acres of Elkhorn Slough property. It planned to build and use a pipeline with a terminus on 5 acres of shoreline property.

The controversy over the proposed refinery split the community around the bay as well as in the Salinas Valley. On the one hand, proponents supported enhancing the industrial corridor with the development of the proposed oil refinery as a crucial step to growing new economic horizons, along with the huge tax benefits to the county that would have accompanied it. Those who sought to protect Monterey Bay's existing economic base against such industry, and the environmental consequences it would bring, opposed the proposal. These consequences included both air pollution from refinery operations, with its potential impact on agriculture and tourism, and the all-too-real potential of oil spills and other impacts on the marine life in the bay.

Ansel Adams, the world-renowned photographer, lived in the area and joined in the effort to stop the refinery. He made public appearances, wrote, and urged people to "Oppose this refinery project with all your strength of mind and heart." He had established a reputation as an ardent environmentalist, and is reported to have said that it was "not just the Humble Oil refinery we are fighting at Moss Landing, it is the whole industrial complex which will inevitably follow and change the whole complexion" of Monterey County.

Fig. 4.7. A snowy egret grabs a sardine.

By a close vote, the Monterey County Planning Commission sided with opponents and denied approval of the refinery project. But in an unusual move, the commission's decision was rejected by the Board of Supervisors, which had the ultimate authority. The board approved the refinery. Members of the public petitioned to reverse the board's vote, trying to stop the refinery, and ultimately Humble Oil backed away and dropped the project. It later relaunched the refinery proposal, with twice the capacity, in another location. It successfully landed the refinery in Benicia, a community located upstream from San Francisco Bay.

Ansel Adams believed the Humble Oil pullout was at least in part due to a frank conversation he had with the president of Humble Oil in which he described the potentially devastating consequences of air pollution on coastal agriculture. There is little doubt that his personal engagement played a role, along with the more than 15,000 local

Fig. 4.8. An adventurous adolescent sea lion owns a small boat at Moss Landing harbor.

citizens who quickly signed petitions following the board's vote to reject the Planning Commission's recommendation. The fact that the board meeting lasted more than 17 hours, until three in the morning, bears witness to the highly controversial nature of the issue and the strength of the opposition to the proposal. So too did the lawsuits that were filed challenging the board's actions. Opponents of the refinery even attended Standard Oil's annual shareholders' meeting to make their voices heard, using a novel tactic that has become more common today.

Environmental regulation

The demise of the refinery reflected a growing shift in attitudes toward development of the slough and the region, with an increasing focus on preservation. These efforts were part of the larger environmental movement emerging across the country in the late 1960s and early 1970s. These times saw the first Earth Days, the passage of the National Environmental Policy Act (1970), the 1972 Clean Water Act (the first major rewrite of the 1948 Federal Water Pollution Control Act), the Marine Mammal Protection Act (1972), the Endangered Species Act (1973), the Clean Air Act (1973), and the official formation of the National Oceanic and Atmospheric Administration (NOAA) and more.

It is an irony of history that much of this landmark environmental legislation that was created and passed by Congress—and that has stood for more than 40 years as a cornerstone of conservation policy—was signed into law by Richard Nixon, a president not initially

Fig. 4.9. Brown pelicans and a snowy egret find a moment of plentiful food, as steel culverts force sardines into higher density in a small area.

known for his environmentally protective inclinations. At the outset of his presidency, he was critical of the growing environmental movement. But he faced a Democratic Congress that would have overridden his veto of this type of legislation, as well as a growing public environmental awareness. His political calculus was that it was better not to engage in a losing veto override battle when, by signing such laws, he could curry much needed favor with a constituency he desperately wanted in the wake of his hugely unpopular Vietnam War policies (and later, the Watergate scandal that ended his presidency in disgrace). He later began to include environmental concerns into his public messaging and policy agenda.

This trend toward using the law to help protect the environment manifested itself along the edge of California when the citizens of the state passed an initiative known as the California Coastal Zone Conservation Act of 1972, which led to the creation of the California Coastal Commission a few years later (see Chapter 14 for more on the Coastal Commission). New, tighter controls over the permitting process along the coast were designed to further a long-term plan for coastal zone management with an eye toward stewardship. As a result of stringent restrictions on coastal development and the demise of the proposed oil refinery, the rest of the Salinas–Moss Landing industrial corridor vision collapsed. No nuclear power plant. No condos. No freeway over the estuary. No deep-water tanker port.

Some of the land that had been bought in anticipation of all that industrial, commercial, and residential development was put back on the market—and this time some of it was purchased solely for preservation. Beginning in 1971, the Nature Conservancy, followed by the Elkhorn Slough Foundation and others in later years, began accumulating land that now totals more than 8,000 acres of privately and publicly held, protected property. In turn, this led to the eventual creation of the Elkhorn Slough National Estuarine Research Reserve, permanently preserving 1,700 acres of this unique region.

This turn of events was fortunate for the slough's health and character, and contributed to the survival of a much larger habitat (Figure 4.9). It averted a wholesale change that would have destroyed vast areas that sustain wildlife, fisheries, agriculture, and now tourism. But this hardly means Elkhorn Slough and Moss Landing are untouched by the human hand. The relationship between humans and the slough had long been strained even before the aborted development plans of the 1960s.

Human-made channel between ocean and slough

The single biggest human impact on the slough came in the 1947 coastal "management" decision by the U.S. Army Corps of Engineers to cut a channel through the sand spit between ocean and slough to create the harbor we now see at Moss Landing. This opened the slough to direct tidal action from the ocean, meaning that the once semi-enclosed estuary, with its brackish waters, was now open to the ocean's saltwater from incoming and outgoing tides. That change began to inexorably alter the characteristics of the slough, its shape and location, and the life it could support.

Until 1908, Elkhorn Slough had been adjacent to the Salinas River, which at that time emptied into the ocean north of Moss Landing, more than 5 miles up the coast from its present mouth. This river had assured a large freshwater source bordering the slough, and the sand barrier to its west insulated the slough from direct saltwater contact and tidal action. A barrier beach and sand dunes still partially protected the slough from saltwater and the ocean even after the river mouth was moved south (with a little help from local farmers who were annoyed at the meandering river regularly flooding their farmland and apparently breached the sand spit to open up a new exit).

But in 1947, once the corps had rerouted the river and dredged the channel, the slough began to show telltale signs of its newer character, now fully exposed to the tides. The initial indicator of things to come appeared on opening day of the new harbor when the first low tide drained much of the slough. No one had ever witnessed such a dramatic drop in water level, and most of the slough's muddy bottom was completely exposed. One local resident recalled that low tide as the most startling event he had ever seen in a lifetime living along the slough. "I watched as thousands of squirts of water arose from the bottom of the slough, which had now exposed shellfish for the first time."

The dozen or so dairies that had ringed the slough since the 1920s built additional levees to protect the edges of their land because once the seawater infiltrated into the slough and the outlet was steepened through a more direct connection to the ocean, erosion began to expand and accelerate along the edges of the estuary. Building these levees had its own impact on the habitat. And on it goes, like a series of dominoes, starting with the decision to create the harbor and breach the natural barrier to the slough.

The decision to remove the sand barrier and create the harbor had been part of a plan to increase fisheries production that had been set out in 1943 by the U.S. secretary of war, who had envisioned a large, permanent harbor. But the impact on the slough and its wildlife was further compounded immediately upon harbor completion in 1947, when Pacific Gas and Electric began building its power plant, which opened just three years later. The threat posed by the power plant with the intake and discharge of large volumes of warm water became part of the complex human footprint that was rapidly expanding.

But 65 years later, we see the footprint also includes some hopeful signs: the efforts to protect and restore the slough and the sensitive surrounding coastal areas, the purchase of land to create a protected area, and staving off the oil refinery and the industrial/commercial corridor. It is possible to view the existing power plant as just a shadow threatening the slough, but the proposed nuclear plant and accompanying development that came so close to fruition would have had a much more far-reaching and extensive impact.

And after all these years, once a visitor passes the power plant, passes the antique stores, passes the restaurants and fishing docks, it is still possible to embark on an adventure that blends the thrill of exploration with the best the coast has to offer—heading out into Monterey Bay in a small boat. That journey begins in Chapter 5.

It's really a primal connection. No matter what is happening in my life, I can count on the ocean; it makes me happy. I'm always intrigued by the surface, the mystery, and I feel connected to it. But also there is so much going on beneath the surface that we don't know, so much of an opportunity to learn. Along with the beach, what I like about it is that it's always changing. It forces you to be observant, watching the tides, watching the way the waves are moving, for safety, for animal life, for birdlife, for sand, and the water. It is so dynamic.

I grew up in the valley, and I remember coming to the coast with my family during the summers. I remember being on the beach, and swimming. When I was pretty young, I recall being caught up in a wave, forced into a somersault and I was slammed onto the sand underwater, spinning. My head hit the ocean floor really hard with a thud. I didn't know if I would come up and I should have been afraid, but I wasn't. Luckily, I came up. But I'm glad it happened when I was so young, because in a second I got to see the power of the ocean and I got over the scary thing. And it taught me to be respectful of it.

Living near the coast now, I look at the ocean in awe every day, and I feel every day is fresh. I wonder what can I see today? The coast sort of seeps into the unconsciousness. I am very fortunate.

I think it is such a great place for children. I see people from all different cultures coming to the coast for the day, playing with abandon in the sand or in the water. It's very nourishing for so many ages and so many cultures.

—Coastal resident, age 62

5

MONTEREY BAY

In this moment, we find ourselves part of a classic seascape, human intruders on an ancient ritual played out over and over again throughout the ocean, throughout time.

Leaving close to dawn is best. Sunrise offers a powerful glowing light on each new day of coastal awakening.

Clambering aboard the boat may mean interrupting a hefty sea lion or two that have taken up station right on the docks (Figure 5.1). Unfortunately, these 600- to 800-pound creatures have recently become acclimated to humans around these docks, and there is little left of their normal, healthy survival instinct to jump back into the water when confronted on the docks. More often than not they stubbornly remain, often partially submerged under their weight. They bark and resist until finally, grudgingly, they may clear the way for a boat owner to pass and board their craft. Or not. They can be fearsome.

Everything on the boat must be carefully checked before departure. Safety concerns must be taken seriously even on a short day's expedition out into Monterey Bay. Because the shape of the bay is a shallow crescent moon, it is wide open to the ocean with the swells, surf, and related hazards to show for it. In this way it is unlike a more enclosed embayment such as San Francisco Bay, which has the protection of the narrow Golden Gate entrance, although it, too, has its boating hazards. The coast is both beautiful and perilous, and more than a few unprepared mariners have died here, tragically—sometimes even entire boatloads. For even though we may have the best of

Fig. 5.1. A sea lion finds a resting place near the Moss Landing harbor entrance, out of the way of passing boats.

preparation and experience, the coastline can explode with sheer, natural power that dwarfs our human capabilities.

After warming the diesel engine and casting off the thick lines, we carefully pull away from the dock. A glance at the depth finder tells us that 10 feet of water lies beneath the boat while still inside the harbor.

DEPTH: 10 FEET
TIME: 7:10 A.M.

Calm water. Cool air, light fog. No breeze. Powering slowly past the rows of docks of the inner harbor at Moss Landing, it is apparent that commercial fishing is not an easy life. We pass fishermen—and a handful of fisherwomen—preparing for the day ahead, clearing the decks, stocking up on supplies, refueling, repairing, tending to the many details of a working life on the water. They will be heading out for squid, crab, salmon, mackerel, halibut, sand dabs, ling cod, anchovies, sardines, whatever is in season . . . Monterey Bay and the ocean beyond offers one of the most diverse arrays of seafood in the world. The sheer number of boats we pass that are arming for squid reveals why, among California fisheries, squid stands out as the state's most valuable in economic terms and highest in catch volume.

Passing through the inner harbor, sea lions are spread along the other docks in twos and threes, barking loudly and jostling for position, and a little more. The sounds of sea lions, gulls, boat engines, forklifts moving bins of fish, and the clanking of repair work are familiar coastal harbor music to be found in the ports up and down California's edge.

A lone southern sea otter makes her way around the stern of a docked vessel, holding a large Pismo clam in her paws, readying to crush the shell on a small rock she has retrieved from the bottom to serve as a chest anvil (Figure 5.2). A nervous, passing glance at the boat going by is all it takes for this vulnerable otter to reassure herself she can continue her morning dining chores without threat from our noisy vessel. Our maintaining a steady course is helpful in minimizing any disturbance to the marine mammals. They like predictability (and distance) when it comes to objects so much larger than they.

A noisy western gull has the sea otter in sight and won't stray too far away. Squawking and swooping down, landing next to the otter, this gull awaits the loose morsel lost or left behind. Experience has shown this kleptoparasite that patience often brings a bit of a crab, or a scrap of shellfish. It must be worth the wait. This gull will bob on the surface alongside the otter for hours. Eternally hopeful.

DEPTH: 20 FEET
TIME: 7:15 A.M.
Still seeing calm water. Cool air, light fog. No breeze. As we leave the inner harbor and pass the last of the docks, we see dozens of Brandt's

Fig. 5.2. Southern sea otters use tools to crack open their prey on rocks they carry on their chests.

cormorants sitting on the posts and pilings at the inner end of the jetty. Although at first glance it appears to be pure chaos, a closer look reveals several young cormorant chicks in half a dozen nests tucked away atop the piles. Much of the activity is parental: retrieving goodies for the chicks, feeding them beak-to-beak, distracting would-be predators, sounding the alarm, and fending off other curious and sometimes threatening visitors.

In the golden light of the early morning sunrise, as the thin strands of fog melt away, more noisy sea lions can be heard. They come into view hauled out on the large rocks of the jetties. There are about three dozen. Combined with the smaller groups in and around the docks, on this day we see around 50 or 60. This number is down from the more than 250 that lived mostly in the harbor for several years, frequently hauled out on a large municipal dock. Piled up in a small living, breathing mountain. Noisy. Smelly. Active and competitive. Pushing each other around, climbing around on top of one another, and vying for the best position . . .

These large animals are comfortable enough in their size and numbers that they don't get too agitated by a lone adolescent sea otter trying to climb out of the water to join them. The otter's challenge is finding a pathway through the shoulder-to-shoulder mass of much larger sea lions. Sea otters aren't equipped with the right muscles and legs or flippers to smoothly haul themselves out of the water. Otters are awkward on land; sea lions appear far more capable.

In comparison to the large group that recently occupied this area, the fewer remaining sea lions are younger and thinner—many showing signs of emaciation—and clearly not doing well. The National Oceanographic and Atmospheric Administration (NOAA) labeled this phenomenon a "sea lion mortality event" during both 2013 and 2015.

The sea lions suffered huge losses in population, and adolescents have been deeply affected. The sea lion rookeries are off the Southern California coast near the Channel Islands. The adult females who normally supply food for their young have been preoccupied with saving themselves—the put-your-oxygen-mask-on-first strategy applied to marine mammals. The small fish they feed on have moved farther and farther offshore due to warming ocean temperatures. Thus, the females have to swim long distances out to sea, taking extended trips to get the food they need. This has left inadequately fed and ill-prepared pups stuck in the rookeries. In many cases, the young population that typically migrates several hundred miles to Monterey Bay has had to leave the rookery too young, underweight, and without the skills needed to survive on their own. Still noisy and smelly. But not happy. And definitely not as many.

Today, in sharp contrast to the shrinking group of sea lions, there is a raft of perhaps 20 sea otters across the channel. These mostly adolescent males are healthy, the shelter and bounty of Elkhorn Slough evident in their condition and behavior. They are resting, grooming, and playing at this point in the early morning light, waiting for the fog to lift and be replaced by welcome sunshine.

The sea lions are starving while the sea otters on the other side of the channel are thriving.

The differing plights of various species living in the same environment is one of nature's perplexing phenomena. The sea lions are starving while the sea otters on the other side of the channel are thriving. On the other hand, the overall sea otter population along the California coast is just over 3,000, and they are listed as threatened under the Endangered Species Act precisely because of the various hazards the species faces. The California, or southern, sea otter was thought to be extinct as the result of the fur hunters in the 1700s and 1800s. But in 1937, a small raft of sea otters was discovered off the Big Sur coast. They have been making a very slow comeback, but faltering increases in their numbers over the past decade gives rise to concern (for more on this, see Chapter 8).

In striking contrast, today there are about a hundred times more sea lions than otters throughout their respective ranges. Despite the current mortality event, from a long-term perspective, these sea lions have done very well in the past several decades. In the 1950s, their total population was estimated at about 10,000. By 2015, the population of the California sea lion had ballooned to 300,000 with animals found from the southern tip of Baja California to southeast Alaska, and as far as 145 miles upstream in the Columbia River (at the border between Washington State and Canada), where they feed on salmon. Many experts believe that the species is now at the carrying capacity for their habitat—that is, all that the environment can sustain. When their food goes elsewhere, which periodically happens, a wave of starving pups and emaciated adults is the result.

There are many other examples of different species experiencing remarkably different plights, like the 2015 crash in sea stars (the creatures often called starfish) along the coast, juxtaposed against the boom in sea urchins. The sea stars are urchin predators, so when a virus took out the vast majority of sea stars along the West Coast, the sea urchin population exploded. Ironically this, in turn, led to higher growth in the sea otter population because sea otters thrive on urchins.

> **When their food goes elsewhere, a wave of starving pups and emaciated adults is the result.**

Another case: the 2015 depression in anchovy population off Southern California contrasted with the simultaneous anchovy boom in Monterey Bay. The ocean and its conditions are constantly changing and not always well understood or predictable. The base of many species problems often involves the food supply, which is dependent on oceanic conditions. These, in turn, often move in natural cycles. But sometimes they are the result of our activity on or near the ocean, and sometimes even great distances away, on land.

We motor pass the end of the sheltering jetties, with a marker light blinking 24 hours a day to provide a comforting beacon for all vessels approaching the harbor and to serve as an entrance guide to the channel. We take a last look inland, toward the slough, to see the many birds vying for food. Near Highway 1, a Cooper's hawk silently alights atop a power pole, watching for mice or other small rodents that might hazard out into the open as the morning unfolds.

DEPTH: 50 FEET
TIME: 7:20 A.M.

Calm water turning to light chop. Cool air. Fog beginning to thin. The breeze is picking up. Since leaving the shelter of the jetties and the smooth channel they protect, the low waves of the bay have begun to churn against the bow of the boat. A look either to the right or the left, upcoast or downcoast, allows for a view of the long, wide sandy

Fig. 5.3. The remnants of the concrete ship SS *Palo Alto* rest in shallow water off the pier at Seacliff State Beach, where it has been since 1930 when it was towed to this location to become a visitor attraction.

beaches stretching away until they disappear in the fog. On a clear day, the pier and the cement ship (SS *Palo Alto*) of Seacliff State Beach are visible in the distance upcoast (Figure 5.3).

The piers at Fisherman's Wharf in Monterey are visible downcoast. Once out of the harbor, the surf is already higher, as waves pile up and crash on the beach in long lines. The mist sprays off the tops of the waves as they curl and break, blending into the strands of fog even as the early morning sunlight begins to catch the spray, making it sparkle and releasing an occasional rainbow. The din of surf is beginning to grow louder and starts to drown out the sounds of the squawking birds and barking sea lions.

The chill of the morning, the distinctive smell of the salt air, the golden sunlight with its grays and velvet blues in the sky, the white of the spray, and the green of the waves are the essential California coast, the edge of beauty.

A handful of kayakers make their way out of the shelter of the harbor channel and into the open waters of the bay. Whether they are hearty and brave, or merely foolhardy, depends mostly on your view of life . . . as well as on their individual skills, their respect for the animals, the condition of the waves and wind, and even the choice of kayaks.

Fig. 5.4. This 40-foot-long humpback whale propels itself up through the water's surface, despite weighing 40 tons.

It is a risky proposition out here in what has now become the open sea. On this day, the goal of the kayakers is to get out on the water and try to find whales, up close and personal. To experience the largest marine mammals on the earth in a way that will be unique and unforgettable. But experienced kayakers are respectful of these creatures and mindful that human activity in proximity to marine mammals can be disruptive and dangerous to the animals as well as to humans—and in some cases, it is unlawful.

The whale's vulnerability is masked by the relative disparity in size between a 12-foot-long, 60-pound kayak with its 160-pound human cargo on the one hand and a 50-foot-long, 80,000-pound adult humpback whale on the other. A large humpback is about the same length and weight as a loaded Greyhound bus (Figure 5.4).

Between a kayaker and a whale, it is not an even match, and we have been fortunate there have not been more disastrous incidents from these close encounters, as whales have been coming farther into the bay and more kayakers have sought this thrill in recent years. It's easy to forget whales are wild animals—and neither the whales nor the kayakers are entirely predictable. But there is an impact on the whales, as well, which is of concern, less well understood, and currently being studied.

At this point we pass through a distinct patch of ocean water that is curiously swirling in a way unrelated to the regular motion and direction of the waves. It also appears to be slightly different in tone and color. This is the surface plume of warm water above the discharge outlet for the cooling water from the Moss Landing Power Plant. Changed temperature. No jellies in this area. No other activity. Eerily empty and barren of birds on this day.

No whales are visible yet, and as we head farther offshore we leave the kayakers behind. Plenty of stray sea lions are plying the nearshore waters, feeding on anchovies. They congregate in small groups around schools of fish, leaping in dolphinesque arcs as they dive quickly for their prey.

From a distance they can be mistaken for dolphins, but closer in it is easy to see they do not have the power and grace to achieve the classic leap, nor do they have the dolphin's dorsal fin; it's really a cheap imitation jump. Because of their proximity to the active schools of anchovies, the sea lions are tracked from the air by brown pelicans, cormorants, and the ever-present gulls.

At a glance, this food fest looks like something straight out of a wildlife documentary. Surface waters roil visibly with anchovies or sardines. A dozen sea lions leap and dive for their catch. Pelicans perform their dramatic, sharp dives from high in the air, wings tucked back, each targeting a single fish, hitting and breaking the surface with a grand, high splash. It takes incredible eyesight to spot a single, small fish under the surface. With a surprisingly high degree of accuracy and success, they emerge with that fish in their oversize bills and work it into their expandable throats. Gulls and cormorants fill in the picture around the edges, getting plenty of leftovers out of the chaos of the feeding frenzy.

The tableau is suddenly broken by several arched backs and tall fins piercing the surface. Despite first impressions, these are not great white sharks, although they occasionally appear in these waters. This time, four common dolphins have joined the feeding fest—three adults and one youngster about half the adults' size. The dolphins are the natural leaders of this pack of feeders, moving more slowly, gracefully, more efficiently, and almost in a line. The exception is the adolescent, who darts in and out and is less directed, more into a morning of wide-eyed exploration.

The dolphins break the surface with their heads, with backs and fins arching, and they occasionally spout, creating a balloon of mist as they exhale. They reverse their direction periodically, returning over the same area to continue to track the same dense school of anchovies that is not yet depleted.

These Common dolphins are not the "spinners" found in certain other parts of the world, the ones whose dramatic, full out-of-the-water twists and turns make for exciting video clips and TV commercials. But these dolphins hold their own with the occasional surprise leap out of the water. It gives them a breath and takes yours away.

All of this activity is taking place in only 50 feet of water and just 20 minutes offshore from the harbor. The light fog continues to burn off as we watch the feeding from an increasing distance, continuing our progress farther out into the bay.

Without fanfare or other cue, in the midst of fish-roiled waters, a giant humpback whale makes its debut. Not content with just slipping quietly into the scene, it emerges seemingly out of nowhere from beneath the waters into full view with a straight-up leap. It first breaks the surface with its enormous head, mouth wide open and throat expanded to dozens of feet, taking in thousands of anchovies in one big gulp. Water explodes and cascades off its head and out of the sides of its mouth, before this massive cetacean thunderously crashes back down, scattering gulls, cormorants, sea lions, and even the nearby dolphins—but fortunately no kayakers.

But that was only the beginning. As if on cue, in identical fashion, a second 50-foot-long humpback breaks the surface right next to the first, doing exactly the same thing. It too takes a huge gulp on the way up with mountainous splashes and thousands of anchovies, and then returns into the depths with a crash to swallow its supersize mouthful (Figure 5.5).

The marvel of this particular day, at this spot, at this time, is that yet a third humpback whale joins the first two and also emerges for its share of the bounty. In its short but spectacular appearance, you can clearly see the jawline, with its long lines of ivory-like, tinted baleen gleaming, the many large white barnacles around its head, and the massive, accordion-like expansion of skin around its neck to

Fig. 5.5. Humpback whales sometimes hunt together as a team, breaking the surface with giant mouths full of anchovies after herding them with streams of bubbles into a tight ball.

accommodate the volume of water and fish. And its eye, large as a basketball. Wide open. Keenly surveying all around.

These three whales are engaged in what is known as "bubble feeding" or "bubble netting." They are working as a coordinated team beneath the surface chasing their prey, moving in a circle, creating wide curtains of bubbles by exhaling. The frightened anchovies react to these bubble streams by gathering together and then the whales, like cowboys herding cattle, draw the fish into tighter and tighter arcas. As this large ball of anchovies becomes highly concentrated within the bubble net, the whales prepare for their simultaneous attack. On a signal between them, one of nature's more remarkable communications, they all launch themselves skyward through the densest part of the anchovy ball with mouths wide open, breaking

> The humpback whales work as a coordinated team chasing their prey. The whales, like cowboys herding cattle, draw the fish into tighter and tighter areas.

the surface with their share of the school of fish now trapped within monster-size jaws.

The other predators retreat in this moment, clearing the way for the whales to settle back under the surface, leaving a telltale slick, smooth, sheen on the water—a whale print on the ocean. The sea lions and birds quickly return, well aware that while the anchovy jackpot has been somewhat depleted by three whale gulps, it's still a rich dinner buffet. The dolphins will return more slowly, since they are larger and had to give wider clearance to the giant whales. The bounty awaits.

We press onward farther into the bay.

DEPTH: 150 FEET
TIME: 7:33 A.M.
Calm water is gone now. The light choppy waves have been replaced by the beginnings of the larger, smoother ocean swells. The air is still cool, and a mild breeze off the ocean has picked up. The drop-off in depth from 50 to 150 feet seems quick, suggesting a steep seafloor below. But it barely hints at the sharp drop-off ahead and the unimaginable depths yet to come.

The water gradually changes color. In this part of the bay, it's a murky blue, not the crystal blues and brighter greens visible just a few miles to the south, closer to Monterey. The northern edge of Monterey Bay is backed by sedimentary rocks. That sandstone and mudstone, and the silt and clay derived from erosion of these younger and weaker rocks, tend to cloud the nearshore waters reducing visibility. At the opposite end of the bay, the coastline from Monterey to Point Lobos and beyond is backed by older and more resistant granitic rocks. Erosion is minimal and the sand produced is coarse, leaving the nearshore waters clear and ideal for snorkeling and scuba diving.

The granite and other older and more resistant rocks have been sculpted into a rugged and ragged coastline that stretches for a hundred miles from Monterey almost to Cambria. This steep coast was essentially impassable from the time of the expedition of Gaspar de Portolá in 1769 until State Highway 1 was blasted through the Big Sur area in the 1930s.

We are rejoined by sea lions and cormorants, searching for their prey from the water and the air. Now hundreds of common murres are noisily diving for their share of fish and demonstrating for their young how to make those deadly dives. Helping train the next generation.

There is so much churning of the water with this feeding that the air takes on a unique odor that combines saltiness with many other scents not ordinarily part of open sea breezes. It is a breeze that reflects a lot of work.

We have spotted a half-dozen whale spouts farther offshore, on the horizon. These appear to be more humpbacks. It is possible to tell the type of whale from a great distance by the size and shape of its spout. Each species has a distinctive spray, heart shaped for the gray whales, tall and wide arcs for the humpbacks, much taller columns for the elusive and more rare blue whales. Depending on the time of year, Monterey Bay may be host to humpbacks, gray or blue whales, orcas (sometimes still sensationally referred to as "killer whales"), even the less frequently found minke and fin whales, and others. Orcas used to dine primarily on whales (such as migrating gray whales) and still do when they have the opportunity. This is the behavior that gave rise to people referring to them as "whale killers."

As commercial whaling in past centuries decimated the whale population, however, orcas looked down the food chain and began to hunt seals, sea lions, and even sea otters, which required much larger numbers to satisfy their appetites. This dietary change is believed to be responsible for catastrophic declines in both Steller sea lions and some northern sea otter populations.

> It is possible to tell the type of whale from a great distance by the size and shape of its spout.

DEPTH: 250 FEET
TIME: 7:55 A.M.

The weather has stabilized, but the swells have increased in size, reflecting the strength of the open ocean we are now approaching. We pass through a cloud of thousands of small, black birds known as sooty shearwaters. They migrate from their New Zealand breeding grounds each year in a circular, cross-ocean, endless-summer migration. These birds leave their rookeries in the southwestern Pacific and make the nearly 20,000-mile trek around the entire northern Pacific, via the Arctic, to Monterey Bay. While traveling along our coast, they feed on small fish for several months before taking off for the return flight. But during the few months they are here, these pigeon-size travelers are an unforgettable sight, literally darkening the skyline over the waters with their sheer numbers wherever they gather in low-flying brigades just above the surface.

There is evidence that Hollywood filmmaker Alfred Hitchcock based his popular 1963 thriller *The Birds* on a well-documented, freakish incident involving hundreds of sooty shearwaters along the northern Monterey Bay coastline. Director Hitchcock had a summer home in Scotts Valley, a small city just inland from the Monterey Bay coast. During one of his frequent vacations from Hollywood, there was a frightening, real-life episode in which these birds were seen flying into people and windows of houses, shops, and cars.

Years later, through some careful detective work on plankton samples collected at the time, researchers discovered an unusually high level of the neurotoxin domoic acid during that unusual event. For some not well-understood reason, this toxin is produced by a diatom with the interesting name of *Pseudo-nitzschia*, a neurotoxin that, while harmless to the shellfish and small fish feeding on the algae, is concentrated in marine mammals and birds that feed on the fish.

> **Alfred Hitchcock based *The Birds* on a real-life episode in which birds flew into people and windows of houses, shops, and cars.**

The sooty shearwaters were seen flying in confused and erratic patterns, crashing into walls and windows, and dying out in the open, because of the impact of the concentrated toxicity on their central nervous systems. Entire streets and yards reeked of rotting fish the next morning. Out-of-control, maniacal black birds—why not make a movie?

We're still heading offshore, and the depth to seafloor drops rapidly from 150 to 250 feet in a matter of minutes, revealing the edge of the continental shelf and the beginning contours of a remarkably steep and very deep underwater canyon. At this point, if you could drain all the water, fish, a few hundred whales and some dolphins and sea lions out of the bay, the edge of a vast canyon, going down farther and stretching out wider than the Grand Canyon in Arizona would appear. Hard to believe, difficult to imagine, and impossible to see.

Another surprise. Risso's dolphins appear out of nowhere, jumping and racing in groups of a half dozen or more. These are unusual and not nearly as plentiful as the common or white-sided dolphins, two of the other most frequently seen dolphins in the bay. The Risso's have very flat faces and splashes of white across their slate gray bodies and faces. They're readily distinguishable because of their coloring as they rush forward, splashing and diving, giving only glancing attention to the boat as they speed past. In brief flashes while they are out of the water, it's possible to see the scars from their encounters with their primary prey, squid, as well as other dolphins. It is this scarring that contributes to their lighter color.

Plenty of murres are still screeching in the air on their way to hitting the surface and propelling themselves beneath with their momentum, sometimes as much as several feet underwater, to catch up with a targeted anchovy.

We are far beyond the sooty shearwaters when we begin to see common dolphins again, this time more than a handful. Dozens quickly turn into 60 or 70, then several hundred.

Although their lives are deadly serious and they must regularly kill and eat to survive, these dolphins give every appearance of being "playful." They seem to enjoy both the bow and stern wakes of our boat. They rush around the bow, surfing alongside the boat and then disappearing as quickly as they appear. They crisscross underneath and ahead and behind the boat, apparently fascinated and remaining engaged. But after three or four minutes they tire of this and one group peels off for parts unknown, while another takes its place wrapping around the boat. They are towering energy sources, quick jumpers and divers, and seem to know how to create their own turmoil and excitement.

After the energy and excitement of the dolphins dissipates, we encounter a single, large mola, or ocean sunfish, which is an almost inert animal. It simply drifts in the water, seemingly without purposeful direction, although it is, in fact, doing exactly what it needs to do to survive, thrive, and feed itself. The mola is one of the ocean's oddest looking creatures. Up to about 10 feet across (sometimes reaching 14 feet from fin tip to fin tip) and weighing up to 2,000 pounds, this fish can't propel itself like an ordinary fish, and mostly drifts along in the currents as it preys on jellies, which are so abundant in Monterey Bay. It is a drifter, like plankton.

The mola looks like half a fish, starting off with the head looking as you might expect. But as you look along the body it abruptly ends, no ordinary tail, and fins wrapped in way you wouldn't expect. It's as if the designer quit partway through the design phase. The mola drifts by as we slowly move onward.

DEPTH: 2,000 FEET
TIME: 8:05 A.M.

Less than an hour out now. The morning fog has already lifted and the swells are now smooth, regular, and large. The offshore breeze is intermittent, putting a light chop and some whitecaps back onto the swells. If you're prone to motion sickness, this is when you're grateful you took those precautions before you left shore. The bottom has now dropped off 2,000 feet into the depths of the submarine canyon, a real edge. It invites questions like: Why so sharp a drop? why here? how far down will it go? what life is down there?

But for now, the surface exploration continues, our journey remains focused on what lies—or shows up—at the sea surface.

The half-dozen or so distant humpback spouts are gone now, but they have been replaced by others, closer, in small groups of two or three. These are now near enough to be able to see that the spouts are followed quickly by the rise of smooth, dark backs with the abrupt hump in the middle, as the whales glide slowly through the water, feeding. These creatures are not setting up bubble nets. They are merely cruising beneath the surface, gathering mouthfuls of anchovies, breaking the surface periodically to breathe and monitor their surroundings. Every few minutes they make a deeper dive, which tips up their tail fluke in a signature flourish before quietly, gracefully—if a 50-ton whale the size of a bus can be graceful—submerging.

The powerful 12-foot-wide tail flukes have patterns that are unique to each animal, like fingerprints. Their exact shape, their scars, their barnacle clusters, and their other markings all make it possible under good conditions to distinguish one humpback from another. As these massive tails lift up out of the water before the dives, water cascades off the back edge in a magical, thin curtain of spray and bubbles.

Fig. 5.6. The humpback whale (background) and a sea lion (foreground) hunt in the same waters, for the same prey.

Then they're gone, slipping beneath the surface leaving only slicks of calm water, traces of just-vanished 40-ton leviathans. It is remarkable that such large creatures are able to silently slip under the water with so little disturbance.

As the nearby waters begin to roil again with small fish that we can see at the surface, the sea lions begin to appear again, as do the diving birds and a handful of dolphins. The food fest has begun in this target-rich spot. Soon enough, more humpbacks emerge in the midst of the turmoil, although they move slowly. One sea lion swims directly in the shadow of a humpback (Figure 5.6). Humpbacks now appear to our west, to our east, and north (Figures 5.7). All visible, all at once. Within minutes, we are nearly surrounded by 17 whales.[1]

The surreal transformation into an extravaganza of nature is aided by the appearance of a black-footed albatross, like an asterisk to add to the wildlife inventory. This is a dramatic bird that you can't miss—it has the largest wingspan of all birds, at 11 feet. It can live for 50 years,

---

1. All photographs of marine mammals in this book were taken with telephoto lenses to assure maintaining a safe distance away from these animals in order not to disrupt or disturb their activities, and to comply with important protections under state and federal law.

Fig. 5.7. A horizon full of humpback whales taking full advantage of an anchovy-rich summer's day.

a remarkable life span for any bird, and makes the ocean its year-round home.

The whales lead the charge in the feverish excitement, with the birds flying and diving to catch what they can around the edges. The dolphins maintain a strong, flashy role in the craze. The sea lions hang tight in the center of the water just above the whales, taking advantage of the herding of the prey that the whales inevitably cause. The humpbacks' sheer size creates tight schools of fish, even without the bubble nets. But this sometimes means that when a whale unexpectedly emerges from beneath the surface, it catches sea lions off guard, and they then cascade off while flailing to avoid being flipped into the air. With all the other loud outbursts of activity, this just highlights the chaos.

But everybody is eating! And the seemingly endless bounty of anchovies takes a hit.

It is now a true feeding frenzy. Pelicans are relentlessly aiming from high above and suddenly diving at their targets. Sea lions are sliding off the backs of the humpbacks as the giant whales break the surface. The whales blow salty spray 15 feet into the air before diving in a tireless quest for thousands of anchovies. The sound of that loud blow is distinctive. The repeated intense bursts are a surreal percussion accompanying the pelicans with their noisy, splashing aerial dives and the distinct sound of dolphins breaking the sea at its roiling surface. The spray from so many whale spouts drifts on the breeze, building into an eerie mist that challenges the sunlight. As the boat smoothly rises up the face of the now-larger swells, we find ourselves part of a classic seascape, human intruders on an ancient ritual played out over and over again throughout the ocean, throughout time.

As the exhaled air of the humpback's breath wafts over the boat, there is no mistaking the horrific stench. These creatures are magnificent, but their breath reeks from their diet of anchovies. It lingers, taking several minutes for the stifling air to clear.

Fig. 5.8. Slapping their giant flippers on the water may be a form of communication among humpback whales.

One of the more distant whales begins to slap at the water with one of its pair of powerful, arm-like pectoral flippers, each of which is 15 to 20 feet long (Figure 5.8). While not known for certain, some experts believe this slapping is a form of communication to other whales, signaling by making loud, unique noises that carry many miles underwater. This long-distance underwater talk is one reason why the issue of noise interference and disturbance by the U.S. Navy's use of sonar and loud underwater explosions raises such important questions about harmful impacts on marine mammals.

Some experts believe that whales' tail slapping is a form of communication.

The dramatic flipper-slapping behavior is usually carried out by a single humpback among a group, but today it is different. Within minutes, three other humpbacks appear and also raise their long flippers, repeatedly slapping them noisily on the surface. Today at least, it certainly seems likely there is more possible evidence of an active "conversation."

Another whale suddenly emerges within the feeding group in a classic breach. This leap from the depths brings its entire massive body out of the water and into the air. It hangs for just a few seconds, white water cascading everywhere, its eye clearly visible, before gravity takes over and it comes crashing back into the sea. The resulting splash is so large it can be seen with the naked eye from the shoreline more than a mile away.

The reasons for these spectacular leaps and the energy output required to propel the body into the air remain something of a mystery. Perhaps it's for fun, perhaps to signal others, perhaps to shake off parasites, perhaps to get a better view of its location and surroundings. Whatever the reason, it is one of the most beautiful and dramatic sights of the journey across Monterey Bay.

DEPTH: UP TO 12,000 FEET
TIME: 8:30 A.M.

At this point, we are far beyond the reach of a depth finder. We are more than 2 miles above the seafloor, suspended above the deepest part of the submarine canyon, like flying over the Grand Canyon but without the ability to see the landscape below.

That underwater terrain is, however, "seen" by researchers who are carefully studying many of the submarine canyon features primarily by using sound. This bay with its canyon may have more research institutes, scientific organizations, and educational and governmental entities poking and prodding, monitoring and measuring, than any other body of water in the world. The location of the canyon makes it a rich source of life and therefore a rich source of information about life, the ocean, and the effects of our interactions with the ocean, its denizens, and our planet.

How did such a canyon come to be?

Monterey's submarine canyon has been known for over a century, but there has been considerable speculation over the years as to why we have this chasm slicing across the seafloor. Most submarine canyons align with river systems on land, but the nearby Elkhorn Slough and the small Carneros Creek hardly provide an adequate onshore source for such a massive geologic feature. Even the nearby, much larger Salinas River is not of the scale that would support an offshore feature as large as this underwater Grand Canyon.

Research in the bay combined with other geological and geophysical observations on land strongly suggest that this canyon was eroded by an ancient river drainage system that played a critical role in the initial formation of the canyon. This buried canyon, named Pajaro Gorge by some, was the route that the drainage from California's vast Central Valley followed to the ocean for millions of years. It is only for about the last 600,000 years that the large Sacramento and San Joaquin river systems, which drain the Sierra Nevada and most of the interior of California, have discharged through the Golden Gate. Before, they worked their way to the ocean much farther to the south.

Further complicating the history of this interconnected terrestrial and submarine drainage system is the San Andreas Fault, which cuts through the Santa Cruz Mountains just behind the city of Watsonville, a few miles inland from the head of the submarine canyon. Everyone living on the west side of the fault is heading northwest toward Alaska at about an inch and a half a year as the Pacific Plate slowly grinds its way past the North American Plate to the east. Every million years or so, we move another 25 miles away from the location on the opposite side of the fault in our northwesterly journey. Monterey's submarine canyon is moving along with the western side of the fault, which over time has taken it farther and farther from the original inland drainage system that initiated this offshore canyon.

Ten million years ago, ancestral Monterey Bay and the canyon's sediment sources were 250 miles to the south of where they are today. Cores taken from the deep-sea fan that has formed where Monterey Submarine Canyon ultimately deposits its sediment reflect the changes in the geology of the source areas where sediments have come from over time.

What we see today is an old submarine canyon, formed millions of years ago under very different geologic conditions than those we see now. But it is that formation that gives rise to the abundant life we see today.

DEPTH: 12,000 FEET HEADING TO 10 FEET
TIME: 9:30 A.M.

The return to harbor takes less than 45 minutes and is relatively uneventful. Well, if you count seeing six orcas, thirty more humpback whales, and a few dozen dolphins as uneventful.

That's the abundant life we have seen today.

When I was 8 years old, we moved to La Jolla. From where we lived we still had to get a ride to the beach, but it wasn't far. I remember the sea animals, the jellyfish and all, the sea life was different then, there was a lot more of it. As kids, we ran into things you never see now, things you might not even see in an aquarium.

And I love dunes. Good sand dunes with sunset, heavy shadow, not a lot of footprints . . . You have to walk a long way to get out there. I sort of like some of these knife-sharp edges, typically with a lot of softness, from wind gusts?

Learning to respect the ocean also means learning to respect the rocks. They can be very sharp. As a kid, when I would go out to swim, by myself, I remember one day, a rough day in the cove, I was trying to come back onshore via some rocks. I didn't time the waves right, and I just got rolled onto the rocks. I felt pummeled and bloody. But I always felt really close to the ocean.

I love to see all these people here, especially seniors, getting out to the beach. I've seen that more in the last 10 years. I love spontaneous things, like the driftwood sculptures people have put up from the big trees that washed up on the beach after these recent storms.

I know there are a lot of people who care a lot about the environment, and I'm happy to be in a place where people care about that. I try to be aware of my own treatment of the beach, to treat it well. I love the ocean, but I really have a lot of respect for it.

—Beach visitor, age 45

Lost Neighborhoods of the California Coast

Sliding Off the Edge

By 2015, only 10 of the original 21 homes were still livable, and most of these were literally dangling over the cliff edge, with Highway 1 as their front yard and a 50-foot drop to the Pacific Ocean one step out of their backdoor.

California is an infant in the long history of civilization, scarcely out of the crib. You only have to spend a few days in Europe, the Middle East, China, or Japan to see buildings and cities many hundreds or even thousands of years old. A historic building in California might be 150 years old. The California missions, among the state's oldest permanent structures, only date back to 1769. This is like last week in the big picture of things.

Those other older and more worldly civilizations have had far more time to learn about safe building sites based on their long history of natural disasters: floods, earthquakes, and tsunamis. At least that would seem to be a logical conclusion, and a sign of intelligent life. But it's been said that there are those who make mistakes, and those who make the same mistake more than once. We have lots of examples of the latter group, and no region or country has any monopoly on a type of collective amnesia, the memory loss of past disasters.

Although "coastal retreat" doesn't have the same emotional impact on people as earthquake, tsunami, or flood, the record of past shoreline losses is not difficult to locate. A little over a century ago (1912), Thomas Shepard wrote a fascinating book entitled *The Lost Towns of the Yorkshire Coast and Other Chapters Bearing Upon the Geography of the District*. Mr. Shepard had some interesting abbreviations after his name on the book's title page: F.G.S., F.R.G.S., and F.S.A. In this volume, Mr.

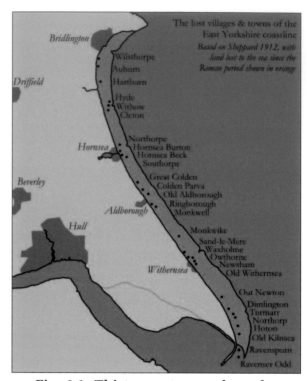

Fig. 6.1. Thirty-one towns along the Yorkshire coast of the United Kingdom have been lost over the past 2,000 years. *courtesy Caitlin Green*

Shepard, F.G.S., writes "that the sea has been encroaching upon the land is well-known, and the voluminous reports of the recent Royal Commission on Coast Erosion will speak fairly forcibly as to the importance of the subject. Unquestionably whole towns and villages have been washed away, and the loss of land and property is still going on." When an issue rises to the level of a Royal Commission, it is serious business indeed.

The Yorkshire coast, along the English Channel, has had a very long battle with the sea, and it's not over. Records of the locations of coastal settlements there go back almost 2,000 years to the time of Roman occupation. Shepard's book documents the progressive disappearance of 31 complete towns and villages during the previous 2,000 years (Figure 6.1). Very weak glacial clay, left behind by the melting glaciers of the last ice age, underlies the bluffs there and does

Fig. 6.2. The Yorkshire bluffs are retreating at an average rate of 6 feet annually and the mobile homes or caravans are simply moved landward to new pads as erosion threatens.

little to resist the relentless North Sea wave attack and gradual sea-level rise. This is an impressive list of lost settlements, and it does make one wonder if there is any collective memory in the region.

In recent years, however, the English seem to have found a solution in mobile home or caravan parks. The bluff top for miles along the continuously collapsing Yorkshire coast is now mantled with literally dozens of mobile home subdivisions. These have become weekend holiday parks and affordable coastal vacation homes for the United Kingdom's city dwellers. When the bluff gets close to the outer row of trailers to the point where bluff failure is imminent, owners just hook the mobile homes up to a truck and tow them inland a few hundred yards to a new site (Figure 6.2). No damage or harm done, no disaster relief or insurance payoffs. It's an interesting and resilient concept and one of the few land uses, besides sheep pastures and hay fields, which can tolerate the 6 feet they lose in average annual bluff retreat.

Disappearing neighborhoods

California has lost not only homes, streets, and land to bluff retreat; complete neighborhoods have disappeared from the state's edge.

From the redwoods of Humboldt County to the palm trees of San Diego, entire blocks of cliff-top homes have been lost to the sea over the past 50 years, and more are on the chopping block. The Big Lagoon/Ocean View subdivision in Humboldt County, Gleason Beach in Sonoma County, Bolinas Bluffs in Marin County, the Esplanade and Moss Beach in San Mateo County, Depot Hill in Santa Cruz County, Carpinteria in Santa Barbara County, and west Newport Beach in Orange County have all been victimized by the continuing disappearance of California's outer edge. The inland march of the coastline isn't a process that started yesterday, and it's going to plague and challenge us for a long time to come. Oceanfront homes are among the most expensive in the state, and few of the owners, understandably, are the least bit interested in letting the ocean have its way.

Most of the state's early coastal residents weren't obsessed with having an oceanfront house and being "steps from the sand," which has become a common real estate advertising theme in coastal towns today. Certainly the Native Americans who populated the coast in small numbers for some 8,000 years before the 1700s and 1800s concerned themselves primarily with proximity to the coast for purely functional reasons—access to the resources the shoreline and nearshore waters provided. Fishing and gathering shellfish were critically important for survival, yet many of these communities were mobile so that they could retreat from the shoreline, seasonally, and pursue other food resources farther inland when the ocean pushed the shoreline landward.

Not unlike the approach of the Native Americans, for most of the last 300 years early settlers usually built well back from the edge of the coastal bluff or cliff and generally avoided building on the sand. However, in the mid-1900s, following World War II, California's population exploded, particularly in coastal counties. The state's population doubled from 8 million in 1945 to 16 million in 1960. The subdivision and subsequent development of coastal cliffs, bluffs, and beachfront areas attracted new residents and immigrants who were delighted to trade the weather elsewhere—in fact almost anywhere else—for the sunny skies, sparse rainfall, and agreeable climate of Southern or central California.

Fig. 6.3. Broad Beach in Malibu has now been armored with emergency riprap until a sand nourishment project can be implemented.

But there was a little understood quirk of historical timing, a natural curveball, which went undetected until after this population explosion: the rapid growth years between 1945 and about 1978 occurred simultaneously with a period of relatively calm climate. This meant fewer and smaller El Niño events and the near absence of the natural coincidence of damaging coastal storms, large destructive waves, and elevated sea levels. In short, it was a developer and real estate agent's dream. Coastal land was subdivided, development occurred right up to the edge, and people flocked to buy their own piece of paradise.

All was well until 1978 when the climate shifted to a warm but stormier cycle with more frequent and damaging El Niño events, which lasted for about the next 20 years. The winters of 1978, 1982–83, and 1997–98 were particularly disastrous and woke the oceanfront home and business owners out of their endless summer. Many private property owners, as well as local government and state agency staff, who hadn't experienced such events in their short memory, were understandably surprised. For the first time they had to consider the long-term stability or survival of their property, businesses, and infrastructure. Coastal roads and parking lots, as well as campgrounds and restrooms, were damaged or destroyed, and the amount of coastline protected through armoring with seawalls and rock revetments[1] increased dramatically. The appearance of the state's coast was changing rapidly. The previously calm and peaceful shoreline became a war zone as bulldozers, front-end loaders, and cranes were imported to stack large rocks and build structures of all shapes and sizes designed to hold back the relentless attack of the Pacific Ocean.

Today, roughly 110 miles, or 10 percent, of the entire coast of California is armored or protected with some sort of structure, usually a seawall or rock revetment. Along the more urbanized Southern California coastline, 33 percent, or one-third, of the entire shoreline of San Diego, Orange, Los Angeles, and Ventura counties has now been armored (Figure 6.3).

Castles in the air

In times past, the earlier residents of the Yorkshire coast of England took their losses, whether castles, churches, or cemeteries, and relocated farther inland. And they did it repeatedly, for hundreds of years. As coastal property has become more valuable in California and the desire and ability to built larger protection structures have grown, the tendency has been to spend large sums of money, whether public or private, draw a line in the sand in an effort to resist nature, and then hold on and pray. The Army Corps of Engineers has made a business of this for decades. This has all been to the delight of

> There are many scenic but absolutely ridiculous cliff-top locations along California's edge where development took place but never should have.

coastal communities, property owners and elected officials who were frequently the beneficiaries of these massive public works projects, which guaranteed at least short-term protection for their investments.

---

1. A revetment is a sloping stack of large rocks placed at the base of a cliff, bluff, or dune in order to protect the coastline or development from direct wave attack.

Fig. 6.4. This apartment building and two homes on Depot Hill in Capitola are at the edge with a 70-foot-high unstable cliff for a backyard.

Some critics note that this also guaranteed the ongoing survival and expansion of the Army Corps of Engineers.

There are many scenic and nearly irresistible, but absolutely ridiculous, cliff-top locations along California's edge where development took place but never should have (Figure 6.4). Most of these sites were subdivided decades ago, when the coastal climate appeared more amenable to building, when there was no California Coastal Commission for permits, no geologic hazard investigations required, and when development wisdom was apparently in short supply but opportunities for profit were abundant.

Fifty miles north of San Francisco along the Sonoma County coast, Gleason Beach, sometimes referred to as "Malibu North," provides a case study that illustrates all these issues, particularly the clash of wisdom and profit incentive. Beginning in the 1930s, 21 homes were built on a very narrow strip of coastal cliff perched between State Highway 1 on one side and a steep, 50-foot drop to the ocean on the other. There was no local sewage system to hook up to, but this constraint didn't deter local developers. They built septic tanks on the beach, perched behind concrete seawalls; not the best solution but apparently acceptable at the time.

Fig. 6.5. Ongoing bluff retreat at Gleason Beach along the Sonoma County coast has led to the loss of over half of the original bluff-top homes. *photo courtesy Kenneth and Gabrielle Adelman, California Coastal Records Project, www.CaliforniaCoastline.org*

This stretch of California coast is underlain by a complex jumble of rocks, known geologically as the Franciscan mélange, which was scraped off the seafloor millions of years ago as one tectonic plate (the Farallon Plate) slid under another (the North American Plate). That collision resulted in churning up all the rocks and sediment and then plastering them onto the edge of the state. Some chunks of this rock are quite hard and form resistant sea stacks or small islets offshore, but others are quite weak, not really rock at all, and offer little resistance to erosion. Many of the Gleason Beach homes were built on the weaker rock. Over the subsequent 75 or so years, the winter high tides and storm waves, as well as rainfall and runoff, have led to landslides and slope failures that have taken large bites out of the cliff. Timber retaining walls, blankets of shotcrete (a special, blown-in form of concrete), and other approaches have been used in a desperate effort to halt cliff retreat and house collapse, but with little success. The cliff was too unstable, the houses were too close to the edge, and the seawalls on the beach holding the septic tanks were too low and inadequate to resist wave attack.

By 2015, only 10 of the original 21 homes were still livable (some marginally so), and most of these were literally dangling over the cliff edge, with Highway 1 as their front yard and a 50-foot drop to the Pacific Ocean one step out of their backdoor (Figure 6.5). It's hard to imagine the residents of the remaining perched houses relaxing with their stunning ocean view when they look to either side and see only the remnants of their neighbors' foundations left behind. To make matters worse, the San Andreas Fault runs virtually along the coastline, within a stone's throw. It's difficult to see a bright future for the houses remaining at Gleason Beach.

It's hard to imagine the residents of the perched houses relaxing with their stunning ocean view when they look to either side and see only the remnants of their neighbors' foundations left behind.

Fifteen miles south of the Golden Gate lies the city of Pacifica, which sits right next door to Daly City, a development of nearly identical houses that was immortalized by Pete Seeger in Malvina Reynolds' song about "little boxes on the hillside . . . and they're all made out of ticky tacky, and they all look just the same." Over the past 50 or so years, Pacifica and Daly City have both become commuter towns for San Francisco. Ironically, these bedroom communities have also been identified as planned evacuation routes in the event of a feared nuclear attack on San Francisco. A dubious honor at best.

Like Gleason Beach, Pacifica and Daly City straddle the San Andreas Fault, more or less uncomfortably. Over the years, homes, apartments, condominiums, and mobile home parks were built in Pacifica on a 70- to 100-foot-high bluff with splendid views out over the sometimes angry and unpredictable Pacific Ocean. The bluff here doesn't contain any rock; it's essentially dirt, although it's designated on geologic maps as "unconsolidated alluvium," which gives it a more permanent-sounding air.

In 1949, when houses were first built on one oceanfront street, The Esplanade, the edge of the bluff was about 160 feet away from the curb. Waves were slowly chewing their way into the weak bluff materials, however, and then the storm climate intensified. During

Fig. 6.6. Erosion of these high, weak bluffs in Pacifica led to the red-tagging of the apartments, first as unsafe to occupy and then for demolition.

the memorable and destructive 1982–83 El Niño, the bluff at Pacifica was repeatedly attacked by waves and retreated 40 to 80 feet.

The first row of coaches in a cliff-top mobile home park had their wheels put back on and were promptly towed inland, giving them a new lease on life. Tons of rock were placed at the base of the bluff at the end of the winter, which, for a while, managed to hold off any additional failure.

Fifteen years later, however, the next large and also memorable El Niño struck with a vengeance. The protective rock had by now settled deep into the sandy beach, leaving the base of the bluff at the mercy of elevated sea levels, high tides, and wave attack. By May 1998, with continued bluff retreat, the neighborhood was gone, as 10 of the 12 homes ended up on the beach. Over the next decade, erosion continued on the adjacent bluffs. Three large apartment buildings now found themselves clinging to the edge, with backyards, patios, and decks gone and backdoors opening onto emptiness. Because of their precarious position and uncertain stability, some of the apartments have been "red-tagged for six years," that is, posted by building inspectors as unsafe to occupy. The expensive emergency efforts to stabilize the bluff failed and erosion and undermining continued (Figure 6.6). Given the unstable and weak bluff materials underlying the apartments, the lack of any buffer zone, and the impending 2015–16 El Niño, it seemed like only a matter of time until demolition was the sole remaining option. Indeed, in February 2016, neighbors across the street awoke to an ocean view they had never enjoyed before, as the first of three 12-unit apartment buildings was demolished and trucked off the site.

The Pacific Ocean is 8,000 miles wide and doesn't care too much about a few feet on either side, whether it's Pacifica or Gleason Beach. When the last ice age ended 20,000 years ago, the shoreline at Pacifica was 28 miles to the west of where it sits today. In the subsequent years, as the glaciers and ice sheets gradually melted and the oceans warmed, sea level rose about 400 feet and the shoreline continued to move inland. On average, the march of the shoreline to the east advanced here at over 7 feet a year. With the well-documented increase in the rate of global sea-level rise, Pacifica is already on its way to becoming another disappearing neighborhood.

The narrowing of Broad Beach

Sixty years ago, in 1955, my parents took a big gamble, or at least it seemed so at the time to me. They had the odd idea that Southern California coastal property was going to become more valuable in the future. So they invested virtually all of their savings, and borrowed some more, and bought a lot on a coastal terrace about an hour's drive from where we were living in the San Fernando Valley. The area was simply called Trancas Beach at the time, and there really wasn't much there. Today it's better known as Malibu, or the western end of Malibu, and more precisely Broad Beach. They bought the lot for about $2,500 and a few years later were offered $4,500. Thinking they had hit the jackpot, they accepted the offer and nearly doubled their investment.

If you pick the name of a Hollywood movie star at random, chances are good that they live either in Beverly Hills or somewhere in Malibu. Broad Beach Road is one of those Malibu addresses "to die for" and that people spend a truckload of money to acquire. Today there are 114 individual beachfront homes with an average price estimated at about $8 million. One at the upper end recently went on the market with an asking price of $57.5 million. If you can't afford to buy, there is also a house you can rent for $125,000 a month. A lot of movie folks live along Broad Beach Road in modest obscurity. The problem is that Broad Beach is no longer broad. It has become Narrow Beach, and for much of the year, it's now become Not Much Beach at All.

> **Broad Beach is no longer broad. It has become Narrow Beach, and for much of the year, it's now become Not Much Beach at All.**

This formerly long, gently curved, sandy beach owed its existence to a resistant promontory of volcanic rock, Point Dume. British explorer and naval captain George Vancouver named the point in 1793 in honor of Father Francisco Dumetz of Mission San Buenaventura. Unfortunately, he misspelled it "Dume" on his map, and the name stuck, leaving Father Dumetz out in the cold. This point forms a littoral barrier or dam for sand moving eastward along the rugged Santa Monica Mountains coast. Just as a collision on the (the) Highway 101 backs up cars quickly, Point Dume halted the littoral drift of sand until a beach nearly 4 miles long and 250 to 350 feet wide had formed. Over 2 million cubic yards of beach sand, enough to fill 200,000 dump trucks, collected to create Zuma Beach to the east and Broad Beach, next door to the west.

Beginning in the late 1940s, small beach cottages were built in the dunes on the back of this historically broad beach. Gradually, they were replaced by larger homes, many owned by people in the entertainment industry. All of the homes are built on beach sand, and the septic systems were all installed beneath the sand in their backyards. The west end of Broad Beach began to narrow in the early 1990s, however, to the surprise and anguish of the residents. This beach loss has gradually progressed to the east in subsequent years, further increasing the nasty problem of exposing septic systems and threatening homes. It appears that the beach has been narrowing due to a reduction in the upcoast supply of sand, which, unfortunately for the homeowners, appears to be quite permanent.

In 2008, in order to protect the beach-level septic tanks and leach fields and also the homes (these can't any longer be described as small beach cottages), hundreds of very large sandbags were installed to

Fig. 6.7. One-third of the coast of the four southern California counties (Ventura, Los Angeles, Orange, and San Diego) has now been armored. *photo courtesy Kenneth and Gabrielle Adelman, California Coastal Records Project, www.CaliforniaCoastline.org*

provide temporary protection. They were temporary indeed, as they didn't survive the first winter. Sandbags, no matter how large or what they are made of, are not a good match for large Pacific Ocean winter waves. After considerable discussion, consulting, proposals, meetings, and finally consideration by the powerhouse of coastal permitting in California, the California Coastal Commission, the homeowners received permission in 2010 to construct a temporary rock revetment while they worked with consultants to develop a permanent protection plan (Figure 6.7).

The homeowners are clearly between a rock and a hard place, so to speak. The wide beach has narrowed to the point where any additional loss would likely put their wastewater on the beach. And it doesn't matter whether you live in Malibu or Monterey, having your sewage on the beach is neither a pleasant nor a desirable outcome. After many months of study and consideration, a proposal was approved to import sand—a lot of sand, 600,000 cubic yards of it—from an inland quarry in Ventura County. With a touch of irony, such beach sand sources, whether onshore or offshore, are typically called "borrow sites," giving the very misleading impression that at some future date, all of the sand will be returned to the lender.

The sand would be used to cover the rock revetment, giving it the appearance of a sand dune, and also to widen the beach, with the hope that Broad Beach would return at least temporarily to its previous robust condition. When all is said and done, this would be a $30 million project, paid for completely by the homeowners, who aren't excited or enthusiastic about doing this again anytime soon. The big unknown, however, is how long the imported sand will last. One very large storm at high tide or a major El Niño could ruin your whole beach, and a rising sea isn't going to make things any better.

> **Sea level is rising at an increasing rate, 8 inches over the last century and likely 3 feet or more this century.**

Sea level has oscillated throughout the ocean's entire history, which goes back well over 3 billion years. It's gone up and down hundreds of feet, thousands of times. The level of the ocean was relatively stable for about the last 8,000 years, essentially the entire duration of human history and civilization. The shoreline was a line you could count on. But it's not staying still any longer. Sea level is rising at an increasing rate, 8 inches over the last century and likely 3 feet or more this century. California isn't alone in having to face this problem. It's happening globally and those who are already being hit the hardest or facing the greatest future risks are the people, communities, or cities that are at the lowest elevations—closest to sea level. Somewhere around 150 million people live today within three feet of high tide. And lots of those people and places are already getting wet at extreme high tides and during hurricanes (like Sandy and Katrina), typhoons, or tsunamis. They won't have to wait until 2100 to be inundated. Many of the world's megacities, including Mumbai, Kolkata, Dhaka, Ho Chi Minh City, Guangzhou, Shanghai, and Tokyo, and a handful of smaller mini-cities, places like New York, Miami, Yangon, Bangkok, Jakarta, Alexandria, and San Francisco, all are within a few feet of sea level and will feel the impact of a rising ocean in the decades ahead.

Broad Beach isn't unique, except that many of the homeowners have names we recognize. There are no simple answers or easy choices for anyone living on the shoreline, whether Malibu or elsewhere. But decisions will have to be made in the not-too-distant future, and the options are quickly becoming limited.

I don't get to the shore as often as I would like. I try to come here at least once a week, to take my shoes off and get my feet in the sand, and get my toes wet. What has always attracted me is the sound of the waves, the smell of the ocean, the salty air and the great life, the birdlife, the ocean life. The ocean has always had that attraction for me, ever since I can remember. I don't know why: it's very magical, mystical, that connection.

My first recollection of the coastline was when I was 3 or 4 years old, I believe, and my parents were visiting my grandfather in Walnut Creek. We had come down to play, actually at this beach, where there is the cement boat. That was like 1963 or '64. We did a little bit of everything. I ran into the water, splashed in it, made sand castles, forts, dug holes, digging for seashells, watching for birds, looking for dolphins and porpoises.

For the future, I hope that we are able to correct and reverse the damage that we've done. Or at least attempt to start that move forward in that direction. It's very sad, the disasters that we've created that have affected the ocean, and the ocean life. I think that it will survive. It does tend to somehow come out ok at the end. Whether we do or not is another question.

I always encourage people to get out and volunteer to help protect the ocean and the shoreline, like for the days that they're collecting trash along the shore. Like the sticker says, "Take care of our coast."

—California resident, lives 10 miles from the coast

FISHING THE EDGE

*I have a vivid memory of an overpowering smell, and then the
sight of a massive whale being pulled up a ramp from the bay.*

The fertile waters along the edge of California have been fished
for as long as humans have occupied the coast. Before that,
seals, sea lions, whales, and a menagerie of other marine
mammals and larger fish took advantage of the fertility of these coastal
waters. It was a dinner plate of massive proportions.

The Native Americans stayed on the rocks or close to the shore
for the most part, fishing in the bays, estuaries, and tide pools. In
the nineteenth century, with the progressive arrival of the Russians,
Chinese, Japanese, Italians, Azoreans, and Portuguese, each group of
immigrants discovered a different resource they could harvest from the
nearshore waters to make a living. At different times over the past 250
or so years, these have included abalone, albacore, anchovies, crabs,
rockfish, salmon, sardines, sea otters and sea urchins, shrimp and
squid, whales, and just about everything else that had any value to
humans. Some were eaten fresh, some were dried on racks or packed
into cans and shipped elsewhere, and some, like the whales, were
boiled for oil or cut up for poultry and pet food, their bones ground up
for bone meal.

A half century ago, the city of Monterey changed the name of
Ocean View Avenue to Cannery Row in honor of John Steinbeck's
classic 1945 story. The sardine fishery made Monterey one of the
largest fishing ports in the world through much of the first half of the
1900s. The right combination of sunlight, nutrients, plankton, and the
fact that sardines are filter feeders that eat plankton directly formed

Fig. 7.1. A label from one of the many brands of sardines that were canned along Cannery Row in Monterey during the peak of the fishery of the 1930s and 1940s.

the foundation for a sardine industry that stretched from Southern California to British Columbia.

The fishery flourished from the mid-1920s to the late 1940s and, for a while, California's sardine fishery was the biggest in the Western Hemisphere. Over 700,000 tons of sardines were landed in California in 1937. During World War II much of the sardine catch, painstakingly packed into cans by a mostly female workforce, was shipped overseas to feed hungry soldiers (Figure 7.1).

During the peak of Monterey's sardine fishery, over twenty canneries employed as many as 8,000 people, stuffing fish into cans each year. We have nothing that compares with that today; in fact, nothing even comes close. The best we can do is the 114,000 tons of market squid, the no. 1 commercial species landed in 2014, which is just one-sixth of the tonnage of sardines at the peak of the harvest.

Sardine decline

Since the late 1920s, the culture and economy of Monterey's Cannery Row developed around sardines, as Monterey became the heart and soul of the fishery. From about 1945 onward, however, the sardine population started a precipitous decline. The fishermen didn't think that they could ever overfish the sardines, although harvesting too many fish was the initial conclusion on the cause for the decline. But Doc Ricketts, John Steinbeck's buddy who had been studying Monterey Bay and its marine life for years, had observed that many species seemed to follow cycles of boom and bust, somehow connected to changes in ocean conditions. Doc was right, although it took several decades for the rest of us to understand why.

Fishing boats brought back smaller and smaller catches until they finally reached a point where it wasn't worth the cost of fuel to go out after the few remaining silvery fish. Canneries shut down one by one, until the last lingering plant closed on Cannery Row in 1973. The Monterey Bay Aquarium opened in 1984 on the old Hovden Cannery site, using parts of the old building as exhibits that give millions of visitors every year a glimpse into the past.

During the peak of the sardine fishery, about 650 million fish were landed each year. If they were lined up head to tail, these little fish would have stretched around the world at the equator two and a half times. In short, a lot of fish were being caught. Following the collapse of the sardine fishery, several theories or explanations competed to explain what caused this economic disaster.

Perhaps foremost among explanations was the widespread use of purse seiners, the fishing boats known as Wolves of the Sea, which lowered nets a quarter of a mile long that reached hundreds of feet into the water. They simply overfished the population down to the point where the fishery wasn't sustainable. We have, unfortunately, now done this with many other fisheries as well, such as the Atlantic cod, the abalone, and many of our rockfish. The California sea otter and the northern elephant seal fell into this same unfortunate category. However, the latter, a rather odd-looking pinniped, has rebounded dramatically from what may have been as few as 20 animals over a century ago to over 150,000 today. The southern sea otter has been much less successful, having been reduced to a few dozen in the early 1900s and now numbering only a little over 3,000.

Another popular argument for sardine disappearance was the widespread use of the pesticide DDT on the crops of the adjacent Salinas Valley. During winter rains, residual pesticide washed off the fields into the Salinas River, making its way into Monterey Bay. Plankton concentrated the DDT and the pesticide was magnified, progressing up the food chain, which was believed to have ultimately affected the sardine population.

It turns out that Doc Ricketts, a keen observer of the natural world, pretty much had it right. Although these other explanations no doubt had impacts on the fishery (and in the case of DDT, devastating impacts on such spectacular birds as the California condor, the peregrine falcon, and brown pelican), his personal observations were

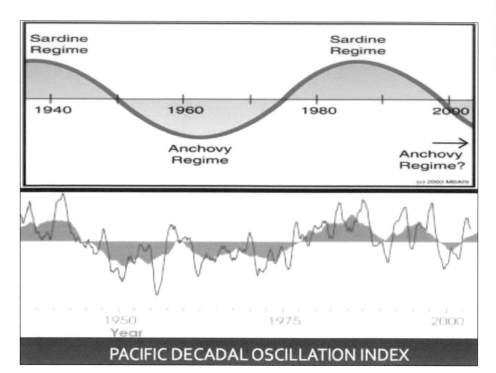

Fig. 7.2. The abundance of sardines or anchovies along the central coast (top) has oscillated over the past 75 years in response to changing oceanic conditions, which are represented by the Pacific Decadal Oscillation Index (bottom). *sardine/anchovy cycles modified from an original graphic by MBARI*

right on target: the oceans do go through periodic cycles. Through years of ocean observations, from ships and satellites, from the shore and at sea, we have discovered that there are major shifts in ocean climate and temperature. These changes can have big impacts on the abundance and distribution of marine life, particularly along our coastline.

In the Pacific Ocean these shifts or cycles have now been recognized as lasting several decades. They have even been given a name and an acronym, which of course elevates them to a new level of importance: Pacific Decadal Oscillations, or PDO cycles. Changes in ocean temperatures over large areas affect atmospheric pressures and this, in turn, affects wind patterns. The storm climate, ocean surface temperatures, intensity of upwelling, and availability of nutrients all fluctuate over cycles that may last 20 or 30 years.

These changing ocean conditions have a heavy influence on which species thrive and which decline in their abundance. So sardines come in cycles that may last 20 or 30 years, and in Monterey Bay they seem to alternate with anchovies. From about 1925 to 1945, in what is now known as a warm phase of the Pacific Decadal Oscillation, the sardines dominated, the fishery expanded, and the number of canneries increased. Cannery Row was on a twenty-year roll (Figure 7.2).

About 1945, the climate in the Pacific shifted abruptly to a cool phase of the PDO, the sardines were gone and replaced by anchovies, and Cannery Row came to a grinding halt. There was nothing left to can. This cool phase continued until about 1978 when the sardines returned again, although the market for sardines was much different than it had been 30 years earlier. In 1977, the last year of the cool phase, the commercial catch of anchovies reached 110,000 tons, while only 5 tons of sardines were caught.

In 1978, the Pacific pendulum swung back and there was a pronounced shift to a warm phase of the PDO, which lasted about 20 years. During the middle of this warm phase, about 30,000 tons of sardines were caught each year, in contrast to about 7,000 tons of anchovies. These population shifts are believed to be due to the types and sizes of plankton that thrive under warmer or cooler regimes and that are favored by either sardines or anchovies.

Fishing industry pioneers in San Pedro

Historically, the hub of commercial fishing traces its roots a little farther south than Monterey. San Pedro could be thought of as the Monterey of Southern California. Although in 1883, when two brothers from Italy, the Diroccos, sailed into San Pedro Bay (now Los Angeles–Long Beach harbors, one of the largest port complexes in the world), it wasn't much more than a dingy waterfront with a few buildings and dirt streets. The similarity of the San Pedro and Palos Verdes coast reminded the brothers enough of their home in Italy that they stayed and bought a small fishing boat. Two years later, in 1885, they started the first wholesale and retail fish market in the region.

Over the next 50 years, as the fishing enterprise expanded, San Pedro became the country's largest fishing port. Fifteen canneries were busy on Terminal Island and the port sheltered 125 fishing boats. The fishing and canneries were made possible by the experience and

Fig. 7.3. The Cohn-Hopkins tuna cannery in San Diego in 1933. *courtesy San Diego History Center*

knowledge brought by immigrants first from Italy and in subsequent years from Japan, Croatia, and Portugal.

The tuna fishery was at the core of a thriving community that evolved because of this unique set of immigrants. Many of the innovations that are used today by global fishing fleets to catch tuna were pioneered by these San Pedro operations. Fish canning began in the late 1800s, initially with sardines and mackerel. Not until 1903 was the process of canning albacore tuna perfected, and two of world's largest tuna canneries, Van Camp and Starkist, opened their doors in San Pedro (Figure 7.3). For the casual individual who goes out on a charter fishing boat today, there are even canning-while-you-wait businesses that will immediately process the catch you may be lucky enough to bring back to port.

Why California?

Why is the coast of California, indeed, the entire West Coast of the Americas, such a biologically fertile area? What has attracted sardines, tuna, squid, seals, whales, and dozens of other species and supported a coastal fishing-based economy for over a century? It's really all about something to eat.

The waters off the western edge of the Americas, North, Central and South, are some of the most productive on the planet because of the process of upwelling. During the spring and early summer, and

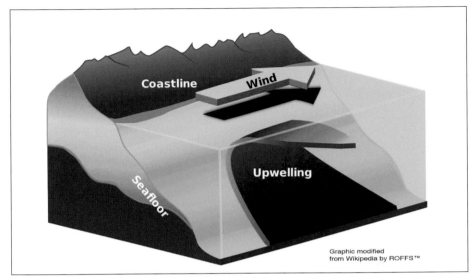

Graphic modified
from Wikipedia by ROFFS™

**Fig. 7.4. The process of upwelling is a major factor in the high
biological productivity of California's coastal waters.**

often in early fall, winds from the northwest dominate along the West
Coast of the United States and Central America, and help drive the
broad and sluggish California Current southward.

There is a mirror image in the Southern Hemisphere. It is known
as the Humboldt Current, named after Friedrich Wilhelm Heinrich
Alexander von Humboldt, a naturalist, geographer, and explorer from
Prussia (which is a very difficult country to find on a map of the world
today). His botanical work through extensive travels in Latin America
over 200 years ago laid the foundation for the field of biogeography.
But, with all due respect for Alexander, the current is more commonly
known as the Peru Current and was named after that small country on
the west coast of South America.

The surface waters of the ocean in both hemispheres are driven
primarily by the dominant wind patterns but are also influenced by
the earth's rotation in a somewhat complex process known as the
Coriolis effect. Gaspard-Gustave de Coriolis, a French scientist, first
explained this process in 1835, but then he was all but forgotten. In
its essence, the rotation of the Earth on its axis—at about a 1,000
miles per hour at the equator—causes ocean surface currents in the
Northern Hemisphere to be deflected 90 degrees to the right of their
flow direction. As a result, thanks to the observations of Gaspard-
Gustave, we know the surface waters off California, which are flowing

south, tend to move to the right, or offshore to the west in the spring and summer. We can't have the ocean level lower along the coast than elsewhere, so bottom water rises to replace the surface water through the process known as upwelling (Figure 7.4).

This deeper upwelled water is typically rich in nutrients, such as nitrates and phosphates, from the decomposing organic matter from life and death in the surface ocean that is constantly sinking to the seafloor. In the Southern Hemisphere, in contrast, the Coriolis effect causes surface currents to move 90 degrees to the left of the direction the wind is pushing them. So off the west coast of South America, the surface waters that are flowing north in the Peru Current are directed offshore to the west, away from the coast, also causing the upwelling of bottom water.

The combination of the nutrients, which serve as fertilizers for plant growth, and the exposure to the longer days and more hours of sunlight in spring and summer lead to enhanced photosynthesis or blooms of the phytoplankton, the microscopic floating algae, in those seasons. These microscopic plants, such as diatoms, are in turn fed on by the zooplankton, or the small floating animals like krill. The growth of the small plants and animals serve as the base of the food chain that provides for all of those marine animals higher up in the food pyramid: fish, seabirds, marine mammals, and us.

Globally, there are other upwelling regions off northwest Africa and also along the equator. All these upwelling regions taken together constitute only about 0.1 percent of the total surface area of the oceans. Yet they account for an astonishing 95 percent of the global production of all marine life and about 21 percent of the world's fishery landings.

It's all really rather simple: start with wind blowing over the sea surface, add in the earth's rotation, and you get upwelling that fertilizes the pastures of the sea, and everyone drops in for dinner. Once this abundance of marine life along the edge of California was discovered, immigrants who came from regions of Europe and Asia with long traditions of fishing realized that they could make a living here, at least for a while. Some understood there were limits to what could be sustainably extracted, and they respected those limits because their livelihood and lives depended on it. Others may also have understood there were limits but acted out of short-term necessity. Still others were hungrier for the quick buck, it appears, and either didn't understand or perhaps just didn't think or much care about the future.

Competition between immigrant groups

There was a lot of competition between immigrants from different countries for the water, the waterfront, and the catch, and most of it wasn't particularly friendly or polite during periods of deep hostility. Over time, each group usually found a niche, or moved elsewhere, and managed to survive, if not thrive. In some cases, the damage done still lingers.

For a variety of reasons, many fisheries that flourished for years and supported entire industries and cultures have now been relegated to the history books. Each fishery or resource has its own history and reasons for decline, although in too many cases it was overfishing, taking out more of the resource than could be sustained.

FIGURE 48. Monterey Chinese sacking squid for shipment to China. The squid, in the round, were sun-dried by spreading on ground. *Photograph by the author, May 21, 1924.*

Fig. 7.5. Chinese fishermen drying squid in Monterey for shipment to China 1924. *courtesy California Department of Fish and Wildlife and Scripps Institution of Oceanography*

The life span and reproduction rate for any of the marine animals harvested or hunted offshore also play a role here. The California market squid and the large whales are two extremes on the list. The market squid range from southeast Alaska to the tip of Baja California and are usually found within 200 miles of shore. These slimy little guys have made up one of California's largest fisheries in volume and revenue for years. From 2010 to 2015, they averaged 64 percent of the total commercial fishery, about 123,000 tons annually.

Asian and European immigrants first commercially exploited calamari along California's coast in Monterey Bay in 1863. Chinese fishermen rowed out in small sampans at night and used burning torches to attract the squid to the surface where they were netted. The catch in the earliest days was dried on racks along the shoreline and sold for export to Asia as both a food source and for fertilizer (Figure 7.5). The Chinese fishermen faced competition at the turn of the twentieth century, however, when Italian fishermen from Sicily brought their own methods, which expanded the fishery. Market squid soon became Monterey Bay's biggest catch.

At the same time, a striking example of the ugly underbelly of our history of cultural resource competition and the discrimination and outright racism that sometimes accompanies this dynamic was playing out at California's edge. In 1880, the California State Legislature passed several bills to implement new provisions of the state's constitution that required cities and towns to take steps to discourage Chinese immigration and to remove Chinese immigrants who were already within their jurisdiction.

> **One of these bills effectively banned Chinese fishermen from plying their trade along the coast.**

One of these bills effectively banned Chinese fishermen from plying their trade along the coast. They were prohibited "from fishing, or taking any fish, lobsters, shrimps, or shellfish of any kind, for the purpose of selling or giving to another person to sell." Another bill prohibited counties, cities, or towns from granting business licenses to these same individuals.

Three Chinese fishermen who were imprisoned for fishing in the face of the new ban filed a legal challenge in a habeas corpus action. The court responded by overturning the ban and releasing the fishermen, finding they were being held in violation of the U.S. Constitution. The court concluded the legislative prohibition violated the Constitution's equal protection provision, noting that subjecting "the Chinese to other and entirely different punishments, pains, and penalties than those to which others are subjected, [is to deny] them the equal protection of the laws, contrary to those provisions of the Constitution."

This victory for the principles of equality came too late for these fishermen. By then they had been forced to move on to find other livelihoods along the coast. Some turned to reclaiming submerged shoreline marshes and planting crops. In many instances that new coastal acreage remains under cultivation to this day.

Before long, word got out about abundant squid along the coast, and fishermen from Italy and Yugoslavia immigrated to the San Pedro and Santa Barbara areas and began to harvest squid and then sardines. Over time, based on the peak in the squid spawning periods, one fishery developed north of Point Conception, primarily in the Monterey Bay area, operating from April through September. Along the Southern California coast, the squid-spawning period and fishery generally runs later, from October through March. Squid fishing is still a nocturnal business, and the boats use very bright lights to attract these cephalopods to the surface where they are netted. Today, sometimes on a clear dark night, you can see the eerie blazing lights of a group of a dozen squid boats tracking their prey in and around Monterey Bay.

Almost the entire global market squid catch is from California's shallow offshore waters. A small amount goes directly to fish markets or is sold as bait, but the great majority is frozen and shipped overseas where it appears on plates as calamari, sliced, diced, breaded, and deep fried.

California calamari are very sensitive to water temperatures. The harvest typically drops abruptly with the warmer water temperatures and reduced upwelling that accompanies El Niño conditions, but then rebounds when cooler La Niña waters return. In strong El Niño years with particularly warm water and nutrient poor conditions, there may be no squid catch at all.

The market squid, like a number of other "forage fish" species, including sardines, herring, and anchovies, are also an important food source for many marine mammals and seabirds as well as a number of fish species. Sadly, the life of a squid is quite short, about ten months at best, so they have to pack a lot into that short life. They grow up fast, reach maturity quickly, and spawn, laying thousands of eggs, and then it's all over for your average market squid.

Whaling

At the opposite end of the size spectrum, whales take years to reach maturity, five to ten years for many species. They give birth to only a single calf, generally every two to three years. Whales can live for 50 to 90 years, depending on whether they are blue, gray, or humpback, etc. But because of their low reproduction rate and a gestation period averaging about twelve months, populations were seriously depleted during the peak of the whaling era.

Shore whaling in California began in 1854 in Monterey, when Captain John Davenport, an immigrant and whaler from Rhode Island, looked offshore one clear morning and noticed whales spouting almost in his backyard. More likely than not, Captain John was witnessing the annual migration of gray whales. Each fall they swim 5,000 to 6,000 miles south from their summer feeding grounds in the Bering Sea to the shallow lagoons of Baja California, where they give birth to calves and then breed. Gray whales when born typically weigh 1,000 to 1,500 pounds and consume copious amounts of milk, up to 300 gallons a day, for their first year of life. Several months after birth, mothers and calves, with a few fathers thrown in for good measure, swim the 5,000 to 6,000 miles back to the Bering Sea off Alaska, hugging the California coast the entire way and passing right by Monterey again.

Whaling in Captain Davenport's native New England began way back in the 1600s, not long after the Pilgrims landed. Once the whalers depleted the local animals, however, whaling vessels headed farther offshore and soon were sailing to equatorial waters where whales were still plentiful. Ships were usually out for months at a time, until their barrels were full of oil. But whaling in the days of Captain Ahab and Moby-Dick was a difficult and dangerous life. Whalers spent long periods at sea, rowing after large and increasingly angry whales in longboats

Whaling in the days of Captain Ahab and Moby-Dick was a difficult and dangerous life.

using hand-thrown harpoons. Sometimes hunts didn't go as planned and whalers didn't all come back alive.

A light went on as soon as John Davenport discovered that whales were passing within view of Monterey. He soon recruited a dozen Portuguese men to hunt humpback and gray whales using hand lances and harpoons thrown from small boats rowed from shore. Thus began the enterprise known as shore whaling, also dangerous, but most of the time, the men got to return home at night.

Even when they successfully harpooned a whale, their job wasn't over. They still had to get a 15- to 40-ton animal back to the beach for processing, by rowing, or if they were lucky, with the aid of a sail. Not an easy task. A fairly large percentage of the harpooned whales, especially humpbacks, were lost when they sank. It wasn't particularly pleasant for the whales or the whalers.

Davenport's business proved to be economically marginal at best, although it soon attracted considerable competition. The Portuguese whalers who had taken over shore whaling from Captain Davenport were evidently more successful as they gradually moved north and south to establish a series of whaling stations along the state's entire 1,100-mile-long coast. From the mid-1850s to about the 1880s, as many as eighteen stations were processing these behemoths along the California shoreline—at Crescent City, Bolinas Bay, Half Moon Bay, Pigeon Point, Soquel, Monterey (which had two stations), Carmel Bay/ Point Lobos, Point Sur, San Simeon, Port Harford (Avila or Port San Luis), Cojo Viejo (Point Conception), Goleta, Portuguese Bend and Dead Man's Island (San Pedro), and San Diego Bay, which also had two stations.

The world of whaling suffered a dramatic change following the discovery of oil in Titusville, Pennsylvania, in 1859. The oil was refined to produce kerosene for lighting and heating, virtually eliminating the most important use of whale oil, and the economics of whaling quickly declined, along with the value of whale oil. By 1886, only five of California's whaling stations were still operating. While the shore whalers certainly reduced the number of whales along California's coast, it's not clear that this reduction in their numbers was the most significant factor in the decline of the industry. Simple economics played a key role. The availability of kerosene as a source of light and heat, refined from oil pumped somewhat effortlessly from

**Fig. 7.6. Sperm whale being brought into Frederick Dedrick's
Moss Landing whaling factory in 1919.**
photo courtesy Monterey County Free Libraries

the ground, at lower prices than whale oil, essentially pushed the
whaling business over the edge, globally.

Despite the economic challenges that the industry faced, in the
early 1900s new whale-hunting technologies—steam-powered chase
boats and the harpoon cannon—led to a brief resurgence in whaling.
In 1919, the California Sea Products Company and a Norwegian
whaler, Captain Frederick Dedrick, selected Moss Landing as the
site for a new commercial whaling factory (Figure 7.6). Two new
steam-driven boats with bow-mounted harpoon cannons would
make whaling in the bay much easier for the whalers but much more
dangerous for the whales. Whalers used harpoon cannons and also
shoulder-held harpoon guns to get a line on the whale. They usually
followed this by a bomb lance shot from a gun, or in some cases, the
harpoon and bomb gun were mounted together on a pole and thrown
as one would an ordinary harpoon. The harpoon penetrated into the
whale a certain distance, engaging a trigger and firing the explosive.

While whales stood a reasonable chance of evading the older
shore whalers who had to row for all they were worth, steam-powered
ships and the harpoon cannon and bomb gun led to much higher kill
rates. An interview with one of the harpoon gunners who worked
out of the Richmond station, the last whaling facility on the West

Fig. 7.7. Humpback whale brought in to Richmond Whaling Station, the last operating whaling factory in California.
photo courtesy John Caito Sr.

Coast, described the injuries that befell many of the gunners as well. Whaling has always been a risky and tragic business, no matter what technology or tools have been used.

Data from logbooks of whaling stations at Moss Landing (1919–22 and 1924) and also Trinidad on the far north coast (1920 and 1922–26) record the taking of 2,111 whales, including 1,871 humpbacks, 177 fin whales, 26 sei whales, 3 blue whales, 12 sperm whales, 7 gray whales, and 15 others. This works out to bringing in a whale every four or five days for each of these two stations, with almost 90 percent of them humpbacks whales.

Within several years of the whaling resurgence in Monterey Bay, the new tools were proving very deadly and effective and the whales had become both scarce and wary. We know today that whales are intelligent creatures and have well-established forms of communication that reach over hundreds, even thousands, of miles. By 1924, the last whale had been brought ashore and the Moss Landing site was closed, bringing an end to 70 years of whaling in Monterey Bay.

There was one final and somewhat surprising chapter in the history of California's whaling. In 1956, 32 years after whaling in Monterey Bay ended, a station opened for business in Richmond along the eastern shoreline of San Francisco Bay. Perhaps the whale population had recovered sufficiently for whaling to become profitable again, or perhaps some new markets, like pet food, spiked the economics.

The Richmond Whaling Station's boats harpooned whales offshore along their California coastal migration routes and towed them through the Golden Gate, across San Francisco Bay to reach Richmond (Figure 7.7), where they were pulled up a ramp by their tails with huge hooks. Station records indicate that in a typical year they brought in about 175 finbacks, humpbacks, and sperm whales. Using very large knives, huge slabs of the blubber were cut off and then cooked down in big pots, which produced a very strong stench. Nearby waters were usually filled with blood, brine, and the remains of the processed whales.

The end of whaling

These are the memories I have as a young boy seeing the Richmond Whaling Station on the second day of our annual summer camping trip. My dad drove our trusty overloaded station wagon onto a ferry for the trip across to San Rafael and the beginning of the Redwood Highway. This was in the early 1950s, well before the Richmond–San Rafael Bridge was built. Driving the car onto a ferryboat with the sound and smell of the diesel engines, the boat rolling with the swell, the whistle as we cast off, and then standing on the upper deck in the salty air for the bay crossing was about as good as it got in those days.

On one of those early trips, I clearly recall my dad stopping the car along the waterfront area of Richmond and saying "Hey I want to show you guys something." My two brothers and I were always up for getting out of the car and seeing almost anything, so we jumped out and followed my dad across the highway. I have a vivid memory of an overpowering smell, and then the sight of a massive whale being pulled up a ramp from the bay. I was 13 or 14 at the time, yet the sight and smell that morning is still pretty clear in my mind.

We were seeing that Richmond Whaling Station, one of the last two whaling stations in America, which was active until 1971. The Del Monte Fish Company opened it in 1956, not far from the Point San Pablo Yacht Harbor. During its fifteen years of operation, the forty-man crew boasted that they could reduce a humpback whale to oil, poultry meal, and pet food in an hour and a half.

It's impossible to imagine this happening today as values have changed, but those were different times and the whaling station crew was working every day to make a living, just like everyone else. We didn't have widespread support for the protection of the whales. We didn't have NOAA, the Environmental Protection Agency, Environmental Impact Reports, the Endangered Species Act, or the Marine Mammal Protection Act in 1970. In 1971, however, Secretary of Commerce Maurice Stans signed the paperwork that ended whaling in the United States once and for all, and the Richmond Whaling Station was abandoned, ending 120 years of whaling along the California coast.

Today, whale populations have slowly rebounded but are still not believed to be anywhere near the numbers that passed along our coast before human intervention. In fact, several species of whales— including some humpbacks—are still protected under the Endangered Species Act because their populations are not at sustainable levels.

The edge of California has always been a hot spot for marine life from the bottom to the top of the food chain. This has translated to lots of stuff that we can potentially eat or use, or that at least one group of pioneering immigrants or another found tasty or worth harvesting. The abundance of some of these marine animals, whether fish or something else edible, not only has fluctuated over time because of natural climate or ocean cycles, but also has been profoundly affected by the top dogs on the planet, us.

There are a lot of people on the earth, about 7.4 billion today, and we have developed tools, technologies, appetites, and, unfortunately, the ability to harvest just about anything in the ocean down to the edge of extinction. There are lots of examples of species that were overharvested or overexploited, but we have learned a few lessons. Now there are some protective measures in place, like the Endangered Species Act, fishing and hunting quotas, and other important policies. Some animals have made or are making slow comebacks as a direct result of these efforts. But we have also learned that it takes constant vigilance, research, and action to keep the balance from tipping against the vulnerable members of the animal kingdom.

I was first introduced to the coast on a vacation, and I fell in love with the natural beauty, and the culture, too. There is a confluence of mountains and sea, of redwood forests and ocean kelp forests. There's a beauty of nature and an interconnectedness of life that is something that I never fully appreciated before in all its complexity. I don't think I understood the true interwoven nature of the environment. But people understand that here in a different way, in a way they don't in other places, I think.

The ocean supports us all, the ocean protects us, and we are better off; without it we all die. But beyond that the ocean and the ocean ecology is almost spiritual, it is like a life force that deserves preserving for its own sake. It is a beautiful, wonderful thing—the strength of life is more apparent here. The concept of preserving that space and by doing that hopefully preserving the greater world really appeals to me so it feels like it is something I need to do.

The coast has an enormous natural energy. It's a compelling natural environment to enjoy and spend a lot of time outdoors, and seems like one of the finest places to be able to do that. There is a vitality, with the pounding of the waves and the big storms that sweep in off the Pacific, but also there's a strength of life that is more apparent here on the coast than it is in a lot of other places, I think, and you can get caught up in it.

The culture is part of it. But above all else it is simply a beautiful place.

—Coastal docent, age 50

THE SEA OTTER
SURVIVAL STORY

Superstars in Trouble Again

The appetite for this rich, dense fur was insatiable. Throughout much of the 1800s, seafaring expeditions plied the ocean waters along the northern coast and relentlessly hunted these beautiful creatures. There was no effort to restrain the bloody harvest. No effort to limit the take to sustainable levels in order to assure a future harvest. No restrictions on number, size, season, or even on the taking of moms and pups. You don't have to be a marine biologist to understand that this is a recipe that pretty much eliminates the future of a species.

And so it was that by the end of the century, this species had been hunted to extinction. Not close to extinction, but fully extinguished. Its great commercial value had, in a very short time, brought about its demise. Now all that remain are sketches. Impressions from another era.

Such is the story of the Atlantic Ocean's sea mink, a close relative of the mink and the sea otter. It can happen.

Since the first time I spied a sea otter in the kelp, I was hooked. This smallest of marine mammals was bobbing its furry head in the bright sun just above the water beyond the surf

Fig. 8.1. In order to stay warm, the sea otter has the densest fur of any animal, with up to a million individual hairs per square inch.

zone a few miles north of Big Sur. At the time, in 1966, southern (or California) sea otters were rare and hard to find. I didn't know much about them. But to me they were playful, mysterious, and beautiful. I did not know then that the otters I was seeing were just in the early stages of a halting recovery from near extinction.

Victims of their own success

Sea otters have been the victims of their own success. Twice.

The sea otter we know today as a creature of the ocean (the species *Enhydra lutris*) has adapted from a terrestrial otter and in this way is like all the other marine mammals. At one point, whales, sea lions, seals, dolphins, and the other marine mammals were land creatures, and they evolved into the sea. Sea otters are merely the most recent to make that transformation, somewhere in the range of 5 to 7 million years ago. But unlike the other marine mammals, all of which meet the challenge of surviving in the freezing-cold ocean water with a thick, insulating layer of blubber, sea otters rely on a completely different mechanism for insulation. Its successful adaptation from a land animal to a sea creature was only possible because of the development of the most rich, dense fur known in the animal kingdom

(Figure 8.1). They also have extremely high food consumption requirements to fuel the energy needed to survive in the cold and the voracious appetites that go along with those demands.

Despite their vital adaptations, the success of that marvelous fur has been both their salvation and their curse. At the same time that it protects them from freezing to death in the chilly ocean waters, our insatiable appetite for the fur's beauty and inherent warmth brought the species nearly to extinction during the eighteenth and nineteenth centuries. After the sea otter had thrived in the ocean for nearly 5 million years, 200 years of exploitation by human contact decimated the sea otter population, killing more than a million animals. It isn't an exaggeration to say this very effective survival mechanism nearly backfired on the species.

Given the luxurious, fine texture of the sea otter's fur, it is not surprising humans coveted the fur for its beauty and warmth. It consists of two layers, with up to a million individual hairs in every square inch at its most dense. The longer guard hairs protect the shorter and more dense underfur in a complex structure designed to keep water and cold out and warmth in. Today, because of its remarkably effective structure, there are even budding commercial efforts in wetsuit design that emulate the fur, using synthetic materials, in what may be a superior approach over traditional wetsuit technology.

For sea otters, the double layer of fur is still not enough to stay warm in the ocean. They also must spread some of their own natural oils onto the fur to help repel water, and they blow small bubbles of air into the underfur to create yet another layer of insulation close to their skin. When you observe a sea otter rolling around in the ocean, looking as if it is chasing its tail, or nuzzling its own fur—like a dog or cat might chase after fleas—it is actually grooming and trying to force more air into its fur or to spread the natural oils. This vital act of grooming accounts for an important part of an otter's typical daily activities. The failure of any element of this delicately balanced anti-freezing design will quickly become a threat to the otter's survival.

It is primarily for this reason that concern over crude oil spills, among other threats, is so high when it comes to sea otters. Any damage to the insulating capacity of the fur, or to the otter's ability to effectively tend to the fur, can prove quickly fatal. Harm can come by

Fig. 8.2. A sea otter mom grabs her pup to pull it away from danger.

way of thick crude oil damaging the fur directly, or the sea otter may ingest the toxic oil or powerful fumes during its extensive grooming. Any wound or other form of injury that impairs its ability to groom can be equally dangerous.

Sea otter pups, as with the youngest members of so many species, are even more vulnerable. For added protection, pups have their own special twist on the fur design. For the first couple of months of their lives, they have a longer, shaggy outer layer of fur that has the effect of creating so much buoyancy, like an air pocket surrounding them, that they can't dive beneath the water's surface for more than a few seconds. This furry life preserver is necessary to prevent them from drowning, since they are not born instinctively knowing how to swim or to dive. They must learn these survival skills from their moms, and until they can safely stay on the surface without sinking, they rely on their fur to keep them afloat. The adult females must always be vigilant, keeping a close eye on their vulnerable pups. They often carry the pups on their chests to keep them close and out of the water (Figures 8.2 and 8.3).

During this early stage, watching a pup try to dive to follow its mom into the depths is pretty comical. It is easy to see that a pup desperately wants to follow its mom down to that fascinating place where she so often goes, but each effort to dive is thwarted by the shaggy life preserver. The pup will start to dive only to bounce right back up to the surface in a splash of bubbles and foam—and frustration.

Deadly harvest

Even sea otter pups were hunted for their fur along the California coast up until the 1830s, when the newly-in-place Mexican government imposed restrictions over the great sea otter hunt to prohibit the taking of pups, among other limits. This was part of a mostly losing

Fig. 8.3. A lost pup triggers a frantic search, and the pup's mom cries out.

battle to gain control over commerce in the vast waters of California's shoreline. Hunting sea otters around the northern Pacific Rim had begun in earnest in the early 1700s when Russian fur traders began to realize the enormous commercial value of these animals' pelts. They were viewed as the finest of all furs, ownership of which served as an important indicator of social status. China was Russia's primary otter-trading partner after some earlier, less commercially significant trade between China and Japan that had gone on for centuries.

As has so often been the case throughout the recent human history of ocean resource exploitation, this trade was driven by the unrestricted aim of maximizing the dollar (or yen, or ruble, etc.) return without regard to any limits on the target wildlife population or consideration of the ability to sustain the population for future harvests or for reasons other than economic value, such as biodiversity. At best, this form of exploitation leads to boom and bust cycles; at worst, it leads to dramatic crashes, sometimes ending in the elimination of a species, such as was the case with the Atlantic sea mink in the 1800s. From the standpoint of taxonomy, sea otters and sea minks fall into the same furry family, the *mustelids*, and as such, it's worth noting the sober reminder that one member of this family has already been hunted to extinction for its luxurious fur.

The need to find ever newer hunting grounds to support the trade, a hallmark of the progressive elimination of a target species, was part of what led to Captain Vitus Bering's crossing from Russia to Alaska in 1741 (the second of two pioneering crossings). Although Captain Bering was Danish, he served in the Russian Navy. This dangerous crossing—which led to Bering's death while shipwrecked on an island on the return voyage—followed the path of what had once been the land bridge between the two continents thousands of years earlier. Despite the shipwreck and the captain's death, a harvest of some 900 pelts eventually made it back to Russia for market.

By coming into contact with Native Alaskans, Captain Bering and the Russian traders opened a new door and a new approach to hunting sea otters. They took advantage of the superior hunting skills Native Alaskans possessed because of their familiarity and experience with sea otters over the course of thousands of years. What began as "trade" evolved quickly into a relationship better characterized as "indentured servitude" in which Russian traders forcibly coerced Native Alaskans, along

> **What began as "trade" with Native Alaskans quickly developed into indentured servitude.**

with their canoes, to accompany them as they progressively hunted southward along the Pacific Rim. After eventually reaching the Northern California coast, in 1812, the Russians established Fort Ross as a fur trading post along the Sonoma shoreline.

By that time, the Americans, British, Spanish, and Mexicans were also involved in the fur trade, some also using Native Alaskan labor and forcing the hunters with their canoes to accompany the ships on their months-long expeditions. These other countries became involved during some of the trade's peak years, in the later 1700s and even in the early 1800s, which hit the sea otter population hard.

Several thousand sea otters could be taken by one ship's voyage, which sometimes lasted more than six months. For example,

Fig. 8.4. A sea otter mom keeps her pup close by her side until it is old enough to fend for itself.

handwritten ship logs tell us that in 1802, the ship *O'cain* out of Boston, with a complement of Native Alaskans and twenty of their canoes, took 1,800 furs. The same ship, with its complement of Native Alaskans and fifty of their canoes, took 4,819 furs in 1806–07, and 3,953 furs in 1810–11. It has been estimated that from 1803 to 1806, some 17,000 pelts were taken along the Pacific coast by all fur-trading ships.

During the peak years of the hunt, there are records of American ships' captains trying to gain a trading edge by picking up hundreds of keys made of brass, copper, or iron in New York and Boston to trade with Native Alaskans, who valued the metals. It is even reported that one captain had 10,000 keys made and imported from Holland for trading during a sea otter–hunting voyage. Toward the tail end of their voyages, a captain and crew would often trade away any iron parts of their ship that could be spared. Anything of value was fair game to squeeze in a few more pelts before the long, ocean-crossing voyage to markets in Asia and, later, Europe.

As this wildlife population crashed because of the unchecked harvesting of pelts, the trade inevitably changed. Where captains once used every possible trick in the book to increase their trading leverage with Native Alaskans and others, there came a point when

Fig. 8.5. A female sea otter uses the placement of her paws to regulate her temperature.

the diminishing catch meant that very few captains would venture into this business because of the shrinking return on their investment. The long, seafaring hunting expeditions were expensive, difficult, and dangerous for those who undertook the task. With so few animals remaining, the value in hunting them all but disappeared.

By the 1830s, around the time of the Mexican government's attempts to limit and license the dwindling take, ships could go for months and come away with only hundreds, not thousands, of sea otter pelts (Figure 8.4). Reports from San Francisco Bay, previously teeming with sea otters and once the site of bountiful catch, reflected hundreds, not thousands, taken after weeks of hunting.

During that same period, hunters began using muskets, rather than spears, to kill sea otters. This technological advance in weaponry contributed to the final demise of the trade, the decimation of the species. With the musket's increase in reach and lethality, hunters could stretch the range in which they posed a threat to the sea otters. Animals that might previously have outrun a chasing canoe to remain out of range of a spear thrown by a hunter were no match for the newer weapon's extended range. Hunters could chase an otter over great distances, inevitably exhausting the small creature, and then make the kill from the weapon. These furry little creatures really didn't stand a chance (Figure 8.5).

Russian hunting spurred Spanish settlement

The Russians essentially abandoned Fort Ross in the 1840s because of the reduction in the otter population and the lack of what the business world might now term "sufficient ROI," or return on investment. They and the other countries involved pulled back from sea otter hunting along the California coast, as well as farther south to Baja California.

The Russian foray into California, chasing sea otter "gold," left a cultural legacy. Ironically, it is not in the form of a dominant Russian influence on California; it is the Spanish influence. Although the Spanish controlled Alta (Upper) California from the early 1600s, it was not until 1769 that they made any serious effort to actively populate the area through land grants and other means. The primary reason for this turnabout in the Spanish hands-off policy was defensive, a concern that the Russians posed a territorial threat as they moved into the region and established a presence in their quest for sea otters.

The sea otter had an outsize influence in geopolitics, shaping the culture of California as we know it today.

So it was that the sea otter, the little marine mammal that has long been threatened along the California coast, has had an outsize significance in geopolitics, shaping the culture of California as we know it today.

Looking at the overall impact of the fur trade on the sea otters as a species reveals an unfortunately all-too-common pattern of boom and bust, technological advances, and belated conservation efforts. When trade began in earnest in the 1700s, hundreds of thousands of sea otters (including all subspecies) were thriving in the coastal waters along the Northern Hemisphere's Pacific Rim. They stretched from Japan in a great arc to Baja California. Once hunting them became an unrestrained commercial business, their days were numbered. The luxurious fur that kept them warm and safe in the water was the very reason they were hunted.

The result of this pattern of commerce in wildlife was that by the end of the nineteenth century, with an estimated 1 million killed, fewer than 2,000 remained across all subspecies. By 1911, as the entire species neared extinction, sea otters were finally afforded legal protection under the North Pacific Fur Seal Convention signed by the United States, Russia, Japan, and Great Britain.

But, of course, that protection was too little and far too late. This once abundant creature had all but vanished from the ocean. The southern sea otter subspecies, within just a few years, had collapsed from a population of 30,000 or more and was widely believed to be extinct.

Sea otter resurgence

This is where the sea otter story has a twist that sets it apart, at least for now, from a lost species such as the sea mink and other creatures taken by humans for various reasons. Incredibly, unknown to all but a handful of people, one small colony of about 40 or 50 southern sea otters survived in the surf and kelp off a remote stretch of California's Big Sur coast in the early 1900s. In this isolated environment, where almost no one was aware they existed, the uniquely resilient otters began to mount a slow recovery. Only a few local residents knew the sea otters were there, but they didn't advertise what they knew.

Over much of the twentieth century, the southern sea otter population grew from this small, hearty group. It slowly but surely expanded its range north and south along the coast. It wasn't until 1937, soon after the opening of coastal Highway 1 near Big Sur, that the public became aware of the nearly 300 sea otters in existence by that time. The northern sea otter, too, recovered in larger numbers, primarily along the Alaskan coastline, throughout the 1900s.

The last several decades have seen a much more troubled growth pattern for the southern sea otter. Today, the population is showing spurts of incremental annual increases as its numbers are now just over 3,000. The number of pups and females has had some fits and starts over the last several years. Over the long-term span of a hundred years or so, the sea otter population numbers have gone up and down like a roller coaster at the Santa Cruz Beach Boardwalk, and they still remain in deep trouble.

During the 1970s, when the southern sea otters' then-blooming recovery had just begun to slide, American awareness of environmental issues was growing. In 1972, the first Earth Day was held, and Congress passed the Marine Mammal Protection Act. In

1973, Congress passed the Endangered Species Act. By 1977, sea otters were included as a "threatened" species under the Endangered Species Act. Listing them under the Endangered Species Act provided special protections and was in part a recognition of their vulnerability, their small numbers and narrow range, and their significance to the marine environment (as a keystone species).

At the time, one of the primary problems for the sea otter population along the coast of California was the large number of otters unintentionally killed, having been caught or injured in gill and trammel fishing nets. Californians went to the polls in 1990 to pass Proposition 132, a citizen-initiated state constitutional amendment that banned gill and trammel nets from central and southern California waters within a newly created Marine Protection Zone extending 3 miles from the shoreline, which encompasses the primary sea otter habitat. The ban was to take complete effect by 1994 following a transition period and included lump-sum compensation payments to ease the burden on those in the commercial fishing industry who were affected by the ban. This important step in preserving the sea otters passed handily, by a 55 percent to 44 percent margin (see Chapter 14 for more on this ban).

The entire sea otter population lives in a small habitat that stretches for a few hundred miles.

Once these forms of commercial fishing were banned in the primary habitats of the otters, their population numbers again began to grow.

Oil spill danger

Along with increasing awareness of the direct threats from fishing, there was also increasing interest in addressing the dangers posed to marine species and shorelines from the massive transportation by sea along California's coast of crude oil from Alaska. The sea otter's heightened risk because of its natural vulnerability to oil put it high on the list of concerns. But perhaps even more critically, it is especially at risk because the entire population lives in a relatively small habitat that stretches for just a few hundred miles along the central California coast.

The risk of an oil spill, the small number of sea otters remaining, and their narrow habitat combine for an explosive recipe for disaster, making it possible for even one large spill to wipe out the entire subspecies. The statistical possibilities of such an event are not as far-fetched as we might wish to believe.

The catastrophic *Exxon Valdez* oil spill in Alaska on March 4, 1989, is a case in point. In that disaster, the huge tanker carrying crude oil crashed on the rocks as a result of a human navigation failure, made all the worse by the captain's many-hour delay in reporting the crash and resultant oil spill to authorities. As a result of the accident, the tanker poured 11 million gallons of crude oil into Alaskan waters, seriously affecting wildlife and humans, including killing thousands of northern sea otters, other marine mammals, and countless birds, and destroying and damaging vital habitat, fisheries, and the livelihoods that depend on them.

Of course, more recently we have seen other oil spills that have eclipsed even the *Exxon Valdez*—most notably, the 2010 *Deepwater Horizon* oil rig in the Gulf of Mexico, a deepwater oil well blowout and explosion that killed 11 workers on a British Petroleum offshore platform. It spilled over 200 million gallons before finally being (mostly) capped but only after nearly three months of failed efforts. However, the *Exxon Valdez* was the first giant spill along the West Coast and served as an early wake-up call. That experience provided a real-life laboratory that tested hastily devised approaches to clean up during and after a spill, to rescue and care for oiled otters, birds, and other wildlife, and to try to deal with the enormous economic and social consequences of such a disaster.

If an oil spill similar to *Exxon Valdez* happened along the California shoreline, it would more than encompass the entire southern sea otter habitat.

The distribution of oil from the *Exxon Valdez* reached such a wide area that if the same thing were to happen along the California shoreline, it would more than encompass the entire southern sea otter habitat from end to end. It may seem that large oil spills are less likely off the central California coast than in Alaska, or off Southern California's oil rigs than in the Gulf Coast. But virtually

Fig. 8.6. The success of the Sea Otter Translocation Program relied on the hoped-for ability of sea otters to populate the small colony off San Nicolas Island. Seen here is a nursing sea otter pup.

all Alaskan oil transported by sea is brought either into San Francisco Bay for refining or to Long Beach, farther south along the coast. In either case, the crude is moving through or near the sea otter habitat. More than a thousand tankers pass under the Golden Gate Bridge each year with millions of barrels of oil and other petroleum products. Even in the last few years, and even with improved safety standards and technology, we have witnessed several smaller oil tanker accidents in San Francisco Bay, as well as pipeline ruptures along the Southern California coast.

The no otter zone

Concerned about the sea otters' vulnerability to spills, Congress passed a bill in 1986 (three years before the *Exxon Valdez* disaster) charging the U.S. Fish and Wildlife Service (USFWS) with creating a Sea Otter Translocation Program. Under the regulations proposed and adopted pursuant to that law, USFWS began to relocate some of the sea otter population outside their existing central California coast habitat in order to create a separate, isolated colony that could survive a local crisis and be used to repopulate in the event of a disaster. Under this program, between 1987 and 1990, 140 otters were captured, transported by air, and released in the nearshore waters at San Nicolas Island, which is one of the smallest of the Channel Islands off southern California (Figure 8.6).

In part to keep this colony intact, but in part for political reasons having to do with opposition by Southern California shellfisheries to moving sea otters into Southern California waters, USFWS created a No Otter Management Zone in a large portion of the waters outside of the vicinity of San Nicolas Island. The shellfisheries had been the beneficiaries of increased quantities of shellfish in these waters for more than a hundred years due to the hunting that had wiped the sea otter out of the area. This No Otter Zone was more than 200 miles long, stretching roughly from just south of Point Conception near Santa Barbara all the way to the Mexican border. The USFWS was charged with removing any otters found in this zone by "nonlethal methods" and returning them to the island or to the central California coastal waters.

Another significant and seemingly counterintuitive element of the political deal that resulted in the Translocation Program legislation was the concession to suspend various penalties within the No Otter Zone, including criminal sanctions, which had been in place for injuring or killing sea otters. These sanctions had applied, for example, to "takings," including killings that might be incidental to commercial fishing activities, such as when sea otters are trapped in nets intended for other creatures. Since otters were protected under the Endangered Species Act and the Marine Mammal Protection Act, harming them would ordinarily carry serious legal consequences. But the creation of the "No Otter Management Zone" suspended the framework of penalties.

There is, of course, a certain not-too-subtle irony in a program that was set up for the specific purpose of protecting sea otters having a component that suspends the strong protections that had been put in place for the sea otters. This exemplifies some of the two-edged-sword type of complexity in trying to *manage* nature through legal and political means.

It quickly became apparent that the program was doomed to fail: after the first three years, 80 percent of the otters that had been translocated either disappeared, died or were killed, or swam back "home" to the central California coast. Returning to the central coast was a remarkable feat in and of itself, since these sea otters had been flown to the island in the first place. Sea otters are typically not long distance travelers, they weren't dropping breadcrumbs, and they certainly don't have GPS devices. Sea otters usually live out their lives within a few miles of where they are born. It turns out that it is much harder than people think to manipulate the behavior of sea otters, or other creatures for that matter, even when motivated by the best of intentions.

> **It turns out that it is much harder than people think to manipulate the behavior of sea otters.**

After many years of inaction regarding the No Otter Zone, and in belated recognition of the failed relocation efforts, USFWS finally acted to formally end the program in 2012. The agency's action came only after litigation by sea otter conservation advocates urged termination of the program, and it held public hearings along the coast after a detailed study. The original legal penalties for sea otter takings were restored with the termination of the program, thus returning sea otter protection to its former, stronger status within the former zone.

The USFWS action triggered several new lawsuits, this time not by sea otter conservation groups but rather by representatives of several Southern California commercial shellfisheries and others. These contentious legal challenges centered on whether USFWS had the authority to terminate the No Otter Zone. The shellfisheries' position in the litigation is that even though everyone agrees the agency had the authority to *create* the zone, it could never *terminate* it.

Like the argument that the sea otters should be exempt from the Endangered Species Act protections, this argument, too, has its not-to-subtle irony. It would effectively mean that the Translocation Program, intended to help preserve a threatened species, would be started and kept permanently on autopilot, even though it was implemented in a way that would prevent the species from expanding its current range southward into its historic range—where it existed prior to hunting by humans decimated its population. And it would lift the criminal penalties in place for harming them. With protections like that, who needs enemies?

It was the sea otters' fur, that successful cold-water survival mechanism, that gave rise to the first existential threat—the decimation of its numbers for the lucrative fur trade. But it is the second successful survival mechanism, its voracious appetite, that gives rise to the second threat. It fuels a perception lying at the core of the shellfisheries' litigation.

The concern expressed in the lawsuits by the abalone, lobster, and urchin fisheries is that at some future time, despite current bleak sea otter population trends, the termination of the No Otter Zone might allow otters to naturally expand into their historic Southern California range and eat their way through the now-commercial food supply.

The commercial activities in that zone, such as sea urchin harvesting, have operated for many years without any competition from sea otters, since the otters were long ago eliminated by hunting. They are, very slowly, expanding into that region. But no scientific evidence has been offered in the litigation to demonstrate that sea otter recovery and expansion into Southern California's waters would alter the current conditions in any meaningful way from a commercial standpoint. Despite this, that fear is still expressed in the lawsuit.

The sea otter's voracious appetite, which the shellfisheries put forward as a fundamental rationale for this litigation, is an undisputed fact. What is in dispute is when, if, and how this appetite would have any negative impact on hundreds of miles of coastline that was inhabited by sea otters until they were hunted out of the zone. In reality, there is ample evidence the sea otters' presence is beneficial to ecosystems such as the life-sustaining kelp forests. Beyond the litigation, we must also ask whether humans have any legitimate business in trying to manage the biodiversity of such an area by placing artificial (legal) boundaries against a species' natural recovery into its former range using a baseline that was created by 200 years of hunting that eliminated a once-vital apex predator.

The delicate food chain

These types of questions take on new meaning in light of the lawsuits. But they are not the first questions that come to mind while watching a sea otter engage in this allegedly devastating activity, eating. This is an activity they do for a surprisingly large part of their day, as well as at night, because they forage as much during the night as during the

Fig. 8.7. Although this hungry pup can forage for itself, a
protective mom still shares a mussel with it.

day. If you are ever on the shoreline after dark and otters are nearby,
by listening carefully you may hear the unmistakable sound of shells
being cracked on their rock anvils.

The immediate questions that come to mind are: How did they
learn to use tools—to pick up and use rocks as anvils on their chests
so they can smash open their shellfish prey? How do they have the
energy to make the many, many daily, one-clam-at-a-time dives to
sustain their need to eat 25–30 percent of their body weight every
day? Do they specialize in one type of food, such as mussels, clams,
crabs, urchins, octopus? By the way, yes, they do: while they will eat
anything based on availability, all else being equal, researchers have
found that individual otters tend to specialize or prefer one form of
food over another, and that this preference is handed down from mom
to pup (Figures 8.7 and 8.8).

This food specialization is further evidence of the great efficiency
designed into the sea otter's survival framework. Being familiar with
and experienced at catching and preparing one type of shellfish means
they expend less energy in order to obtain their needed nutrition. And
for sea otters, it is all about the caloric intake. As with the fur, stoking
the metabolic fires that generate the substantial heat and energy they
require in the cold water is the hallmark of the sea otter functional
design and its survival.

Fig. 8.8. A gooseneck barnacle bonanza will save this sea otter a few dives and preserve precious energy.

In the same way they are vulnerable to damage to their fur, any injury that impairs an otter's ability to dive, catch prey, or break open a shell can quickly become life threatening. An otter can lose 10 or more pounds a day if it cannot eat and will die within a few days. This, of course, makes rescuing an otter a very shaky proposition. Few injured otters will be lucky enough to be discovered within hours of injury, and within reach of one of the few organizations capable of handling the injury and the subsequent recovery, to say nothing of the difficult process of preparing an otter for release back into the wild. With only a little over 3,000 remaining, every single otter is important to the survival of the species, and every injury can contribute to the high annual mortality rate—which has been in the range of 10 percent for several years.

Watching an otter eat is also a reminder of how delicate the food chain can be. Because of pollution and discharges of contaminated water into the ocean, it is easy to understand how in some cases toxins are first concentrated in shellfish and then by sea otters consuming that contaminated shellfish. This sensitive food chain gives us strong impetus for taking steps to reduce these threats, but it also means the sea otter is an excellent indicator of the health of its habitat. For this reason, like the canary in the coal mine, sea otters are known as an "indicator" or "sentinel" species. We can learn a lot about ocean conditions from studying sea otter health.

Fig. 8.9. As human development and sea otter habitat increasingly come into conflict, roadways along the shoreline near Highway 1 pose a deadly threat to sea otters who may infrequently cross the road.

Sea otter research

Understanding the threats to our nearshore ocean waters has led to action, even if sometimes it is in how to be well prepared to respond to catastrophic problems once they occur. In part as a legacy of the *Exxon Valdez* spill on Alaskan sea otters, the state of California passed legislation that mandated a plan and created facilities capable of responding to a major oil spill impacting sea otters and other marine life along the waters of the coast. There are several locations, but the facility in Santa Cruz is known as the Marine Wildlife Veterinary Care and Research Center. Constructed in 1997, it is operated by the California Department of Fish and Wildlife on the Coastal Science Campus at the University of California, Santa Cruz. It houses emergency treatment and care resources, but it is also a center for sea otter research. Among other research efforts, staff at the facility perform necropsies on all dead sea otters that are brought to this laboratory. A necropsy is the equivalent of an autopsy on a human, an examination to unearth the cause of death. By studying the causes of death and developing a database that now reaches back several years, researchers can identify various trends in the species' mortality and the health of the ocean.

Fig. 8.10. A young sea otter pup experimenting with food, trying to learn what is edible and how to get into it.

Developing and maintaining data on the causes of death of every sea otter found anywhere along the coast is as painstaking as it is critical to unlocking the key to their survival. These efforts go hand in hand with the current field research and other data collection on live sea otters. Cutting-edge catch, tag, and release techniques and extensive monitoring and observation of otters as they move around the Monterey Bay and along the central coast yield a treasure trove of information for study. These operations are conducted by a combination of educational and research institutions, government agencies, and nonprofit organizations. Among some of the leaders in this field, in addition to the California Department of Fish and Wildlife's Marine Wildlife Veterinary Care and Research Center in Santa Cruz, are the Monterey Bay Aquarium with its Sea Otter Research and Conservation (SORAC) program, the University of California Santa Cruz Institute of Marine Sciences and Long Marine Laboratory, and the U.S. Fish and Wildlife Service.

The results of years of study and research have begun to fill in the details of the sea otter survival story. As they have been recovering from the decimation caused by the fur trade, they have faced a litany of newer threats beyond oil spills, including pollution and tainted runoff from the land, parasites and disease, competition for food, predation by great white sharks, range limitation, the impact of fishing, and the impact of land development and shoreline "management" such as armoring of the coastline. Our activities often place greater obstacles in the path of the sea otter recovery (Figure 8.9).

To that list of hazards we can now add the threat from the lawsuits aimed squarely at establishing a limitation on their range—an invisible barbed-wire fence that reads Otters Go Home.

This last threat underscores the importance of the relationship between science, policy, and law when it comes to the California coast. The intersection of these can have critical consequences. The latest research tells us that the current population of sea otters has a healthy rate of reproduction, but that it may have reached something of a carrying capacity problem, a limit on the number of how many healthy otters can live in the current range. So, despite all the other threats, unless they can expand farther into their historic range and habitat along the coast, they will not reach a sustainable population. This means we cannot be assured of their survival so long as humans limit their range, even though they seem as a species to have the capacity to grow in numbers beyond their current range. Thus, the outcome of the litigation to restore the No Otter Zone and other policy choices have wide-reaching consequences.

Another key policy choice on the horizon involves the question of what criteria should be used to evaluate when or if sea otters can be removed from listing ("delisted") under the Endangered Species Act. There are new political pressures to roll back the number of creatures listed in the act and make it easier to delist them. It will require sustained efforts to make sure that good, current science will drive the criteria and policies, not short-term political pressure. We have seen the disastrous consequences of short-term interests shaping policy for sea otters and other wildlife.

The sea otters' first success and the triumph of recovery from near extinction as a hunted target for their incredible fur actually set the stage for their current crisis. That comeback, a measure of their resilience and strength as a wildlife species, is again being tested by human activity.

Their second success, the capacity to eat and extract the fuel necessary to stave off the frigid ocean waters, has brought a perceived conflict with a commercial operation that worries about competition from a species that once inhabited that fishery (Figure 8.10). The use of a law and a program that was intended to preserve the threatened sea otter to create an artificial barrier to the sea otter's survival along California's coast puts the spotlight on the complexity of the relationship between science, policy, and law.

Overall, sea otters have a pretty tough existence as delicately balanced creatures living in a very demanding environment with a variety of human impacts tipping the scales against them even further. Yet in those moments when they are in smooth coastal waters, quietly floating on their backs in the sun (after diving for hours, after eating for hours, after cleaning up, after grooming their fur, after . . .), they appear calm and peaceful, by and large. No sense of urgency evident. Their heads turned skyward.

Mom: We live in the Central Valley. We usually come to the ocean once or twice a year, because California has such amazing beaches and just about anywhere you go it's going to be beautiful. It's either going to be rocky or sandy or there's always something interesting.

I remember first coming out here to the coast when I was very young, with my mom and my sisters. We went to the boardwalk. It was really cold. But it was so special, I've come back ever since, now with my own family. The rest of the family usually comes out here with us as well, but the rest of the kids are older now, not at home. My son here is the last one, but we're still coming out to the shore.

It's absolutely important to get to the coast. My son is learning about the ecosystems, he's learning about the animals, the sea life, and everything that lives here, the resources that we get out of the ocean, and how it's really important to protect that, to keep everything healthy. This is important to us, that it be here.

Son: What I get out of it is the fresh air, just to relax, and throw away all the worries like at work or at school. I like to dig around and find things, like sand crabs. It's like a treasure hunt, whenever the wave comes in I just put my hands in the sand and usually I get one. We've also seen dolphins swimming out here, which is fun. Usually we go over to Monterey and we see sea otters, swimming on their backs.

I remember the first time I actually went out farther into the waves. You know, into the water, not just on the edge. Where the water was up to my chest and my head. Where the waves would actually wash all the way over me. It was scary at first . . .

—Mom and son, age 8

Beaches and Sand

A Soft Edge

If the state's entire population of nearly 39 million people all decided to go to the beach at the same time, they would each have only about a half-inch of beach front to enjoy.

California has some really hard edges, but some much softer ones as well. It's the place where the edge of a huge continent, 2,500 miles wide, collides with the planet's biggest ocean, 7,000 miles across, producing some impressive landscapes.

Two hundred and fifty years ago, Gaspar de Portolá and his crew slogged up the coast on foot from San Diego searching for Monterey Bay as the perfect harbor, "sheltered from all winds," for treasure-laden Spanish galleons to replenish supplies on their return from Manila. At the southern end of the rugged Big Sur coast, north of the Hearst Castle, Portolá ran smack into nearly sheer cliffs and was stopped in his tracks.

Cone Peak, 50 miles to the north, is the highest coastal mountain in the lower 48 states, rising to over 5,000 feet just 3 miles from the sea. It's not quite vertical, but even today it is not for the fainthearted, and it surely made travel with pack animals nearly impossible for Portolá's expedition. Today, as part of the Los Padres National Forest and Ventana Wilderness Area, it is still nearly an impossible grade to hike, along the cliffs of loose slippery rocks, with rattlesnakes, mountain lions, ticks, and endless fields of poison oak creating a

Fig. 9.1. The rugged Big Sur coast was a major barrier to early explorers and settlers until Highway 1 was finally completed in 1937; it was known initially as the Carmel–San Simeon Highway and then as the Roosevelt Highway.
photo courtesy Kenneth and Gabrielle Adelman, California Coastal Records Project, www.CaliforniaCoastline.org

formidable barrier. It is daunting to the most capable explorers, and even for modern hikers with all of their cool gear.

Portolá had two choices: turn around, go back to San Diego, and admit defeat to Spanish authorities, or make a sharp turn eastward to avoid the steepest mountains and drag his crew inland in hopes of finding an easier route north. He chose the latter, found the Salinas Valley, and continued north.

The Big Sur coast, because of its geological origins, has some remarkably hard and resistant rocks, ranging from pieces of ancient volcanoes and old mountain ranges to geologic debris from deep beneath the seafloor. There are no rivers or watersheds of any size to smooth out the terrain. It's about as rough an edge as you can find. In 1937, however, following 18 years of construction and aided by funding and labor during the Great Depression, Highway 1 opened up this stretch of coast for the first time to travelers and visitors (Figure 9.1). It was known initially as the Carmel–San Simeon Highway and later as the Roosevelt Highway. What took weeks of hiking a century ago today takes a few hours of driving today.

Labor for many, coastal access for few

Access to this particular piece of the edge of California was opened partly due to the incredibly hard manual labor of members of the Civilian Conservation Corps, known as the CCC. This Depression-era jobs program for those single, unemployed men on "relief" created a labor pool for many such projects in California, and nationwide, resulting in improvements in access to nature, including roads, bridges, and trails, as well as facilities to support public engagement and comfort. Today, much of the work of the CCC remains as an important part of our coastal infrastructure. If you look closely at various structures, from the most basic park benches to sturdy, well-used buildings, to the most elaborate bridges (think of the iconic graceful arch of Big Sur's Bixby Creek Bridge, immortalized in dozens of auto commercials, along with its two less-well-known smaller versions over nearby creeks), you will usually find a date from sometime in the 1930s stamped or stenciled on the structure.

It's hard to look at the CCC's role in facilitating access to the coast and the creation of infrastructure without also noting that so much of the access to the edge was built by people who culturally were not in the mainstream or who would not necessarily benefit from the tough projects they completed, often at great risk to life and limb. Chinese laborers, for example, hand-dug tunnels that allowed the railroad, the Sun Tan Special, to cross through the mountains and bring summer tourists to the shoreline in Santa Cruz from hot interior valleys. These same workers also managed to bring the Ocean Shore Railroad across Devil's Slide, at least temporarily, on its planned route from San Francisco to Santa Cruz. The line was never completed, owing in large part to economic failure.

So much of the access to the edge was built by people who would not benefit from the tough projects they completed.

The poverty of those who paved the path with their hard physical labor for little or no wages—the CCC workers received $30 per month and were required to send $25 of that to their families—stands in stark contrast with the wealthy homeowners and local businesses, and even the visitors and tourists, who have reaped the long-term benefits. The tension between access to the coast and the barriers of money and landownership put a spotlight on the ongoing need to preserve the coast for everyone, not just a limited few. Government, from federal to state to local, and educational institutions and nonprofits are now grappling with the many ways to assure access for a wider range of people in order to realize the vision of what can truly be called a "people's coast." Income, race, and status still form a significant barrier to access, just as they form the dividing line between many of those who constructed the access and those who enjoy it.

The King Range, which includes portions of southern Humboldt County and northern Mendocino County, was just as impassible as the Big Sur coast, at least in the days before heavy construction equipment was available. The Lost Coast of far northern California is lost for a reason; you can't get there from here. A similarly rugged edge occurs along the western end of the Santa Monica Mountains between Point Mugu and Malibu's Broad Beach. Until the Roosevelt Highway was carved out of the cliffs and opened in that region in 1929, the steep mountains and resistant volcanic rocks made for a nearly impassable transit.

Classic California beach living

But California has some nice soft edges as well, those that we head to on a summer weekend. Those beaches form a ribbon of sand that stretches discontinuously 1,100 miles from Oregon to Mexico. In many ways, beaches define the state, at least for many who live along the edge. The beaches are at the epicenter of a lifestyle that has been glamorized and romanticized for decades in movies, on TV, and in books and music. People come here from California's inland valleys, from across the country, and from around the world to visit the state's iconic beaches, sometimes in massive, noisy tour buses. Tour bus visitors are a recognizable species: they occasionally get out to walk in the sand or wade into the water for a few minutes, snap some photos, and buy a T-shirt with a local logo to take back home to show friends and family that they were here—evidence that they actually got to taste what some think of as paradise.

California's soft edge is the place where millions of people, many between the ages of 15 and 30, come to lie out in the sun on weekends

**Fig. 9.2. Long sandy shoreline at Pacific Beach and
Mission Bay along the San Diego County coastline.**
photo courtesy Bruce Perry, California State University, Long Beach

between June and September. They spend millions of dollars every summer on sunscreen in the hope of getting a golden tan, yet avoiding sunburn—and courting skin cancer.

California has a really long coastline, but only about 320 miles of this edge consists of accessible and usable beaches. These include the long sandy stretch of shoreline from Santa Monica to Redondo Beach, the coast from Huntington Beach to Newport, and the white sands of the Silver Strand in San Diego (Figure 9.2). Far to the north, Monterey Bay is a 30-mile-long, gently curved section of sandy shoreline that extends continuously from Santa Cruz to Monterey. Despite its chilly water and occasional sharks, Monterey Bay beaches attract millions of central California visitors and residents annually.

If the state's entire population of nearly 39 million people decided to go to the beach at the same time—and it seems that they do on Memorial Day, Labor Day, the Fourth of July, and a few other warm summer weekends—they would each have only about a half-inch of beach front to enjoy. To make matters worse and reduce that personal space farther, add those millions of tourists from elsewhere who visit California. And many of them also want to go to the beach so they can soak up some of that glamorous lifestyle, even if only for a few minutes. In 2014, the state had 250 million person trips from visitors, 200 million of which were for leisure, and these folks spent a combined $117 billion. A major destination for many of these people was no doubt a sandy shoreline. Beaches mean big bucks for the state.

Think for a moment what the coast of California would be like without public access to beaches. One long highway filled with cars, the occasional parking lot or overlook for getting a view of the ocean, and perhaps a few motels and fast-food joints scattered along the highway—a bit like the current Highway 1 extending from Cambria to Carmel. Not many places to get out of the car and get sand in your shoes or get wet. Our lifestyles would be very different, indeed, without beaches.

But many of us do want to get out on the beach. The opportunities our beaches provide may not be quite endless, but they are certainly many, regardless of our age and interests—from walking the wild and remote beaches of the north coast searching for treasures to watching wildlife, picnicking, swimming, surfing, paddle boarding, wind and kite surfing, volley ball, or just contemplating the ocean. The list is long, which is why so many people visit them each year.

It's pretty clear that beaches don't occur everywhere along California's edge, or we could just stroll from Oregon to Mexico—well, we could if we were motivated, were in reasonably good shape, and had a few extra months to kill.

Beach formation

Beaches only form where a healthy supply of sand has been delivered to the shoreline, and where the coastal topography is flat enough that sand has a place to accumulate. Because California is geologically quite young, and therefore very active, the presence of uplifted mountains and steep cliffs at Big Sur, portions of the Mendocino and Humboldt coasts, and the Santa Monica Mountains coast, for example, have not allowed space for beaches to form. Many of the state's smaller scenic and secluded *pocket beaches* have formed where streams have cut through the coastal mountains or sea cliffs, or where waves have eroded embayments or small coves in the weaker materials making up the coastline (Figure 9.3).

Fig. 9.3. Pocket beaches in Laguna Beach.
photo courtesy Bruce Perry, California State University, Long Beach

Long, straight or gently curved beaches, occasionally backed by sand dunes, form where there are no mountains or steep cliffs, where the coastline relief is low and ample sand is available. These are the beaches that many residents, visitors, and the movie industry envision when they picture the California coast, a wide sandy shoreline lined by palm trees and convertibles. Somewhat fortuitously, many of the state's long sandy beaches are in Southern California where most of the state's population is concentrated and the weather and water are the warmest. Not surprisingly, these long, wide expanses of sand are big income generators for local economies, supporting a diverse cornucopia of local businesses, from hotels and motels to restaurants and fast-food chains, to surf shops and bikini factories.

Lots of beaches in California form upcoast of the state's many natural headlands, rocky points, or other obstructions, because they trap the sand that is being moved along the shoreline by wave action (Figure 9.4). Point Dume, along the Malibu coast, has backed up millions of cubic yards of sand moving toward Santa Monica, which led to the formation of the mile-long Zuma and Broad beaches. A few miles farther northwest, Point Mugu has had a similar effect and has trapped enough sand to form a beach nearly 2 miles long. Morro Rock in San Luis Obispo County has also collected sand moving downcoast,

Fig. 9.4. Beach fronting the campus of the University of California, Santa Barbara, which has formed as littoral drift, has been trapped by the headland of Campus Point. *photo courtesy Kenneth and Gabrielle Adelman, California Coastal Records Project, www.CaliforniaCoastline.org*

forming an extensive beach. In the city of Santa Cruz, San Lorenzo Point is a natural rock outcrop that traps sand moving into Monterey Bay from the north and has led to the formation of Main Beach, a three-quarter-mile-long, wide strip of sand that has been a popular recreation area and home to the Santa Cruz Beach Boardwalk for well over a century.

Most of our beaches, however, only exist because of a unique combination of mineral properties and wave energy. There are beaches scattered along California's coast that are made up of pebbles, large cobbles, or shells, but these are the anomalies, the oddities, and generally not the places where people spread their towels, play volleyball, or take long quiet walks. Jogging or a pickup game of volleyball or soccer on a cobble beach just doesn't work. If this is what we were faced with each time we arrived at the beach, we might just as well stay in the car and eat lunch.

The pebble, cobble, and shell beaches along California's coast are unique enough that they are often named after these somewhat odd and infrequent accumulations: Pebble Beach, Shell Beach, Sand Dollar

Fig. 9.5a. Large concretions cover the shoreline at Bowling Ball Beach along the Mendocino County coast *photo courtesy Deepika Shrestha Ross*

Fig. 9.5b. Glass Beach near Fort Bragg along the Mendocino County coast, the site of a former city dump.

Fig. 9.5c. A pebbly beach along the San Mateo County coast.

Fig. 9.5d. Granite cobbles form a beach along the 17-Mile Drive on the Monterey Peninsula.

Beach, Glass Beach, or Bowling Ball Beach (Figures 9.5a and 9.5b). Because they are so different, they attract visitors who often load up their pockets or containers with the shells or pebbles (sometimes ignoring restrictions aimed at preserving these unique beaches). Pebble Beach along the San Mateo County coast, often called "the other Pebble Beach," is a good example (Figure 9.5c). Bucket loads, even truckloads, of the beautiful shiny pebbles were being carted off for years. Many of these pebbles would find their way into the stream of commerce, whether for landscaping, construction, or rock collections. Park staff finally had to post a sign specifically asking people to restrict their pebble removal from the beach.

These coarse beaches usually form under a unique set of conditions (Figure 9.5d). The rocks in the surrounding cliffs may consist of pebbles, for example, or there may not be a nearby source of sand. In other places, the wave energy may be so high that sand isn't stable on the beach and doesn't stay put, or the area may be such a rich habitat for clams or sand dollars that their shells accumulate on the shoreline.

The ideal beach for most of us is clean white sand that doesn't get too hot to walk across comfortably on scorching summer days. What is fascinating and what makes sandy beaches around the world possible is that many rocks (granite in particular) consist of minerals that gradually break down over time into sand-size particles. Through weathering in the watersheds that ultimately drain to the shoreline (Figure 9.6), these rocks gradually decompose and break down into small individual mineral grains, quartz and feldspar being among the hardest and the most abundant. Rivers and creeks gradually transport the sand downstream toward the shoreline where waves are then able to move these grains around, sorting, rounding, and polishing them until they are comfortable to walk on. The shoreline is a marvelous grinding mill or rock polisher on a huge scale, as every wave picks up billions of sand grains, washing them back and forth to gradually produce soft, smooth beach sand.

Not all beaches are soft and smooth, however, and they aren't all white either. The color of any beach reflects the mineral composition of its sand grains. Whether derived from the local bluffs or cliffs, the rivers and creeks that drain to the coast, or the organisms that may populate the nearshore area—coral or coralline algae, clams, urchins,

Fig. 9.6. The Santa Clara River discharges about 1 million cubic yards of sand annually on average to the shoreline of Ventura County.

or any of a number of other invertebrates that make hard skeletons or shells—it is these locally derived materials that make each beach a bit different and unique.

Most beach sand looks almost uniform, tan or light gray in color, maybe even boring; but geological conditions coalesced to mix the colors up in some places. Particularly during the winter months, many beaches will have been eroded and narrowed by the larger and more energetic winter waves, leaving behind deposits of black sand, heavier than the more common and lighter-colored quartz and feldspar. The black sand consists of various mixtures of metal-rich minerals, such as magnetite, ilmenite, or chromite, which tend to stick around when the lighter minerals are washed offshore. Typically, the black sand is concentrated in small ripples or channels on the beach face where it can be pulled out with a magnet, as you may have done in the sandbox when you were a kid.

Minerals in sand

California has always attracted entrepreneurs and mavericks, and in the eyes of some early opportunists, these metal-rich black sands looked like money. For a short while in the 1920s, the Triumph Steel

Fig. 9.7. The beach at the mouth of the Big Sur River is unique in being colored purple from the garnet delivered by the river to the shoreline.

Company owned nearly 2 miles of beach along the northern Monterey Bay shoreline and was mining the black sand, which contained 500 to 1,100 pounds of magnetite (an oxide of iron) per ton of sand. They used a magnetic separator to remove the magnetite and then used a furnace to produce a red iron oxide that was used in the manufacture of paint. While this happened in the 1920s without any permit, chances are that mining beach sand and setting up an industrial furnace on a public beach to extract iron would probably not be viewed very favorably today.

In addition to iron-bearing minerals, black sand may contain small amounts of other more valuable but less abundant amounts of gold and platinum. A beach gold rush of sorts started along northern Monterey Bay near Aptos in the summer of 1860. Miles of beach were quickly staked off and 25 mining claims filed. The digging and searching continued for over 20 years with one family tunneling into the bluff and extracting a grand total of $5 in gold for each ton of sand. Doesn't sound too attractive, but if we adjust for inflation and use the present price of gold, this would amount to over $7,000 per day. That's without factoring in the price of an attorney and consultant, however, to get you through the Coastal Commission and other permitting processes that are now in place with regard to such coastal activity, intended to protect our edge (see more on the California Coastal Commission in Chapter 14).

Twenty-five miles south of Carmel, at the mouth of the Big Sur River and at the start of a scenic 20-minute walk from Highway 1 through Andrew Molera State Park, you can find ruby-colored beach sand. The color is from garnet, a very hard mineral that weathers out of metamorphic rocks high in the adjacent Santa Lucia Range, and is carried to the coast by the Big Sur River. Much of today's sandpaper is coated with garnet because it is a very hard and abrasive mineral. Wind and waves have concentrated this ruby-colored mineral in interesting and beautiful patterns along the beach for a considerable distance south of the river mouth (Figure 9.7).

A hundred and seventy-five miles north of San Francisco, on the Mendocino Coast, lies the old lumber town of Fort Bragg. For decades, the local residents used a beach at the north end of town as their city dump. In the days before curbside recycling, anything that couldn't be burned or fed to the chickens or pigs was simply dumped at some convenient and out of sight location. While it sounds shockingly contrary to our values today, this was common practice in rural communities across the country. Over the years the metal rusted away, but the glass survived and was broken up and smoothed by the waves, leaving behind Glass Beach, which has become a popular visitor destination. People young and old, locals and visitors, spend hours on their hands and knees, looking for their own treasures derived from Grandpa's old beer bottles and Grandma's old kitchen jars and medicine vials. Today, these treasures are protected and the state parks warn visitors not to remove or disturb them but to take pictures instead.

Beaches change their shapes

Those wide sandy summer beaches look pretty stable, but there really isn't anything permanent about a beach. Sand grains are only temporary residents, and like a hyperactive 2-year-old, they rarely sit still for very long. Wind blows the sand around on the back beach, usually inland, and the waves are constantly at work, pushing the sand back and forth across the beach face. Every time we have a change in wave conditions the shape of the shoreline changes. These daily and seasonal processes can create both obvious and more subtle features along the beach.

Perhaps the most striking change to the shape of most beaches takes place between winter and summer. The summer beach has a berm—that's the wide, dry, higher part of the beach—where we throw our towels, get sunburned, have picnics, and play volleyball. The berm might be hundreds of feet wide. In winter, much or all of this sand is removed by the steeper and more energetic waves, usually leaving behind a much narrower winter berm. Under heavy wave conditions, the berm and sand may be completely removed, leaving behind a layer of gravel or cobbles.

The sand carried off the beach is transported offshore where it often forms a series of sand bars, or large sand waves on the seafloor, separated by troughs. The height of the waves determines the depth of water where the waves break, so the presence of these sand bars causes the waves to break farther offshore in the winter months. This dissipates more of the breaking wave's energy offshore, which reduces the energy expended on the beach, a natural shock absorber for the shoreline.

In the late spring and summer the less energetic waves will gradually begin to move the sand that accumulated offshore back onto the beach. These more gentle waves will wash the sand up the beach face, building up the berm over the months ahead. By July or August, the exposed beach will usually be at its maximum width again, just in time for the millions of summer visitors.

Going with the flow: littoral drift

Science is odd stuff, and the same could be said for many scientists. While studies have shown that, in general, people tend to have much more confidence in scientists than, say, politicians or even the clergy, when it comes to science, most people don't understand it very well. Why this is the case is another issue, but at the risk of alienating a few readers, even in California, maybe especially in California, there are people holding on to a lot of rather odd beliefs that have no scientific basis. Big Foot, flying saucers, astrology, and dowsing for water with a coat hanger, or anything else that might be handy, are a few examples.

There are people who believe that the water coming out of springs in the mountains of coastal California comes from the Sierras through some amazing secret natural underground passageways. In fact, a fair amount of our water does come from the Sierras, but through human-made pipes and canals along the Central Valley. There are many reasons why this long-distance transport doesn't happen naturally, but people's beliefs change slowly, even in the face of clear scientific evidence.

Another perception existed for years, and perhaps still does, that the sand along California's shoreline moves from north to south (which is generally true), carried by the action of waves, and that the beach sand that has its origin near the Oregon border ultimately makes its way to Mexico. While most sand does moves south along our edge, there are a lot of obstructions along the way. That sand from the beaches of Northern California doesn't even make it to San Francisco, much less Tijuana.

Every time a wave breaks, and it happens thousands of times every day, it picks up billions of grains of sand. I've never tried to count them, but you've got to believe me on this one—it's billions and trillions of sand grains. That sand not only moves up and down the beach face, but depending on the angle at which the waves break on the shoreline, the sand may move some distance along the shoreline as well, up or down the coast, north or south.

Most waves approach the California shoreline at some angle, simply because the storms that generate the waves are usually somewhere else, far out to sea. They may have come from the north or south but rarely from directly offshore. As each wave breaks at some small angle to the beach, it stirs up and suspends those trillions of grains of sand and washes them up the beach face at a slight angle. The backwash flows back down the beach face also at a slight angle, carrying the sand with it. So each wave moves each sand grain a short distance away from where it started. This might not seem like an efficient way to move sand, at least compared with using a huge dump truck, but there are typically 5,000 to 10,000 waves breaking on any beach virtually every day of the year. Granted, they are not all Mavericks-size waves, but during the winter months, most of California's shoreline will have its sand stirred up by a lot of storm waves. They all pick up those grains and help them along on their imperceptibly slow shoreline journey.

Those thousands of waves breaking on the beach every day generate a slowly moving current of water and sand that flows downcoast, parallel to the shoreline. These longshore currents exist along most of California's beaches, and the sand they carry is known as littoral drift, literally a river of sand making its way along the shoreline. The amount of sand carried along the state's beaches amounts to thousands of truckloads every year, and we can't even see the trucks. They just keep on truckin' along, one load at a time, day after day, year after year.

So why doesn't all that sand from Humboldt County end up in Mexico? A lot of obstacles are in the way, much like driving on a crowded freeway, and sand doesn't move too far before it hits a traffic jam or an off-ramp.

Seventy-five or so years ago, when the earliest oceanographic expeditions were just beginning to explore California's offshore area, a number of seafloor canyons, or submarine canyons, were discovered. As ships worked their way slowly along the coastline, the fathometer, or depth recorder, would suddenly show an incision in the seafloor, often crossing the continental shelf and in some cases coming up almost to the beach.

The discovery of these many offshore submarine canyons, and the recovery of cores of sand from the floors of these canyons, led scientists to realize that sand moving downcoast along the beaches was being diverted offshore into these seafloor gorges, which were acting like freeway off-ramps.

Downcoast of many of the canyons, the beaches typically narrow or disappear and are replaced by rocky headlands or points. Dozens of submarine canyons cross California's edge, and each is responsible for draining sand from the upcoast beaches, which is then carried miles offshore into deep water, lost forever to the shoreline. The canyons have names tied to the features along the edge of the adjacent coast, such as Monterey Canyon, Hueneme Canyon, Mugu Canyon, Santa Monica Canyon, Redondo Canyon, and Newport Canyon. These submarine canyons are where most of that beach sand ultimately goes, and why the beaches in the southern part of the state don't continue to get wider—the sand doesn't get that far.

Monterey Submarine Canyon, which slices right through the middle of Monterey Bay and extends almost to the beach at Moss

Fig. 9.8. Monterey Submarine Canyon is the largest submarine canyon along the California coast and is the highway to the deep sea for over 300,000 cubic yards of beach sand each year.
image courtesy David Fierstein ©MBARI

Landing, is one of the world's largest submarine canyons—over 6,000 feet deep (nearly 12,000 feet below the ocean's surface) and big enough to swallow the Grand Canyon of the Colorado River (Figure 9.8). But it is completely invisible to us standing on the beach. Every year, this vast underwater system of conveyor belts carries into deep water offshore almost all of the nearly 300,000 cubic yards of sand being transported down the coast from as far as 75 miles to the north at Half Moon Bay, as well as the sand moving northward from the Salinas River mouth.

Once sand starts moving into one of these canyons, it is permanently lost to the beach. Observations by scuba divers and submersibles reveal that in the steeper canyon heads, this sand simply flows down slope, grain by grain, the same process that occurs when you start digging into a steep sand dune. Transport farther offshore, however, where the slopes are less, is achieved by underwater mudflows known as turbidity currents. These currents can flow many

Fig. 9.9. The dredge in the Santa Cruz Small Craft Harbor removes about 250,000 cubic yards of sand each year from the entrance channel and discharges it on the downcoast beach.

miles down submarine canyons over very low slopes and transport huge volumes of sediment to the deep-sea floor.

The amount of sand carried along the shoreline by littoral drift each year, leaving the beaches and falling to the deep-sea floor through these littoral off-ramps, is truly immense but difficult to see. Only where it piles up in harbor mouths and has to be sucked up and moved by floating dredges do we get some idea of how much sand is really in motion along our outer edge. At Santa Barbara and Santa Cruz, decades of dredging, of moving the sand from one side of the harbor entrances to the other, have given us a good idea of how much sand is on the littoral freeway and ends up in a nearby submarine canyon (Figure 9.9). At each of these harbors, about 300,000 cubic yards, or 30,000 dump truck loads, is dredged in an average year. That's equal to a line of trucks, bumper to bumper, 142 miles long, or one big dump truck full of sand moving down the beach every 18 minutes, 24 hours a day, 365 days a year. At the Channel Islands Harbor, near Ventura, even more sand is dredged, typically 1 million cubic yards, or a line of large dump trucks 475 miles long, moving down the beach, every year.

Interrupting or blocking this volume of sand can have big and expensive impacts. Imagine the pile of sand that would be formed if a line of trucks 142 miles long, each carrying 10 cubic yards, dumped their loads in one place, and how long it would take to move the pile left behind. Many of California's harbormasters and port directors face just this scenario all year long, where a jetty or a breakwater protects a harbor but also interrupts the longshore transport of sand.

Between 1970 and 2001, at a cost of tens of millions of dollars, over 10 million cubic yards of sand were dredged from the Santa Barbara Harbor, nearly 20 million cubic yards were dredged from the Ventura Harbor, and about 28 million cubic yards of sand were dredged from the Channel Islands Harbor. Dredging from just these three harbors totaled over 58 million cubic yards, or 5.8 million dump truck loads of sand over the three decades. This line of trucks would extend the entire length of the California coastline from Oregon to the Mexican border eleven times! These three harbors are just a few of many large sand traps that have been created along the coast of California, where jetties and breakwaters have been built, where annual dredging is a permanent and expensive way of life, and where harbor-masters and port directors usually have permanent headaches as a result.

All of that beach sand doesn't end up in submarine canyons, however. Some escapes the water, turns inland instead of offshore, and is blown into dunes by onshore winds. As a beach widens and the area of dry sand on the back beach expands, a persistent onshore wind can begin to move the sand inland and off the beach. Huge dune fields were formed in the geologic past along California's shoreline; Pismo Beach and Nipomo Dunes are good examples. But others have now been covered with vegetation, graded, carted off in trucks, and so urbanized that they are no longer recognizable as old sand dunes. The coastal plain from Santa Monica to El Segundo, including the Los Angeles International Airport runways, was formerly covered with sand dunes. Sand blown off the beaches of San Francisco's Ocean Beach a century ago formed a huge field of dunes that extended across the entire peninsula from the Pacific to the bay. Today, the entire area is covered with the city of San Francisco.

The last exit

But there is one more off-ramp for littoral sand, this one with human fingerprints all over it. In addition to the natural process of beach sand loss offshore through submarine canyons, and inland losses by wind into sand dunes, sand was historically mined from some California beaches. Three major mining companies took sand directly from the beach in southern Monterey Bay for nearly 75 years. The smooth, rounded, coarse-grained, and amber-colored sand was in great demand for many industrial uses, including water filtration, abrasives, packing of water wells, and various coatings. Year after year, about 20,000 dump truck loads of this valuable sand was scraped directly off the public beach and sold.

Severe wave erosion of the sandy bluffs backing the southern Monterey Bay shoreline during the late 1970s and 1980s, however, raised the question of whether mining 200,000 cubic yards of sand from the beach each year had a role in the ongoing shoreline retreat. The connection made between beach sand mining and bluff erosion led to the termination of all but one mining operation by about 1990. Unfortunately, because of permitting agency jurisdictional issues—and we have a lot of state and federal agencies that could have their oar in the water on this one—the sole remaining sand company *still* dredges its sand from a back beach pond (as of December 2016; Figure 9.10). Worse than that, it not only continued but also increased its annual extraction rate to equal the combined total of all of the previously operating southern Monterey Bay mining operations. As a result of the failure to effectively manage this resource extraction, the removal of beach sand continues while the adjacent shoreline retreats, threatening several large structures and posing a challenge to the health of the shoreline habitat.

Californians love their beaches. While forming a wonderful soft carpet along our shoreline, they are fragile and vulnerable and constantly change size and shape in response to waves and tides, wind, and sand supply and loss. While appearing stable and permanent, they are one of the most dynamic features on the face of the earth and can grow, shrink, alter their shape, or even disappear in a single storm. Having a sandy beach in front of your home in August doesn't guarantee the same beach will be there in January.

Fig. 9.10. Sand has been dredged for decades from this "pond" on the back beach in southern Monterey Bay, the only beach sand mining operation anywhere in the United States.
photo courtesy Deepika Shrestha Ross

Cutting off sand supplies by damming rivers and streams, interrupting littoral drift through the construction of long jetties and breakwaters, covering over a beach or bluff through construction or armoring, and mining beach sand are a few of the challenges that our beaches face. Large-scale changes to the landscape and major alterations and disruptions to natural systems accompany the settlement and development of California. Dams and debris basins have been built, rivers and creeks have been paved or concreted over, sand has been quarried for construction, and harbors and other large coastal engineering structures have been built along the shoreline. Each of these actions has altered the natural flow of sand to or along the state's beaches, particularly in central and Southern California, where the recreational demand on beaches is greatest and continues to grow along with the population. Although there are no simple solutions, we are now recognizing the problems and disruptions we have created and have begun to evaluate and even implement various responses and solutions. The approaches we develop today need to be sustainable and rely as much as possible on natural processes.

I grew up along the California coast. We had fun as kids at the beach. I first went to the beach when I was very young. It was all about looking at sand crabs running away from you, and digging holes, looking at starfish and sand dollars, looking into the tidepools. We had more of them, and it was really just a treasure of marine activities that were transitioning between the sand and the water. It was just at the edge that we would watch and see. We enjoyed the pier, and we could get up real early and get down to the beach before daylight with our little crab traps. We got lots of crabs, and they were very edible.

I love the water. I have two daughters and they were both raised right into the water environment, even though my mother wasn't fond of the water—there was a lot of fear from her, because she didn't swim. But we went as a family, and often with friends.

Later, I went away for almost 20 years, working in the desert. But I came back. So I had an appreciation for the coast from the very young, certainly at a different level than I do now. I understand it now really as a transition zone from an inland dynamic to an ocean-marine dynamic. And it's a critical transition for human responsibility between those two. It's not just that you go to the beach, because it's not just a beach. It's impacted by watersheds; it's impacted by mountain erosion. And also what we do on the beach impacts the ocean. The most difficult thing for me is that most people don't realize that this relationship exists. And they can abuse each one of those individually and not make the connections and realize that you can do one thing that has the impact on another.

—Student of the shoreline

THE FIGHT TO PRESERVE 1.4 MILES OF SAN FRANCISCO BAY SHORELINE

Imagine looking out over the splendid expanse of San Francisco Bay in all its natural wonder and thinking: "I've got a great idea! Why don't we take some bulldozers to cut off the tops of the hills at the north end of the bay and move 20 million cubic yards of dirt into the water so we can create enough new land to build 2,000 homes?"

Someone has had that thought.

Just a short drive across the Golden Gate Bridge to the north end of San Francisco Bay brings you to Richardson Bay, a blue arc of water curving from Sausalito to Tiburon. In the 1950s, the oak-studded grassy hillsides surrounding this waterway were majestic, rolling, and, like the bay itself, teeming with wildlife. The shoreline was punctuated by a handful of homes, some hidden in forest, along the communities of Strawberry Point and Belvedere. Other than these few scattered houses, the area was largely undeveloped.[1]

Richardson Bay consists of about 1.4 miles of tidelands that provided a vital habitat for harbor seals and other marine life. It was

---

1. Portions of this chapter's description of the early efforts to halt proposed development along the northern shoreline of San Francisco Bay are adapted from David Steinhardt's 1996 publication, *Richardson Bay Journal*.

Fig. 10.1 White pelicans hunt for small fish and are among the many varieties of birds and other wildlife that thrive in the now-protected habitat at the north end of San Francisco Bay.

on the path of the Pacific Flyway, serving as a major, safe winter stopover for dozens of species of migratory birds such as ducks and geese heading on their long annual journeys, some traveling as far as 3,000 miles south every winter. It was the undisturbed home to spectacular wading birds such as egrets and great blue herons, as well as others—pelicans, gulls, terns, and many more (Figure 10.1).

The shallow waters at this edge of San Francisco Bay, combined with the action of the tides, created vast acreage that changed from open water at high tide to muddy marshes at low tide. Because of this special dynamic, the bay was a natural sanctuary for waterfowl and marine life traversing the increasingly urban and suburban sprawl that was the greater San Francisco Bay Area. Birds and other wildlife could count on a place to rest and feed; observers could always count on an eye-opening smorgasbord of nature, which changed seasonally.

Richardson Bay was named for William A. Richardson, originally from England and a mate on one of the many square-rigged whalers that sailed into the San Francisco Bay and dropped anchor there in 1822. He had learned some Spanish on his voyages, and legend has it that he jumped ship after meeting and dancing with a local woman, Maria Antonia Martinez, at an all-night fiesta. Richardson remained in the small town then known as Yerba Buena (later San Francisco) and quickly became an influential person in that Mexican territory. The Mexican governor at the time, Pablo Sola, allowed Richardson to teach navigation and carpentry to his local constituents.

In 1825, Richardson converted to Catholicism and married Maria Antonia, one of the nine daughters of the local *alcalde*, or mayor. Richardson carried on a lucrative trade in Yerba Buena (which was at the foot of what would become Market Street). He also filed a claim for a rancho on the headlands across the Golden Gate, to be called Rancho Saucelito. The rancho had a spring that enabled Richardson to sell fresh water to visiting ships, expanding his business enterprise. His land claim was involved in years of legal challenges, but in 1838 he was granted title to the land surrounding present-day Richardson Bay. The bay's proximity to San Francisco has always given it great strategic and commercial value, and its natural beauty, waters, and shoreline have attracted many.

In fact, during the 1940s, the western border of Richardson Bay, known as Strawberry Point, was one of the two sites under consideration to be a "World Peace Center," the permanent headquarters of the United Nations. The history of the coast and the bay might be quite different if New York City had not been the final choice.

Building on underwater land

The 1940s and early 1950s saw cutting and grading for roads on Strawberry Point and elsewhere. This was due to quick growth and a population boom in the San Francisco Bay Area that began during World War II, especially as shipyards shifted into high gear as part of the war effort. The road and development excavations yielded piles of earth that were routinely dumped into the bay, lining the nearshore of Strawberry Point with a thin ribbon of artificially created land that came to be called Eel Island.

It wasn't long before sea grasses and pickleweed covered Eel Island. To harbor seals, it soon became an important hauling out and pupping area. But to at least one real estate developer's eye, this looked like an irresistible invitation to lay the foundation for a massive explosion of housing, a new community, and profitability. The idea of further filling in the bay with earth from the nearby land fueled the vision of building 2,000 or more homes in what was still 900 acres of bay water.

In 1949, in pursuit of that vision, Reedsport Properties, Inc., obtained the deed to 879 acres of submerged tidelands for $36,000. If that same property could be purchased today, the cost would be well over a billion dollars.

The new owners' audacious plan to fill in and develop the bay with homes, boat basins, and yacht clubs threatened to obliterate this critical waterfowl staging area of the Pacific Flyway, as well as displace all the other wildlife in the rich habitat. At that stage of California's coastal development, few were asking the important questions about the impact of this type of construction. In fact, these types of questions were rarely raised at all. Certainly the criteria we use today were not normally being applied to evaluate the wisdom or overall benefits of development.

> **Today, we are only in the early stages of asking key questions about the impacts on habitat, wildlife, the shoreline itself, and the quality of water and air.**

Today, we are only in the early stages of asking key questions about the impacts of development on habitat, wildlife, the shoreline itself, and air and water quality. We have only begun looking at sustaining resources for new communities, such as power, water, waste disposal, schools, and government services, and at the hazards of earthquakes and seismic instability, sea-level rise, flooding, and more. The environmental impact analysis, so common (and often hotly debated) in today's discussion of development along the coastline, was only broadly introduced during the 1970s as part of growing public concern over environmental issues.

One of the key challenges of evaluating any proposed development along the shoreline involves the question of how to weigh—and what if any weight to give to—any short-term economic benefits claimed to be associated with development. This balancing act is often very political, and politics can sometimes trump good environmental science since the short-term dollar benefits of a healthy environment or preservation of ecosystems often are not readily quantifiable—in that short term. It takes long-term vision, and watchful advocacy, to assure that all types of costs are considered and weighed in the decision-making process.

The foundation—no pun intended—for all of the potential Richardson Bay development was the curious legal mechanism by which private property owners in California could own tidelots, the "land" that is routinely submerged beneath the water adjacent to the shoreline. This land might be more realistically called underwater mud.

Even before California achieved statehood in 1850, California's military governor, Brigadier General Stephen W. Kearny, who was put in charge when the territory was acquired from Mexico in 1848, auctioned off much of the waterfront of San Francisco in what now seems a novel, freewheeling approach to raise money. "Land" that was invisible at high tide and exposed only when the tide was low was also sold into private hands after California was admitted to the union. Title to tidelands, from mean-high water lines to mean-low water lines,[2] had passed from the federal government to the state. The state surveyor general ordered the counties to convey land that was "above low tide" to buyers.

In the San Francisco Bay Area, many parcels lying 6 to 18 feet underwater were sold for $1 an acre. These properties skyrocketed in value over time. Imagine San Francisco waterfront property today, purchased at $1 an acre!

Navigation through this area was still controlled at the federal level, but under this framework vast amounts of intertidal land went into private ownership in San Francisco, Marin, San Mateo, Contra Costa, and Alameda counties. For many generations, banks, real estate firms, corporations, railroads, and churches, in addition to individuals, held title to large areas of tidelands.

This unconstrained approach came to a screeching halt when, at California's second constitutional convention in 1878, the laws were changed to stop all tideland sales within 2 miles of any city or town. This restored the historic concept of "public trust" for the shoreline. Before the brief explosion of tideland sales, shorelines

---

2. This means that the tide lines are drawn, for legal purposes, not at any single high or low tide, since they are changing all the time, but rather at the mean of both the high-tide lines and the low-tide lines taken over a 19-year period.

and the immediately adjacent waters were generally reserved for the citizenry and protected for the public good, to be used by all the people, whether for navigation, recreation, or preservation. This system predominated throughout modern history in U.S. coastal states and in many countries around the world. Of course, it would be nearly another hundred years before the California Coastal Commission would emerge as an additional measure intended to assure public access and maximize protection of the coastline (see more on the Coastal Commission's successes and failures in Chapter 14). But doing away with tidelots and restoring the shoreline to the people's trust was an important step.

Although the constitutional change applied to the sale of new intertidal land and for future generations, it was too late for the 50,000 acres of San Francisco Bay that had already passed into private ownership. For Richardson Bay, with its existing tidelots, this meant that the battle over the use of the tidelands was just beginning.

While the Reedsport developers never successfully advanced beyond the planning stage—drawing sketches, making pitches, and purchasing property—the vision of filling in the bay lived on. In 1956, under financial distress, Reedsport Properties, Inc., sold option rights to those tidelands to the giant Utah Construction Company. This company had already successfully filled in 400 acres of the eastern side of San Francisco Bay near Oakland to greatly expand the city of Alameda. It was also the company that built the Hoover Dam, one of the most massive construction projects ever undertaken up to that time.

Utah took an option for a $600,000 purchase of the submerged tidelands of Richardson Bay (with inflation, the equivalent of about $5 million in today's dollars but worth several billion dollars in real estate value). This option was for that submerged mud for which Reedsport had paid $36,000 just a few years earlier. The construction behemoth also acquired options on adjacent Tiburon wetlands and hillsides, intending to level them with bulldozers to provide the fill material to convert the north end of the bay into highly desirable "marina" tracts with several thousand homes.

Fig. 10.2. Janith and David Steinhardt, seen here in a 1997 Tiburon Heritage and Arts Commission ceremony honoring them for the leadership role they played 40 years earlier in the bay preservation efforts and moving the Lyford House.

A backyard battle . . . and a victory

The enormous scope of these plans, along with the potential for devastating impact on the area's wildlife, hit home when my dad, a young surgeon living on the shoreline of the bay, and my mom heard the sound of a diesel engine. They spotted a dredge in the distance slowly working its way along the waters of Strawberry Point, at the edge of the bay. It was scooping up massive amounts of mud and depositing new landfill as it noisily inched its way along. Its smokestack belched long plumes of exhaust into the near-pristine sky above the water and nearby forests. Each huge bucketful of muddy sediment was also full of creatures that lived along and beneath the bottom of the bay (and a few artifacts of prior human cultures).

My parents, David and Janith, were alarmed. They had come to the California coast from New York City, from one edge of the continent to the other. They were passionate about the shoreline and were raising their young family of three children with respect for nature and conservation (Figure 10.2). This was an urgent call

Fig. 10.3. Dredging that would have created landfill for the construction of 2,000 homes at the north end of San Francisco Bay was stopped at the last minute through quick action by a concerned community.

to action. As my dad described it succinctly many years later, "We needed to take action, fast!"

After a crash course in tideland ownership, and seeing the potential it had to create important new leverage against this unfolding threat, David and Janith determined who owned the tidelot that stretched in front of their house and called the owner to make a proposal to buy it. They made a quick deal: in that initial phone call, they agreed to purchase the tidelot for $3,000. Since they didn't just have $3,000 hanging around, they also arranged to pay for it over time.

This quick action changed everything. They had created a strip of private ownership stretching right through the heart of the area of the bay tentatively destined for fill, and they had no intention of allowing development on their newly acquired underwater lot. But the developer did not know it yet.

As the dredge with its giant, hungry scoop closed in on the waters in front of their house one afternoon, Janith ran down to the shoreline calling for it to stop, waving the new ownership papers (Figure 10.3). The vessel's operator refused to back off and continued to maneuver the large barge with its crane and bucket into position to begin dredging into the family's tidelot. After a tense standoff between shoreline and barge, and as Janith threatened to get the local sheriff, the pilot finally gave in and began to back the dredge away.

The line had been drawn. The legacy of tidelot ownership rights had been turned into a two-edged sword, this time to block proposed development of the bay that had been enabled only by the same antiquated legal tool in the first place. For good measure and a degree of permanence, the Steinhardts added a covenant to the deed to the tidelot requiring that it not be developed, thus preserving the gains for that one lot *in perpetuity* . . . just in case.

Utah Construction ultimately dropped its plan along with its option on the tidelots. In addition to the ownership barrier to filling in the bay that had been created by the newly undevelopable strip, Utah faced fierce, growing community opposition to the project. The company also discovered, through its private, contracted engineering study, that there were new problems to face: Based on test borings into the bay's floor, the company determined the volume of fill that would be necessary to support the development would have to be much greater than originally believed. Concrete pilings that were more than 100 feet long would have been required to support each home. Even today, that would be an extraordinarily difficult and hugely expensive prospect for thousands of homes. Converting the bay waters into new, buildable land was not only unwise but also impractical.

Community action creates the Richardson Bay Foundation

However, the longer-term issue of possible development by others still threatened so long as the Reedsport tidelots were still available for purchase, dangling out there like a live wire. So David and Janith, along with other Marin County conservation leaders of the time, began organizing their neighbors, their community, and their county. The neighbors all pitched in to defray the $3,000 cost of that first tidelot and to purchase another two to widen the blockage. But the need for a longer-term fix led David to reach out to the National Audubon Society's New York headquarters to try to involve the society in a plan to reach a permanent solution—to help purchase the whole area's 900 acres of tidelots and to create a protected bird sanctuary in that area.

These efforts led to the formation of the Richardson Bay Foundation to serve as a vehicle to negotiate and secure the transfer of the tidelands, and to the creation of a Marin Chapter of the National Audubon Society. The campaign to raise money, negotiate the purchase, and create a sanctuary moved forward with a supportive and vocal community, with the help of the already existing Marin Conservation League, and with the support of conservation activists such as Caroline Livermore, Elizabeth Terwilliger, Martin Griffin, M.D., and many others. They held evening meetings in local schools and private homes; they canvassed neighborhoods; they lobbied government agencies; they raised money.

As a result of the environmental threat and the local community's mobilization against it, the National Audubon Society agreed to put up $25,000 so long as Marin County would commit an additional $25,000. And the town of Belvedere would be asked to match that combined total of $50,000 with $50,000 of its own. The conditions of this patchwork of interdependent funding required that the title to the lots be accepted by Marin County and Belvedere, and that the 900 acres be leased to Audubon as a sanctuary for 50 years (subject to later renewal).

But there was a giant gap in this plan. That was the hole between the total of $100,000 that could be committed by these three entities, and Reedsport's $750,000 asking price for the tidelands. This price was even $150,000 more than the aborted $600,000 Utah Construction option (quite a bit of quick appreciation in value for what was rapidly becoming unbuildable underwater real estate). Through lengthy negotiations, David and his co-negotiator, Everett Jensen, a former U.S. Forest Service official who had purchased many tracts of land for the Forest Service, succeeded in wresting an agreement from Reedsport on a price of $232,500. In later years, David described how much he enjoyed being the bad cop to Everett's good cop in those meetings because it enabled him to do something he never did—raise his voice and storm out of the meetings. But he also was always quick to admit that their success

This serves as a textbook example of how coastal resources can be protected when committed citizens get involved.

was undoubtedly mostly due to the serious financial distress the seller was under at the time, as well as several pending lawsuits it faced.

Because of the greatly reduced price, the bulk of the remaining cost was found when the State of California committed $100,000 to purchase a right-of-way along one section of shoreline for improvements to an already existing road along the edge of Belvedere. This purchase was the perfect final piece to the puzzle in several ways: it saved the state more than half a million dollars (the state would have had to pay if it had waited to purchase these rights later); it assured that there would be no development along that shoreline; and it was the last needed funding to close the deal to purchase the 900 acres. This serves as a textbook example—modeled by many successful land trusts—of what can be achieved in protecting California's precious coastal resources when concerned, committed, and creative citizens get involved in issues that matter to them personally.

To make it all come together, through education and action, the community organized to make sure that each of the necessary pieces fell into place. The night before the Belvedere voters went to the polls to vote on the $50,000 bond issue for its share, one supporter, who was a former pilot, dropped a series of long-lasting, floating flares into the waters to dramatically mark off and demonstrate the area of the bay that was being threatened, the subject of the bond. The day of the election in November 1957, conservation groups mounted a phone call get-out-the-vote campaign and provided rides to get people to the polls. This was done with hand-posted flyers, lists, and personal phone calls, a far cry from the big data and robocalls of today's elections. With a record 78 percent turnout, the bond measure passed by an 8-to-1 majority.

On January 15, 1958, just fifteen months after David's original proposal to Audubon, Reedsport transferred title to "the whole enchilada" to the Richardson Bay Foundation. In due course, this was transferred to Marin County and Belvedere and then leased to Audubon as a bird sanctuary. Today, this protected area is part of the internationally designated San Francisco Estuary Hemispheric Reserve of the Western Hemisphere Shorebird Reserve Network (quite a mouthful). The reserve lies within California Department of Fish and Wildlife's Mount Tamalpais Fish and Game Reserve.

Fig. 10.4. This decrepit nineteenth-century Victorian house on Strawberry Point was nearly razed by bulldozers in the mid-1950s.

Moving house

The sanctuary's headquarters, located on a pristine, sheltered knoll along the eastern edge of the protected waters, includes a beautiful Victorian-era house with a colorful history that is inextricably tied to the effort to stop the commercial development. Amazingly enough, it was originally built on the opposite shore of the bay, on Strawberry Point, where it remained for nearly 100 years—before the upheaval of the citizen-led effort to create the sanctuary caused some unforeseen and dramatic changes.

During the same months that the campaign for the funding and creation of the sanctuary was under way, David happened to be walking the forested portion of Strawberry Point when he couldn't help but notice several bulldozers clearing the trees to make way for a small housing development. In the path of the bulldozers was an old, dilapidated house that in its earlier years had been a spectacular Victorian-era home, built in the late 1800s. Alarmed that the house was about to be destroyed, he contacted the developer who told him that it was, indeed, set to be razed (Figure 10.4). Unless, of course, if my dad wanted to take it and move it away. "You can have it if you can take it, *quick.*"

Coming back home to the family that day with the possibility of the house was a little like coming home with a new puppy (or a rowboat), except that this "puppy" was a decrepit house in a forest with all of its windows broken out, no paint remaining on deeply weathered and stained wood, and plenty of broken pieces. The family was familiar with the empty, worn building, although not so familiar with its rich history. As young kids, we sometimes crept up to the house, which was darkened by its age and its position in the shadows of the trees, to peer in past the boarded windows. Of course, we always gave it the respect due a house that was rumored to be haunted. Curiosity always won out over caution, however, even if we never dared to go as far as to enter into the forbidding structure. Close was always close enough. That is, until one evening when we approached from the underbrush, got too close, and were shocked to see a light go on inside near a broken window. I don't think we stopped running until we reached home. I know I didn't.

Regardless of how we had experienced this diamond in the rough, the offer to take it set off a series of hurried actions to make arrangements to remove it to . . . somewhere. This is where a romance of more than 100 years earlier guided the house's future in a very real and surprising way.

Built in 1876 by Benjamin Lyford and his wife, Hilarita, the old Victorian and its outbuildings were in an idyllic location on the water's edge. Dr. Lyford had a checkered background—from his medical "degree," granted to him by a shady diploma mill where he studied for six months, to his brush with charges of conduct unbecoming an officer in a Civil War infantry division, to his unethical attempts to withhold from his colleagues, for personal gain, a reputedly remarkable embalming process he had developed. But his fortunes had changed when he married Hilarita Reed in 1872, as she was the daughter of wealthy landowner John Reed, who held the land grants to much of Marin County's shoreline property. Following Lyford's death, Reed's grandson and granddaughter, John Paul and Clotilda, lived in the house. This is where the connections began to emerge for the ultimate movement of the house to its current location based on a lifelong romance.

In 1883, soon after John Paul and Clotilda moved into the Lyford House, a 3-year-old named Rose Rodriguez moved into the house

Fig. 10.5. After volunteers painstakingly loaded the house onto a barge, a tugboat nudged it across Richardson Bay to the Tiburon Peninsula property of Rosie Verrall in December 1957.

along with her parents, who worked for John Paul and Clotilda. As she grew up, Rose (later Rosie Rodriguez Verrall) became Clotilda's servant, and her diaries let us know that her heart belonged to John Paul. He apparently felt the same way. But Clotilda took a dim view of the relationship, and Rose ultimately was forced out of the house and came to live on the opposite shore of the bay. For many years, she lived in isolation, but she was able to gaze across the bay to the mansion where she had once lived and had fallen in love. John Paul died in 1919, but other than the many letters they wrote each other, they never made a life together.

During her later years, I remember visiting "Rosie the goat lady," as she came to be known, playing with and feeding her goats. I recall her visiting our family and sometimes sharing dinner together. My most vivid memory involving Rosie is the sight, on December 4, 1957, of the Lyford House being lifted onto a barge and floating ever so slowly alongside a tugboat three-fourths of a mile across the bay to Rosie's property in Tiburon (Figures 10.5 and 10.6). I can picture her watching intently once the house reached the shoreline destination as

**Fig. 10.6. Something you don't see every day on the bay
(December 1957).**

a group of hearty volunteers rolled it on long timbers partway up the
small hill to the site where it sits today. Fully restored to its former
glory through community efforts, the house now stands as the crown
jewel in the headquarters complex of the Richardson Bay Wildlife
Sanctuary and Audubon Center of Northern California (Figure 10.7).

Although a surplus house and the need for a headquarters
with a hoped-for sanctuary on the opposite side of the bay were
apparently unrelated, they were tied together by Rosie, history, and
an active community. Rosie and the house were reunited as part of
an arrangement in which she donated her property for sanctuary
headquarters, on the condition that she could live out her life there
and that the Lyford House be moved to the property. She got her wish,
and the house is now on the National Registry of Historic Places. In
addition to serving as the sanctuary's headquarters and the Audubon
education center, the building and grounds are the site of weddings
and celebrations for those who wish to embrace romance with the
spirit and history of that spot, and in plain view of the edge. Rosie died
in 1964.

These stories of communities becoming active in protecting
against threats to the coast, to their edge, have been played out in
many places throughout California, both before and after the fight

to save 1.4 miles of San Francisco Bay shoreline. Some have met with success; others have not. Permanent solutions are hard to come by. Through legislation, Californians have provided some level of protection through the creation of a network of nearly 30 Marine Protected Areas. In 1992, the federal government established the Monterey Bay National Marine Sanctuary (MBNMS). That sanctuary affords certain protections for 276 miles of coastal waters running from near Point Reyes all the way south to Cambria, reaching out an average of 30 miles into the ocean (see Chapter 15 for more on Marine Protected Areas and the MBNMS).

Fig. 10.7. Even though fully restored, the mansion still needs periodic TLC (2017). It serves as part of the headquarters for the Richardson Bay Wildlife Sanctuary and the Audubon Center of Northern California.

Not every threat can be warded off by buying tidelots and creating sanctuaries. In part this is due to the dynamic nature of the coast and the forces that drive human behavior, including the urge to develop. But vigilance, leadership, dedication, and creative use of all the available tools remain as bedrock principles despite these changes. These tools include organizing and education, research, law, legislation, and elections. They continue to serve us well, especially through trying times that demand greater participation from each of us.

The events I witnessed as a young child in Richardson Bay planted seeds that grew over the course of my lifetime. I could not have understood the legal or policy details of what was happening, and many years would pass before I became a litigator, advocate, and administrative law judge. But the inspiration of meeting complex challenges with creative and unrelenting advocacy has inspired me throughout the decades.

But even in the case of Richardson Bay, despite citizen efforts that stopped 900 acres of fill in the 1950s, in later years multistoried mansions have sprung up on some of the original, dredged fill just outside the sanctuary. This has become some of most valuable real estate in California. After thousands of years of occupancy, seals and other wildlife have been displaced from their homes and sanctuaries by human intrusion and a few dozen $8 million luxury homes.

Someone has had that thought.

I've lived along the coast all my life and I've loved it here since the day I was born. I wouldn't trade it for anything or anybody. Some of my very earliest, best memories as a young kid are of playing on the beach in the warm sun and the water with my older brother and sister. I've had the opportunity to travel and see a lot of country, been to a lot of spots. But none of it has the moderate climate, the scenery, or the wildlife. You can watch the birds and all the wildlife, there's always something coming by that you can see.

What you have on the coast are your hills, mountains, broken terrain that pretty much leads to the ocean—that alone makes the beauty of the area so much better than waking up in the morning and all you see is flat ground with roads that cross flat fields and the real hot climate in the summer and the cold climate in the winter. I mean, you've got a long way to get to the ocean.

I guess people are drawn to the ocean, drawn to the coast. I sort of get a charge out of it. It has something to pull you here. The ocean is right with you, and the climactic condition is different than most areas. The weather and the scenery, these two together. The coast has everything to offer you.

That's why it is so important to preserve coast. To try to keep it as rural as we can.
　　—Dairy farmer, age 80

SEARCHING FOR THE COAST

Finding human bones on an offshore island provided more credence to the theory that the earliest humans entered North America and traveled down the coast by boat, along what has been dubbed the "kelp highway."

Everyone is an immigrant to California. Some just arrived a lot later than others. There are volumes written by those who came during the past 150 years or so, but the first humans didn't leave a lot of information behind, at least not letters or journals. Thus, their history is a bit sketchy. So much so that the people who study these things can't seem to agree how they got here, or even when. The jury seems to be still out on some of the details.

Immigrants have come to the coast of California from all points of the compass, north, south, east, and west. Some passed through the state, but most fell hard for it and decided to stay. For the same reasons people around the world have been drawn to coastal regions, California's settlers often headed to the coast, and still do in large numbers. Today, two-thirds of our California population has settled in coastal counties. That's 26 million of us, and the numbers continue to increase.

The earliest arrivals and coastal Indian groups

Archaeologists are a feisty lot. Although they had reached a truce of sorts for several decades with general agreement that near the end of the last ice age, the first humans coming into the Americas came from Siberia across a land bridge, that shaky consensus has degenerated a bit in recent years. The problem is that as they have looked harder

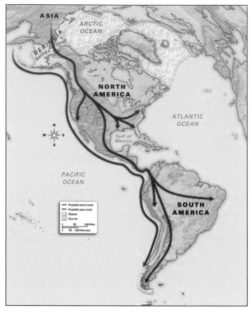

Fig. 11.1. Possible migration routes for the earliest humans into the Americas from Asia.

and dug deeper, they keep finding more "stuff" that appears to have been left behind by early inhabitants. Finding evidence of the oldest or the first human is no small matter for the stature of an archaeologist. It's akin to a geologist's getting credit for dating the world's oldest rock, or a paleontologist's finding the oldest evidence of life. The problem is that the evidence left behind and uncovered is not always as convincing to everyone else as it is to the person who first found it.

Scholars generally agree that the peopling of the Americas took place sometime in the past 25,000 years. The most accepted view at the moment is that a wave of hunters crossed into the New World from Siberia when the continental ice sheets had expanded to the point where the lower sea level exposed a land bridge (Figure 11.1). The first documented and later dated remnants of human activity were found in the 1920s near Clovis, New Mexico. These early humans seem to have settled down here about 13,000 years ago. The Clovis site and projectile points were the gold standard for decades, and any competing theory was usually quickly discredited or not given much credence. There was a lot at stake there in Clovis.

Archaeologists have been down on their hands and knees in the dirt across the Americas ever since, however. The evidence turned up more recently makes it increasingly clear that the Clovis site was not the earliest human record in the Americas and that the history and migration rate was likely far more complex than initially envisioned.

In the late 1970s, an American archaeologist and his Chilean colleagues began excavating what appeared to be an ancient settlement on a creek bank at Monte Verde, in southern Chile.

Radiocarbon dating of organic material collected from the ruins of a large tentlike structure indicated that the site was 14,800 years old, predating the Clovis finds by nearly 2,000 years. Mastodons were apparently butchered nearby, and cordage, stone choppers, augers, and wooden planks were preserved in an adjacent bog, along with plant remains, edible seeds, and traces of wild potatoes. While some have questioned the evidence from the site, they generally agree that humans must have arrived in the Americas earlier than originally thought and that they also traveled farther and faster. To the disappointment of many archaeologists who had staked their reputations on Clovis, the glow was fading.

In the 1980s, below a layer of undisturbed sediment, archaeologists in Florida found stone flakes that are believed to have been chipped from a larger stone in order to make tools and projectile points. A mastodon tusk found in the same location, scarred by circular cut marks from a knife, was dated at 14,500 years old.

In a set of caves in a very dry area of central Oregon (the Paisley Caves), scientists in 2008 discovered dried human feces (fossilized poop, technically known as coprolites) along with lots of animal bones and artifacts. They extracted human mitochrondal DNA, a lengthy and painstaking multistep process you certainly couldn't perform in your kitchen or home lab, dated at 14,300 years ago.

Even more recently—in 2011—at a site in Texas known as Buttermilk Creek, archaeologists discovered projectile points and other evidence showing that hunter-gatherers had reached the area as early as 15,500 years ago.

Based on the number of sites where evidence of human habitation has now been uncovered, stretching from Alaska to Chile, and despite some archaeological arm wrestling over what counts as acceptable concrete evidence and what doesn't, it seems that humans arrived in the Americas at least 15,500 or 16,000 years ago.

But these findings did more than just adjust a date by a few thousand years. They changed everything that had been understood about the arrival of humans because pushing the date back introduced a conundrum, another problem to be solved. Based on sea levels and ice coverage 15,000 years ago, there wasn't an ice-free highway open for traffic yet for these early visitors to follow southward into the rest of the Americas.

The lack of a convenient or even passable route on dry, ice-free land raised the possibility that perhaps the first Americans didn't walk here at all but came from Siberia to the Americas in small boats, following the coastline south. This idea was first proposed in the late 1950s after very old human bones were discovered on Santa Rosa Island, off the coast of Santa Barbara. The bones were initially determined to be male and were named the Arlington Springs Man, after the discovery site. Subsequent reanalysis led to renaming the remains the Arlington Springs Woman, but after a final review, the referees reversed their decision and decided, no, the leg bones were actually those of a man.

The most startling aspect of this find came when the bones were later dated at 13,000 years old, making these *the oldest human remains found anywhere in the Americas at that time*. Although sea level was about 150 feet lower then than today, Santa Rosa Island was still separated from the rest of California by about 5 miles of ocean. Unless this early man was an Olympic swimmer, he and his friends and family must have crossed the deep Santa Barbara channel by boat. Although pygmy mammoth bones of the same approximate age were also unearthed on Santa Rosa Island, indicating coexistence with this early human, it is not believed that this miniature elephant shared the boat.

It now seems highly probable that the earliest Americans worked their way down the coastline.

Finding human bones on an offshore island provided more credence to the theory that the earliest humans entered North America and traveled down the coast by boat, along what has been dubbed the "kelp highway." There was ample seafood and seaweed along the way so they didn't go hungry. The finding and later dating of Arlington Springs Man also altered the prevailing view that the earliest humans reached the interior of North America first and then dispersed to the coast. Based on the Santa Rosa Island findings, it now seems highly probable that the earliest Americans worked their way down the coastline.

The earliest Americans seem to have thrived along the state's ocean edge. The 13,000-year-old man from Santa Rosa Island is the oldest-dated human discovered thus far in California. By about 10,000 years ago, early humans appear to have fairly widely occupied the coastal region, for a number of good reasons. The same climate that draws people to the coast today was, even 10,000 years ago, more agreeable year-round than inland areas. California has long been a fertile and productive region with an unusually rich diversity of plants and animals that provided year-round subsistence for the early inhabitants.

Ultimately, more than two dozen tribal groups occupied the coast, stretching from the Tolowa near today's Oregon border to the Kumeyaay in the San Diego area. These indigenous people suffered much with the arrival of Europeans, including massive declines in their numbers from imported disease like smallpox and from direct efforts to challenge their cultures. Yet despite this there are over 100 federally recognized tribes in California today. California now has the largest Native American population and most distinct tribes of any state in the nation.

Before European contact, Native Americans spoke at least 100 distinct languages and many more individual local dialects, and generally the groups could not understand each other's languages. Because of the rugged topography of much of California, and the abundant food supply from both the land and the water, the indigenous tribes that evolved seemed to be quite isolated and independent of each other, living in many small self-sufficient groups without a lot of resource conflicts.

Because the tribes had no written language, there was no Rosetta Stone for archaeologists or anthropologists to work from. What we know about the earliest Californians has been extracted from several different sources: (1) archaeological findings; (2) the earliest writings of European explorers and colonists who encountered the indigenous people; (3) oral histories from the tribal elders who survived into the early 1900s; and (4) the oral traditions passed down through successive generations of native Californians.

Probably the most reliable sources of information on how these indigenous people lived have been their trash piles or kitchen middens, much like looking in the trash and recycling containers we put out on the curb for collection every week. There's a lot of cultural information buried in the things we toss—pizza boxes and breakfast cereal containers, beer cans and wine bottles, newspapers and junk mail. Although most of this won't survive for 5,000 years, a few remnants will, and we might well be remembered by these varied items.

The native tribes who lived along the coast were mostly hunters and gatherers, and food came from wherever they could find it, on land and underwater. All evidence from their astonishingly large garbage heaps or shell mounds, which are also surprisingly widespread along the coast, indicates they consumed almost everything that was in any way edible and without much regard to size. Although we are a bit picky about what we eat from the littoral zone, they harvested almost anything they could scrape from the rocks, pull from the tide pools, or catch with simple hooks and nets. They left behind huge piles of shells: mussels, limpets, chitons, clams, scallops, snails, crabs, abalone, and barnacles, as well as the bones of seals, sea lions, and sea otters. Clearly, their diets were diverse. The flat terraces that front nearly 60 percent of California's coast along with the stream valleys that have cut through the terraces were also rich with wildlife, and many of the middens contain bones of deer and elk, coyote, rabbits, birds, and even mice and gophers.

Everything was fair game and no fishing or hunting licenses were required. The modest populations along the coast didn't have huge appetites, but hunting and gathering probably took much of their waking hours. While they certainly took their share of natural resources, they seem to have figured out the concept of sustainability and how many people could be supported by any local region. Life was probably reasonably good for perhaps as long as 15,000 years until the Europeans started to arrive.

Europeans begin to explore the Coast

Well before the Pilgrims landed at Plymouth Rock in 1620, ships were exploring the West Coast. In the sixteenth century, Spain was a powerful country with more navy vessels than any other nation in the world, and they were venturing everywhere, searching out new areas for trade and commerce. A handful of expeditions explored along the coast in the 1500s, but because of the rugged nature of much of this uncharted coastline and the frequent blanket of fog, many of the earliest ships stayed well offshore and left very few detailed accounts of their observations.

Juan Rodríguez Cabrillo, who was Portuguese but sailed under the flag of Spain, was the first European to explore the coast of California. On June 27, 1542, he set out from Navidad, on the west coast of Mexico, with three ships. On the first of August, he anchored within sight of Cedros Island, along the west coast of today's Baja California, and then continued north, soon entering completely uncharted waters. By September 28, he landed in what is now San Diego Bay. A little over a week later, he discovered Catalina Island, encountering "a great crowd of armed Indians." Cabrillo progressed north to San Pedro Bay, which was named Baya de los Fumos, "bay of smokes," from the fires being maintained by the local residents. They anchored in Santa Monica Bay for a night, and later sailed along the east–west-trending Santa Barbara coastline, first encountering the northern Channel Islands.

The expedition spent a week exploring the islands, anchoring in a bay on San Miguel Island, and then on October 18, rounded Point Conception, which Cabrillo somewhat curiously named Cabo de Galera, loosely translated from Portuguese as "cape of the guys." They got as far north as the Russian River mouth on the northern California coastline by late October 1542. But, as luck and perhaps fog would have it, they completely missed the Golden Gate, as did many subsequent explorers. Cabrillo sailed right by one of the greatest natural harbors in the world—twice, once heading north and once returning south—and continued down the coast to Monterey Bay, which they named the Bay of Pines. Cabrillo stopped at Catalina Island on November 23 (then named San Salvador after the flagship of his small fleet) to make repairs over the winter.

About a month later, during what he described from his perspective as an attack from local island warriors, Juan Rodríguez Cabrillo is said to have stumbled on some sharp rocks while trying to rescue some of his men. The injury became infected, gangrene set in, and, after leading this first voyage of exploration along much of the Golden State's coastline, he died on January 3, 1543, as a result of his injuries.

Francis Drake was the first Englishman to see the Pacific Ocean, reportedly after climbing a tall tree in the Isthmus of Panama in 1573. He was also the first European to sail completely around the world as the captain and leader of the expedition from beginning to end.

Magellan didn't fare nearly as well on his attempt to sail around the world 50 years earlier. He died in a skirmish in the Philippines, and just one of his five ships actually made the complete global circumnavigation, coming home with only 18 of the original crew of 237. Sailing around the world in the sixteenth century through uncharted waters was truly a risky undertaking with a huge number of unknowns. Magellan never came close to California, however. Drake did.

Sir Francis Drake was a thorn in the side of the Spanish throughout his entire career at sea and a character of the first order.

Sir Francis Drake was a thorn in the side of the Spanish throughout his entire career at sea and a character of the first order, at various times a navigator, slaver, sea captain, privateer, vice admiral, and ultimately, the highest of all callings, a politician of the Elizabethan era. He was born in England, the eldest of twelve sons, about the time that Cabrillo was readying his fleet for his first exploration of the California coastline. Drake plundered Spanish treasure ships anywhere he could find them, ransacked Spanish ports in the Americas, and generally lived a life of adventure and crime, often at Spain's expense, including playing a key role as vice admiral of the English fleet in the defeat of the Spanish Armada in 1588.

His official charge from the queen of England, as he worked his way up the West Coast of the Americas in 1578, was to destroy Spanish ships and plunder settlements as part of his voyage around the world. He encountered neither ships nor settlements along the coast of California, however, and just how far he reached has been argued about for centuries. Historians appear to have some of the same types of long-standing and acrimonious disagreements as archaeologists. Many of those interested in this history, especially those who live in the area, favor Drakes Bay, in the lee of Point Reyes along the Marin County coast (Figure 11.2), as the New Albion embayment where Drake anchored and made repairs on his ship, the *Golden Hind*, before heading out across the Pacific to complete his round-the-world voyage.

Fig. 11.2. The white cliffs of Drakes Bay on the Point Reyes Peninsula. *photo courtesy Bob Campbell, robertcampbellphotography.com*

However, in the interest of truth in reporting, over twenty other places have been put forward as the New Albion in Drake's log. These various harbors span more than 800 miles of the West Coast, from as far south as the interior of San Francisco Bay to as far north as Vancouver Island. Sir Francis and the queen preserved some secrecy regarding his voyage and precisely where he was because of the competition between England and Spain at the time regarding claims for ownership of North American lands. This secrecy is often used to explain the wide discrepancies in various theories on how far north Drake actually sailed.

The voyage of Sebastián Vizcaíno in 1602, 60 years after Cabrillo's initial journey and over 400 years ago, was the first true mapping expedition of the seaward edge of California. Reports from his ships set the stage for the first overland exploration of California. Vizcaíno was a Spanish soldier, explorer, and diplomat who through his coastal mapping played an important role in California's subsequent history. The Spanish viceroy in Mexico City, the Count of Monte Rey, appointed Vizcaíno the general-in-charge of an expedition to locate safe harbors in Alta (Upper) California for Spanish galleons to use on their return voyage from the Philippines to Acapulco. He was given the

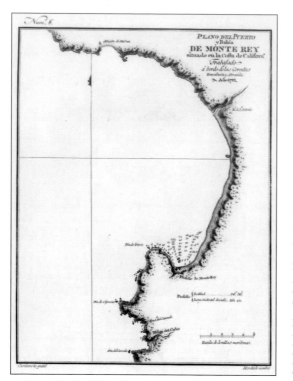

Fig. 11.3. The first map of Monterey Bay from Sebastián Vizcaíno's voyage of 1603.

authority to map in detail the California coastline that Juan Rodríguez Cabrillo had first explored in 1542.

Vizcaíno left Acapulco on May 5, 1602, with three ships. After entering and naming San Diego Bay on November 10, he continued up the coast giving names to, and in many cases renaming, many of the prominent features that Cabrillo had previously named—Santa Catalina Island, Santa Barbara, Point Conception, Carmel Valley, and Monterey Bay. Vizcaíno sailed as far north as Cape Mendocino, making detailed charts of the coastline. There were no cell phones or any other ship-to-ship communications at that time, however, and one of his three ships, the *Tres Reyes*, or "three kings," was separated from the others. That ship continued almost 200 miles farther north, at least as far as Cape Blanco on the Oregon coast, before deciding to turn around.

It was a difficult voyage, as were most at that time, and many of Vizcaíno's crew soon were suffering from scurvy because of a lack of vitamin C. Sixteen sailors had already died by the time the expedition reached Monterey Bay. While he gave new names to many places, the only stretch of coast he apparently actually explored in detail was Monterey Bay, which seemed to satisfy Spain's need for a safe harbor for ships returning from the Philippines. In fact, he mapped the bay's coastline so carefully that his maps were used for the next 200 years (Figure 11.3). Like so many of the other navigators during the sixteenth and seventeenth centuries, however, he managed to completely miss the entrance to San Francisco Bay.

Vizcaíno reported in his logs that Monterey Bay was a safe harbor, "sheltered from all winds." This somewhat idealized characterization of the generally windy and largely unsheltered bay was no doubt motivated at least in part by a desire to file a successful report from his difficult mission. As was discovered in subsequent years, Monterey Bay really has no natural harbors, and considerable effort was expended in the last century to build harbors sheltered from the wind and waves at Santa Cruz, Moss Landing, and Monterey.

Although Vizcaíno spoke in glowing words of the California coast and Monterey Bay as a good port for galleons returning from the Philippines, he was not allowed a return visit. Alta California was ignored for over a century and a half. Escalating confrontations in Europe were diverting Spain's attention and resources.

The global situation began to change in the late eighteenth century, however. The Spanish government, fearing that the Russians, who were engaged in the sea otter fur trade, would extend their empire southward from Alaska, decided it was time to establish a presence in Alta California. The Spanish also had to contend with England, which had recently obtained Canada from France and was starting to look longingly at Spanish "possessions." The world at this time was akin to a huge Monopoly board, where the big players could buy, sell and trade entire regions of the Earth. Or take them by sheer force.

This is an appropriate place to ask the most basic California historical question: where did the name "California" originally come from anyway? The most widely accepted source of the name of the Golden State is a popular early-sixteenth-century romance novel, *Las sergas de Esplandian* (The adventures of Esplandian) by a Spanish author, Garci Rodríguez de Montalvo. The novel depicted the Island of California as being east of Asia and "very close to a side of the Earthly Paradise; and it was populated by black women, without any man existing among them, for they lived in the manner of Amazons. They had beautiful and

> **The most widely accepted source of the name of the Golden State is a popular early-sixteenth-century romance novel.**

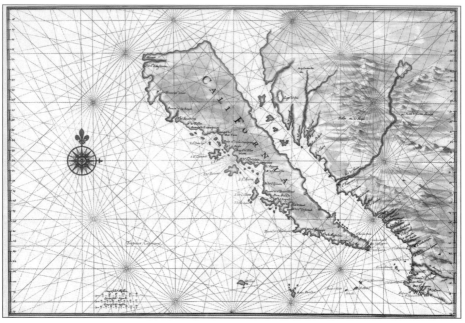

Fig. 11.4. Map of California when it was still believed to be an island, drawn by Dutch cartographer Joan Vinckeboons about 1650. *Library of Congress*

robust bodies, and were very brave and strong. Their island was the strongest in the world, with its cliffs and rocky shores. Their weapons were made of gold, as were the harnesses of the wild beasts that they were accustomed to taming so they could be ridden, because there was no other metal on the island but gold" (translated from the Spanish).

The earliest maps depicted California as an island, separated from the rest of New Spain (Mexico) by the Pacific Ocean. This was an erroneous impression, which no doubt derived from the initial exploration along the coast of northern Mexico that hadn't yet reached the head of the Gulf of California (Figure 11.4).

Spanish inactivity in Alta California was about to end as the king of Spain decided to defend the area by establishing both missions and settlements. The West Coast became a giant chessboard, but with three players making serious moves. An experienced and capable military officer, Captain Gaspar de Portolá, was selected to make the move for Spain and was appointed as the military commander of the first Spanish overland expedition into Alta California.

Portolá was born in Spain into a family of nobles and joined the Spanish army where his skills as a leader and an organizer soon became evident. He came to New Spain as a military officer, and in 1768 was appointed governor of Baja California, which was at that time an almost unpopulated desert. In the spring of 1769, two expeditions, one commanded by Portolá and a second by Captain Fernando Rivera, set out by foot from Baja California to prepare for the military occupancy of Alta California. An important objective was to reach Vizcaíno's famous Monterey Bay harbor. The increasing threats of Russia and England along the coast provided a strong catalyst for a successful expedition.

The Portolá expedition left San Diego almost 250 years ago, on July 14, 1769, heading north along the coast with 64 men, mostly soldiers, and 200 pack animals. With some men on horseback and some walking, they reached Los Angeles on August 2 and Santa Barbara a little over two weeks later. This was the easiest part of the trip. The land was flat, without much vegetation, although probably not much water either in July.

Near what is now San Luis Obispo, they encountered bears and named the area Cañada de los Osos, "valley of the bears." They also encountered the massive rock at the shoreline that Cabrillo had discovered 227 years earlier and named *El Morro*, "large rounded rock." Today this is the site of the city of Morro Bay. The rock is the most westerly of a series of at least twelve volcanic plugs, the remains of the interiors of ancient volcanoes, 22 to 26 million years old, that stretch inland to San Luis Obispo.

Although the trek along the flat coastal terraces was manageable, on September 13, they ran into the southern end of the rugged Big Sur coast, not far beyond San Simeon and Hearst Castle. Driving an automobile north along Highway 1, which was literally chiseled and blasted out of the steep cliffs during the Great Depression, can usually be managed without incident today. But Portolá and his men and mules found the route impassable. They were forced to make a difficult detour inland, through the Santa Lucia Range to the Salinas Valley. Following the Salinas River north and, counterintuitively, downstream toward Monterey Bay, they reached an area between present-day Marina and Salinas on October 1, where they camped.

Fig. 11.5. Mulligan Hill, in the center of the photograph, is an old sand dune at the mouth of the Salinas River that Gaspar de Portolá climbed in 1769 looking for Monterey Bay. *photo courtesy Kenneth and Gabrielle Adelman, California Coastal Records Project, www.CaliforniaCoastline.org*

Portolá and a small group of soldiers headed toward the Salinas River mouth. They climbed a low mound of sand, known today as Mulligan Hill, near the mouth of the river, but failed to see or recognize Vizcaíno's harbor "sheltered from all winds." Mulligan Hill is actually a large old sand dune, and like much of the rest of the central and southern Monterey Bay shoreline, the extensive dune fields bear evidence to a long history of strong winds and an ample sand supply. It's also an area that is frequently foggy, with limited visibility, as Portolá discovered (Figure 11.5).

Another scouting party headed south and explored the Monterey Peninsula but couldn't find the protected harbor there either. Portolá was also eagerly anticipating meeting a ship, the *San José*, which was carrying needed supplies. But the *San José* never arrived. It had been two months since Portolá and his men had left San Diego, and whatever they were eating, it didn't include any or enough vitamin C. Many of them were now incapacitated from scurvy and were being painstakingly dragged behind mules on litters, which didn't help matters or morale.

They continued north, reaching the Pájaro River (bird river), which they named after a large straw-stuffed bird that was left behind in a deserted Indian settlement. The expedition reached the area of present-day Santa Cruz on October 18 and continued north along the coast, paralleling the route that State Highway 1 would follow nearly 150 years later. Finally, after a very difficult and unpleasant journey up the north coast, they headed inland and on October 31, 1769, from San Bruno Mountain, sighted San Francisco Bay for the first time.

Although San Francisco Bay would be recognized just a few years later as one of the greatest natural harbors on the planet, Portolá apparently thought little of the bay and was disappointed in not being able to find the Monterey Bay's supposedly remarkable harbor.

Being a dutiful soldier, he turned the expedition around, dragging the sick and lame, and headed back toward the Monterey Peninsula. Reaching the Carmel Bay area, the expedition's mules and horses found lots to forage on, but the explorers themselves were reduced to eating seagulls and pelicans. Some evidence suggests that local native residents may have saved them by providing ground corn and seeds.

They continued to believe that the San José, the resupply ship they were expecting, would find them. In one last attempt to communicate, they erected two wooden crosses on low hills above the beach and buried notes at their bases, hoping that the crew would see them from a distance and come ashore. It didn't happen.

It was now December, however, and the weather was deteriorating so they decided to head south. The remaining party, minus several deserters, reached San Diego on January 24, 1770, six months after its original departure. The ship that the expedition had been waiting for had initially been forced to return to port in Mexico for repairs shortly after departing. But after setting sail again, it never reached Monterey Bay. In fact, it was never heard from again.

Portolá was a very determined soldier, however, and he walked all the way back the next spring with another expedition. This time he recognized Vizcaíno's Monterey Bay, although it was never really "sheltered from all winds."

Gold changes California forever

By the early 1800s, the stories of mountain men and early explorers of the west were beginning to trickle east. Many adventurous souls, single men at first and later covered wagon trains with families, began to work their way across the plains, hoping to find better opportunities. This migration led to one of the most important events in California history and had a profound effect on the development of California's coast.

On January 28, 1848, gold was discovered along the American River in the Sierra foothills above present-day Sacramento where John Sutter was building a lumber mill. Sutter was from Switzerland and evidently came to the United States with some financial resources and business sense. He gradually worked his way west, joined a party of fur trappers, and in 1838 ended up well north of California at Fort Vancouver on the Columbia River. For some unknown reason, perhaps because he came from Switzerland, he decided to head south and start a utopian colony in California. It seems he was merely the first of many throughout California's history who would get this idea. Exactly what Sutter envisioned as Utopia at that early date in the wild and largely unexplored and unpopulated area that was to become the state of California isn't clear.

Getting to California from Fort Vancouver was complicated at the time. He started recruiting men and then sailed to what were then known as the Sandwich Islands (Hawaii), where he engaged in more business deals and recruiting. Sutter next proceeded to buy out what was left of the Russian-American Fur Company in Fort Ross. By this time the Russians had largely abandoned sea otter hunting along the Northern California coast because of the lack of enough otters to make hunting worthwhile. He then became a Mexican citizen in order to obtain a large land grant near present-day Sacramento. Sutter purchased boats and supplies and worked his way up the Sacramento River to build a fort and start a colony.

In late January 1848, James Marshall, who was building the sawmill for Sutter, discovered gold and the future of California forever changed. The settlement of Yerba Buena near the Golden Gate became the city of San Francisco, as people arrived by land and sea to seek their fortunes in the gold fields. A few found fortunes, but most did not (Figure 11.6).

Fig. 11.6. Sutter's Mill, where James Marshall first discovered gold and set off the California gold rush in 1849. *Library of Congress*

The discomfort and dangers of sailing from New England around Cape Horn at the tip of South America to San Francisco, or crossing the plains and mountains of the Wild West, were recorded in many journals and letters. Unlike today's motorists driving the interstate in an air-conditioned SUV, stopping for fast-food and Starbucks every few miles, the earlier immigrants went through some very tough times. Either way, land or sea, the journeys took months and safe arrival was never guaranteed.

Like many others, I have ancestors who decided to take that leap, hoping to strike it rich in the gold fields. My great-great-great-grandparents moved their growing family steadily westward, initially from Massachusetts, down the Ohio River to Princeton, Indiana, in 1819, where my great-great-grandfather Calvin Goodrich Griggs, his brother, Ensign Bush Griggs, and a sister, Fanny, were all born. Four more children came along as the family built mills, transported goods by wagon and ferry, and ultimately ended up in Rockford, Illinois, in 1835.

Ensign entered college to prepare for work as a minister, which was quite common in those days, but once he heard of the discovery of gold in California, the ministry suddenly seemed a lot less interesting and not nearly as promising. In the spring of 1849, he and several friends started west with their wagon and joined an emigrant train at Council Bluffs, Iowa. His letters tell of the hardships endured while crossing "The Plaines," of danger in swimming the Platte River below the livestock to keep them upstream, as the current was quite strong. He also suffered from "mountain fever" (which may well have been malaria but wasn't recognized at the time), as did many on the wagon train, some of whom died along the way from this and other diseases. Another danger he faced was while guarding the wagon train at night, and he details some encounters they had with Native Americans that led to the loss of life for several night guards. But he and his friends and many others continued west, heading for what they hoped was a brighter future in California.

Ensign and his party reached Salt Lake City in July 1849. His team of horses was failing, so he sold his wagon for $25 and their harnesses for $5. He continued on with his horses for the next 600 miles, but when his horses failed entirely, he decided to leave them behind in Carson Valley, Nevada. He reduced his load as much as possible because he was now going to have to carry all of his gear. Ensign sold his best suit for $1.50, his suspenders for half that, and his pistol for $2 (this may not have been a wise decision at that time) and then gave away what he couldn't sell. He kept two suits, four shirts, and three blankets, along with provisions for the next 200 miles. He also purchased flour and meat for 50 cents a pound.

From here he packed his remaining belongings on his back and headed over the Sierra Nevada. This part of the crossing proved to be the most difficult, although Ensign must have grown accustomed to hiking by this time. He described traveling through snow for many weeks, in some places up to 2 feet thick. Fortunately, it was still late summer instead of early winter, which had spelled disaster for the Donner-Reed Party three years earlier. Ensign Griggs arrived in California on the last day of August 1849, with 75 cents in his pocket. He found work and soon bought the supplies he needed to head to the gold country and, hopefully, strike it rich in California. He bought mining tools, provisions, and a tent. At the age of 31, he had managed to reach what was soon to become the Golden State safely, without fatal mishap, and left for the mines.

Ensign wrote his family from Placerville, describing life of a much different sort than the ministry in Illinois might have entailed. He wrote "miners are tucked in as thick as bugs" and "there are many lawless characters who are determined to get gold by fair means or foul." He wasn't comfortable in his new surroundings, and contrary to the ideas that had been circulating in the east, gold was not picked up off the ground there but had to be dug by hard labor. A fortunate miner might strike a rich vein and take out $150 or more in a day (over $4,000 in today's currency), but most made only a few dollars, if that. Provisions were expensive; sugar was 40 cents a pound, coffee 60 cents, potatoes 25 cents each, and molasses from $3 to $4 per gallon.

Ensign found the California climate delightful, however, and wrote home that he never again wished to live in the east with the freezing winds of winter and hot sweltering, suffocating days and nights of summer. His letters of the next several years describe disappointment in his return from working in the mines, however, and he decided to change course and began to work in the woods to obtain lumber for construction. He soon realized that most of those who were profiting from the gold rush were the merchants who were supplying the miners. After months of hard labor, a fire unfortunately wiped out his lumberyard. To add to his discouragement, smallpox broke out in Placerville, and though he suffered a light case, he was called on to care for others who were much sicker.

He soon realized that most of those who were profiting from the gold rush were the merchants who were supplying the miners.

In Placerville, on March 13, 1853, at age 35, Ensign married Mary Wing Post, a widow, aged 26 years, with a young daughter. With her first husband and baby, she had left home in Indiana a few years earlier to join an emigrant train bound for the gold fields. Her husband died and was buried somewhere along the way, and she had no options but to continue with the wagon train. Several months after marrying, Ensign and his new family left Placerville and headed northwest for Humboldt County, where they settled on a claim on the Pacific Coast, in or near Hydesville along the Eel River. They lived there for a while, but the fog and the nearness of the ocean were depressing for Mary, so they moved 50 miles to the small town of Eel River, hoping that it would be better for her health.

In addition to ill health and the otherwise hard times of pioneering in what was remote California at the time, they experienced continuing problems because of poor relations between newer immigrants and the original inhabitants. Nonetheless, Ensign and Mary remained for several years, and it was here that their son, Charles Ensign Griggs, was born in 1857. He was perhaps the first Griggs born in California, after the long path that Ensign followed west. Clearly the proud father, Ensign wrote to his mother in Illinois: "You would like to know about this little chap. Well, he is as smart as a steel trap, as quick as a cat, and is said to resemble his father in looks." (It's reassuring to see humor under such less than pleasant pioneer conditions.)

In the early 1860s the family returned to Hydesville, where they endured many hardships in the "Godless community," wrote Ensign, who was thought by his neighbors to be too religious. His brother Calvin (my great-great-grandfather) and his son George, from Illinois, came by boat from San Francisco to Eureka to visit in the summer of 1874, no doubt wondering what the west coast offered.

In about 1877, when Ensign was 59 and Mary was 50, having grown a little tired of roughing it, the family moved to Alameda County on the edge of San Francisco Bay, where his son Charles secured work in a printing shop in Oakland. In 1891, he established a music engraving company in San Francisco, which, after the great 1906 earthquake, was moved to Oakland. Mary Post Griggs died in Oakland in 1898, and Ensign died a few weeks later of pneumonia at age 80 years. They were buried in sight of the Golden Gate, both having taken some very long steps across the country to the edge of California.

" . . . we strolled about, picking up shells, and following to see where it tumbled in, roaring and spouting, among the crevices of the great rocks. What a site, thought I, must this be in a southeaster! The rocks were as large as those of Nahant or Newport, but, to my eye, more grand and broken. Besides, there was a grandeur in everything around, which gave a solemnity to the scene, a silence and solitariness which affected every part! Not a human being but ourselves for miles, and no sound heard but the pulsations of the great Pacific! And the great steep hill rising like a wall, and cutting us off from all the world but the 'world of waters'! I separated myself from the rest, and sat down on a rock, just where the sea ran in and formed a fine spouting horn. Compared with the plain, dull sand beach of the rest of the coast, this grandeur was as refreshing as a great rock in the weary land. It was almost the first time that I had been positively alone—free from the sense that human beings were at my elbow, if not talking with me—since I had left home. My better nature returned strong upon me. Everything was in accordance with my state of feeling, and I experienced a glow of pleasure at finding that what of poetry and romance I ever had in me had not been entirely deadened by the laborious life, with its paltry, vulgar associations, which I had been leading. Nearly an hour did I sit, almost lost in the luxury of this entire new scene of the play in which I had been so long acting . . . "

—*Two Years Before the Mast*, Richard Henry Dana, Jr., 1840, recording his observations upon first setting foot ashore on California's edge

Big Sur and the People's Highway

The Road on the Edge

We awoke to the unlikely and terrifying snarling of two mountain lions as they fought each other not 20 yards from where we lay camping in the Big Sur uplands.

Several miles north of Big Sur, between Highway 1 and the seacliff, there's a small pine forest perched above a short stretch of rocky coastline. These large trees might catch your eye because their branches are now gnarled, mostly brown, and unhealthy, and because there are ordinarily no trees along this stretch of coast, only a wide, grassy terrace. The once flourishing pines are nearing the end of their lives, since they live only 35 to 45 years. I have a very personal connection to these trees—40 years ago, my little brother Jeffrey and I planted them.

Together, we spent several summer months painstakingly digging holes in what seemed at the time like solid rock. Slowly but surely we planted about 500 two-foot seedlings as part of a plan that had been agreed to as one of the first actions of the newly formed California Coastal Commission. The trees, along with the creation of a half-dozen easements to allow public access to the shoreline from Highway 1, were part of an overall plan adopted when my parents, along with a group of several friends, pooled their resources to purchase 37 acres of that unique coast. My family named the area "Otter Cove" since that

Fig. 12.1. Brown pelicans take flight along the central California coast.

was where we saw our first sea otters. Little did I know then that we were seeing the handful of otters that were slowly beginning their recovery from near extinction and gradually recapturing their range along the central California coast.

With little precedent to go on, the Coastal Commission was experimenting with landowners in new approaches to coastal management and public access. In hindsight, the choice of these particular trees was a good lesson in less-than-optimal policy. The relatively short-lived, nonnative pines were probably not ideal for the area, despite everyone's best intentions. They grew quickly, but their short life spans wouldn't provide long-term solutions. Because they were nonnative, they were illsuited to support the plants and animals of the local ecosystem. More important, from a policy perspective there are (still) challenges to make effective use of the types of small easements to the coast that were part of the plan. They are often hard to locate, and there was limited public awareness of many of these older easements. There has been some improvement in awareness, although locating them can still be challenging. Some Coastal Commission publications (and the commission's website) are now listing local access points along the state's entire coastline. Perhaps the advent of electronic means to get this information will lead to increased access to the shoreline.

During those months of digging and planting, my brother and I lived in my VW bus, crammed into tiny quarters along with our clothes, food, picks, shovels, and other tools. At first it seemed like a pretty nice place to live and work, out on the rugged coast reveling in the natural beauty and hoping for spectacular sunsets every afternoon (Figure 12.1). But oddly, even in such an isolated place, on just the second night we were there, someone stole the tools we left outside, underneath the van. We had to spend most of our first month's wages-yet-to-come replacing them. From that night on, we slept with all of our tools inside with us, along with everything else we owned.

The physical work was daunting, so we were usually pretty tired by the end of each day, and without any access to running water to clean up, well, we were a sorry lot. But we soon fell into a pattern of calmly living on the edge, contemplating the fog rolling in each evening (rather than spectacular sunsets) and listening to the extraordinary sound of surf. Sometimes soft, lapping at the rocks; sometimes raging, pounding them well through the night. There is nothing like the smell of the salt air along the coast. Our small seashore home was often cold, damp, and windy but always beautiful.

Coastal wildlife

After dark we often heard howls, growls, and hoots, and guessed what animals were responsible, large or small, four legged or flying, furred or feathered. We had some general idea of just what wild things frequented that area of the coast, having spent some meaningful time hiking with our dad in the steep hills and mountains above and in the nearby Ventana Wilderness Area. There were hawks, eagles, and owls. California condors were rare, because they were on the verge of extinction resulting from contamination by DDT, the deadly pesticide that was later banned, leading to a tentative recovery of condors. By contrast, wild boars were not uncommon. In fact, actor-director Clint Eastwood's frequent encounters while hunting such creatures on his nearby hillside land led him to name his restaurant in Carmel the Hog's Breath Inn, with its Dirty Harry Burger, before he became mayor of that small town.

It was on one of those overnight hikes above the Big Sur coastline with our dad that my brother and I found ourselves forced into plunking down our sleeping bags in mid-trail to camp along the edge of

At dawn we awoke to the terrifying sounds of two mountain lions snarling as they fought each other not 20 feet from where we lay camping.

a long, steep stretch of rock cliff. Our evening's forward progress had been halted by the darkness of a rare total lunar eclipse (apparently, we missed that helpful bit of information in the planning stage), and the trail was the only nearly level place to sleep. But it was narrow enough, and the cliff drop-off steep enough, that we considered using ropes to fasten ourselves down to keep from rolling off while sleeping. We had been taking advantage of the full moon's light to try to make our way past the cliff. To make matters worse, tired as we were after an uneasy few hours' sleep, at dawn we awoke to the unlikely and terrifying sounds of two mountain lions snarling as they fought each other on the trail not 20 yards from where we lay. Petrified, we remained silent until the fighting passed. Fortunately, these lions were so distracted and engaged with each other that they never saw us before slinking off into the brush.

At least we had no 800-pound grizzly bears to contend with. Although grizzlies were once quite common throughout California and along the Big Sur coast, their absence is not a happy story. Grizzlies were once so abundant they were considered a fixture in California's landscape, including the coast. There were so many of these bears in the hills near Big Sur that they would often overrun the whaling station at Point Lobos, drawn by the smell of whales being processed. The whalers had to build huge fences to protect themselves and their families, as well as the valuable whales they had worked so hard to capture.

Like many of us, these big bears also had a habit of occasionally preferring beef. By 1922, as a result of humans' protecting their herds of beef on the hoof, as well as unrestrained recreational hunting, almost every grizzly bear in California had been killed.

I've had more than one tick surgically removed, and by that I mean with a hunting knife, sterilized with a match.

But there is still one more grizzly seen from time to time around government buildings, spread across the greater part of our state flag. The grizzly was adopted as the state's symbol and appears on both the flag and the "Great Seal of the State of California." It is seemingly one of the great missed marketing opportunities to have focused on the seal as "great" rather than on the state. But even so, we now have a flag with grizzly bears for a state with no grizzly bears.

Despite our youthful exuberance, based on our hiking experiences around Big Sur we developed a healthy sense of how dangerous this wild and difficult coastal terrain could be. Like mountain lions, wild boars were also not something to be tangled with, although we saw our fair share. There are also smaller, more subtle hazards like the routine but annoying ticks and poison oak. I've had more than one tick surgically removed, and by that I mean with a hunting knife, sterilized with a match. No fancy hospital rooms, no big bills.

There are rattlesnakes, which are especially dangerous during the springtime when the very young ones don't yet have their full set of rattles, making it harder to hear them before stumbling across these deadly snakes. I've had more than one encounter with these quiet reptiles, although I've managed to avoid being bitten. We also discovered, and suffered from, nasty stinging nettles—plants forming a deadly garden that actually seem to sway toward you ever so slightly as you pass. We encountered these pesky plants while trying to approach and fight our way through the thick brush and brambles down into an old mineshaft we discovered one day on a high hillside in plain view of the ocean. Somehow the universal admonition "Stay away from old mines" fell on deaf ears in my case.

Point Lobos State Natural Reserve

Years later I learned that the shaft was the remnant of an abandoned coal mine left from an effort by the short-lived Carmel Land and Coal Company. In the mid-1870s, the company started to dig coal from the hills a few miles southeast of Point Lobos. Horse-drawn wagons were used to haul the coal to an old county road where it was loaded onto ore carts, which used a short tramway to a coal chute in Whaler's Cove. Deep water allowed coastal steamships to get in close to the chute where they could load up.

Poor market conditions and high operating costs, however, spelled a quick end to Monterey County's coal industry and the mine closed in the late 1890s. But nearly 100 years later the entrance remained open, even if obscured by brush. Today, remnants of the machinery from the mine can be found at Point Lobos State Natural Reserve.

When coal mining became unprofitable, the Carmel Land and Coal Company, which owned the land around today's Point Lobos Reserve,

Fig. 12.2. The California shoreline north of Big Sur is one of the most memorable convergences of land and sea in the world.

subdivided the area around Whalers Cove into 1,000 small residential lots. This proposed development was initially named Point Lobos City, but the name was soon changed to Carmelito. Within several years, Alexander M. Allan, a successful engineer from Illinois, recognized the scenic beauty of this unique area and saw the value of its preservation. In the 1890s, he purchased 640 acres of the mining company's land at Point Lobos and soon began buying up the lots that had already been sold. The State of California purchased part of the land with help from the Save the Redwoods League—even though the land has no redwoods. Along with a gift from the Allan family and additional acquisitions, 400 acres of Point Lobos and 750 offshore acres were protected, becoming the nation's first marine preserve.

The Big Sur highway

For many, there is nothing that embodies the California coast more than the drama of sharp cliffs and crashing surf along the Big Sur highway (Figure 12.2, Figure 12.3). But there is a backdrop to this splendor that lies just beneath the surface, literally and culturally.

Apparently one of those cultural bonds is that of the VW bus and Highway 1. We both approached the Big Sur coast in VW buses, Gary

Fig. 12.3. The unusual geological history of the Big Sur region generates perfect conditions for dramatic surf, suitable for photography, though not for surfing.

from the south and Kim from the north, long before either of us had any sense of its earlier history. It would be decades before the two of us met.

Europeans first saw the Big Sur coast 475 years ago. In 1542, Juan Rodríguez Cabrillo sailing under the flag of Spain on his exploratory voyage passed along the shoreline, at least as close as he dared. His journal entry states: "There are mountains which seem to reach the heavens, and the sea beats on them; sailing along close to land it appears as though they would fall on the ships."

In 1769, when Gaspar de Portolá reached the southern end of Big Sur, north of San Simeon, on his exploratory mission searching for Monterey Bay, he quickly realized that there was no way his men and mules were going to be able to continue across this stretch of coastline. So he took an inland detour and headed across the Santa Lucia Mountains hoping to find an easier route. The Salinas River Valley provided that easier passage and allowed them to avoid the treacherous Big Sur coast and ultimately reach Monterey Bay, which he hadn't been able to find on his first visit.

In the summer of 1963, I first drove up Highway 1 through Big Sur in an old VW van, which at that time was seriously underpowered. All these years later, I have two brilliantly vivid memories of that trip. The first is of downshifting repeatedly to get up the endless hills, followed by coasting at breakneck speed down the other side to save gas. Gasoline, at least by today's standards, was pretty cheap at 30 cents per gallon, but as a typical impoverished college student I didn't have any extra change so I was always looking for a way to save a little money. The second recollection is that after passing Cayucos, Cambria, and Hearst Castle and starting up the southern section of the highway, I noticed very few other cars on the road. Almost none, in fact. The drivers of the few cars I did see who had successfully navigated what then was a very treacherous drive all the way south from Carmel enthusiastically waved their arms as they passed, which I took as relief on their part that they had survived. It was also a good luck gesture for the uncertain venture that lay ahead for me.

Even today, it's a rough piece of coast and dangerous stretch of highway if you aren't wide awake and alert. No gasoline or services for many miles; in fact not much of anything commercial for many miles. Topographically, it's a challenge and geologically it's a nightmare. It bears little resemblance to the regions at either end, the flat, mostly undeveloped terraces and open grazing land to the south, or the stone houses and genteel Carmel cottages to the north. It's a place where the southernmost of California's coastal redwoods rub shoulders with a chaparral landscape more reminiscent of arid Southern California. In fact, there is no other place on the planet where fog-dependent redwoods grow, as they do here, in the same narrow canyons as the desert-loving yucca.

Geology of the Big Sur coastline

The Big Sur coastline owes its rough-hewn character to its underlying geology, which has challenged geologists for decades. The topography was so steep and access so limited that until fairly recently large areas on geologic maps were simply labeled as "unmapped." We didn't really know what was there because no one had been to this part of the coast to interrogate the rocks. It's not an exaggeration to say it's about as geologically complex a region as one might find anywhere. At the root of all this lithological[1] complexity is the ancient history of this piece of California real estate, which runs right along a

---

1. The physical characteristics of a rock.

complicated tectonic plate boundary. Millions of years ago, about 130 million years ago give or take a few years, the coast of what we call California was far to the east, somewhere near the Sierras. At that time, the massive North American Plate was moving west and colliding with a now mostly long-lost slab of lithosphere,[2] the thinner offshore Farallon Plate. This denser oceanic plate was sliding under the thicker continental plate and in the process was dragging down the seafloor to create a deep trench. Although that trench consumed the Farallon Plate long ago, today many other trenches nearly encircle the Pacific Basin and are doing their own plate consuming: the Peru-Chile Trench, the Middle America Trench, and the Aleutian and Japan trenches.

The great pile of marine sediments that had been accumulating in the trench off ancestral California was being scraped-off as the Farallon Plate descended, much as a carpenter would create wood shavings pushing a plane over a piece of wood. This scraped off sediment accumulated in a thick wedge along the boundary between the two giant plates, called an accretionary wedge.

As the Farallon slab descended deeper into the hotter interior of the earth, it began to melt, and this in turn led to hot molten fluids or magma that rose back toward the surface. Where the magma reached the Earth's surface, it erupted and formed volcanoes and fine-grained volcanic rock. Where the molten material didn't make it all the way to the surface but cooled deeper within the crust, it formed coarser-grained granite. Over millions of years, this process created the ancestral Sierra Nevada. And over time, all of those sediments that had been scraped off and accreted to this ancient edge were raised above sea level to form the rocks of the Central Valley and portions of the Coast Range, including the Santa Lucia Mountains.

That's the simplest story, but this picture became more complicated about 29 million years ago. At that time, these two huge lithospheric plates underwent some chiropractic readjustment as the collision, or subduction, of the Farallon Plate was completed. The two plates now began sliding alongside each other and the San Andreas Fault system was born. Large exotic blocks of diverse rocks from far to

---

2. The lithosphere is the outer shell of the earth and consists of the crust and upper mantle.

the south began sliding north along this newly created plate boundary to join with the new lithologic neighbors. A large fragment of the southern Sierra Nevada was transported northward along the fault, bringing granite into the Big Sur area. This process continued and introduced other exotic rocks into the neighborhood to complicate—and enliven—the lives of geologists millions of years later.

Today, if you could look carefully out the window as you navigate the 90 miles of sinuous highway from the Hearst Castle to Carmel-by-the-Sea, you would see a mélange of rocks as diverse as you might encounter along any 90-mile stretch of coastline on the planet. They make for a colorful index: maroon-colored cherts from the siliceous remains of ancient diatoms and radiolaria, gray limestone derived from the calcareous skeletons of coccoliths and foraminifera, conglomerates of cobbles and sand, dark volcanic rocks and coarse-grained granites, and then green jadeite from deeper in the earth. These diverse rocks have been uplifted from the seafloor, transported from the south and thoroughly mixed up on arrival, making the job of a geologist more than challenging, just short of impossible.

Human settlement of the Big Sur coast

The earliest dates of sites of human occupancy of the Big Sur coast come from two locations, one dated at 3390 BP[3] near Church Creek and a second near Esalen dated at 4630 BP. It's not known if there were Native Americans in the area earlier, although the same rugged topography and dense vegetation that the Portolá expedition encountered would have also been a deterrent to native peoples thousands of years earlier.

When the Spanish first ventured into the area, three different groups of Native Americans lived along the central coast, the Ohlone, the Esselen, and the Salinian. Between the shellfish in the intertidal zone and the acorns in the interior valleys, supplemented with deer and small mammals, nourishment for these early inhabitants was plentiful, although their populations were not large. The garbage heaps, or kitchen middens, they left behind have provided

---

3. BP refers to Before Present and is used in many areas of science to specify the timing or age of events relative to 1950 when radiocarbon dating became a commonly used tool.

archaeologists, paleoecologists, and historians with an interesting record of the eating habits and diets of these early coastal residents.

Although the early history of permanent settlement in the Big Sur area was not well recorded, we know that by the middle of the 1800s a handful of simple homesteads had been established. The California Gold Rush and statehood brought many new immigrants to the state, and some of these newcomers began to look for land to settle along the coast. While life elsewhere along California's edge proved to be profitable and communities grew and prospered from San Diego to Eureka, the Big Sur coast was steep, rocky, and nearly inaccessible for decades. Life was difficult, and the land didn't provide any excess of resources for the earlier settlers. Hunting, fishing, small farms, and gardens provided little more than subsistence.

> **While communities grew and prospered from San Diego to Eureka, the Big Sur coast was steep, rocky, and nearly inaccessible for decades.**

The steep terrain and deep canyons made transportation and communication difficult at best. A few primitive wagon roads and an occasional ship landing at Gamboa or Lopez Point provided the only way to obtain mail or supplies or export any produce or livestock. There were brief periods when local resources were developed into small industries such as tanbark, used for tanning hides into leather. Lime was also mined, as was gold, even if only for a short time.

That gold rush took place in the 1880s just inland from present-day Gorda, along the southern reaches of Big Sur. The boomtown of Manchester grew almost overnight to a population of about 350 people and included a hotel and dance hall, several saloons and general stores, a restaurant, a blacksmith shop, a post office, and a school. The modest amount of gold was quickly mined by the earliest years of the 1900s, Manchester was abandoned, and in 1909 it burned to the ground. None of these local industries lasted long, and much of the Big Sur area remained isolated from the outside world, essentially an inaccessible wilderness attracting settlers who were, for the most part, independent and self-reliant. Nearly all of the residents lived off the grid until electricity arrived in the area in the early 1950s. Even today, it is a challenge to string cable and maintain utilities along the rugged Big Sur coast (Figure 12.4).

Fig. 12.4. This helicopter, with its spool of cable suspended far below, strings utility lines from pole to pole in remote areas of the Big Sur region in 2016.

Big Sur in the twentieth century

With the coming of the 20th century, California became the Golden State and immigrants began to arrive in greater numbers. As the cities became more crowded, Big Sur's isolation began to appeal to different types of people, artists and writers, adventurers, those seeking to escape something, someone, or somewhere, and then the tourists who had started to read about this mythical and magical place.

Following World War I, as automobiles and travel became more routine and common, interest grew in building a highway along California's coastline from one end to the other. Road building in the Big Sur section proved to be a major undertaking because of its jagged topography and was challenging to highway engineers. In 1919, state voters passed a $1.5 million bond issue to construct what was initially called the Carmel–San Simeon Highway. The project wasn't initially at all popular with local residents as they could see the environmental effects of road construction and also feared the influx of visitors. They feared the ways this would impact their bucolic lifestyle and destroy this still mostly pristine coast.

The project moved ahead, however, with additional state and also federal funds. Three temporary camps were set up for prison laborers from San Quentin, one at the Little Sur River, one at Kirk Creek, and another at Anderson Creek. The convicts were paid 35 cents a day and had their prison sentences reduced. Some of the tough labor involved dangerous blasting: 35 tons of dynamite were used to blast through the marble, granite, and sandstone along the route.

Some of the greatest challenges involved bridge construction across the many steep

Fig. 12.5. McWay Falls in Julia Pfeiffer Burns State Park now falls onto a new sandy beach created in the aftermath of the massive 1983 landslide just north of the cove.

ravines. Thirty-three bridges were ultimately constructed, the famed concrete arch Bixby Creek Bridge perhaps the most iconic and oft-photographed. This bridge required initial forming with 300,000 board feet of lumber, followed by 300 tons of reinforcing steel and 6,600 cubic yards of concrete delivered in 825 truckloads. The initial highway construction estimate of $1.5 million was low, as is nearly always the case. But by 1937, 19 years and $10 million later, the Roosevelt Highway was opened. In 1939, it was added to the state highway system and renamed California State Route 1, or just Highway 1 for short.

The highway through the rugged terrain, with its unstable road cuts, commonly experiences winter landslides and failures, often closing the roadway for months—or for a year. In 1983, a landslide knocked the road off its perch, and it fell 700 feet into the surf below. Considered by some estimates to be the state's largest landslide, this massive failure of earth killed one man and brought down nearly 3 million cubic yards of hillside. So much rock and dirt plunged into the sea, from both the initial landslide and the subsequent year of cuts and fills to rebuild, that a small beach was formed a short distance to the south. McWay Falls in the nearby Julia Pfeiffer Burns State Park had previously cascaded directly into the ocean. But it now falls onto the sand of the newly formed beach (Figure 12.5). It is further evidence of that dynamic movement of sand as it slowly migrates along the coast and of the undeniable power of nature. Of course, it is also further evidence of human impact on the environment.

Ultimately the roads are always rebuilt, patched, and reopened for local residents as well as weekend and summer travelers. Residents and conservation groups have consistently opposed any significant level of development, although the road is always maintained even if at great cost. But the resistance to development more generally has kept the region much as it was in the past. Monterey County has fought to ban all billboards and other visual annoyances. It has also prohibited new construction within view of the highway. The California Coastal Commission has exercised jurisdiction and diligence over this region of the shoreline. This stretch of Highway 1, virtually on the edge, has been largely preserved and protected for everyone to enjoy.

I think the coast is super cool. I like the wildlife—I like learning about that. I think it's interesting how they live, how they adapt to their surroundings, how they're different from other animals. I'd love to be able to help them for the future. I think that I could help in research and figuring out ways to save the animals. So they're not endangered.

I've been to the ocean a lot. We went camping to the beach every year, every summer. We started when I was six months old, and I'm 14 now. My dad and his friends had small boats, so we would go out into the ocean and there were these caves, and there were starfish and, I think, jellyfish. I would help him with the abalone. He would tell me about all the parts of an abalone. At first I didn't even know what it was, I didn't even know it was a living creature. My father told me how it lived, how it adjusted to its life. That was really interesting to me. They're really good to eat, but I feel bad because there's not a lot of them, but hopefully things will get better in that way.

When I first went to the ocean, it was scary, because it was so big and I wasn't really used to it. But it was fun to learn about. Over time, I went into the ocean. But first, I went along the beach and picked up crabs. And shells. My dad would just tell us about the creatures like otters and everything that was in the ocean.

Recently, the last two years, I've taken a friend with me, too. For her it was the first time there. And so I got to tell her all the things my father taught me about it. She loved it. She was super-interested in all the sea life and what we saw.

At the ocean, I feel really at peace, like there's nothing you have to worry about. You're just there. When you're at the beach it's just in the moment, thinking about all the wildlife, nothing else crosses your mind. You're just there at that time with yourself.

—Repeat coastal visitor, age 14

13

OIL ON THE EDGE

As we continued to paddle through the surface oil slick, our arms soon became dipsticks, and had turned almost completely black.

As a geology student at the University of California, Santa Barbara, in the early 1960s, I was intrigued by a massive ship anchored just offshore, doing exploratory oil drilling in the spring of 1964. Any student at UCSB in those days was acutely aware of the globs and patches of tar on the beaches of Isla Vista, next door to the campus. We all usually came back from the beach with feet covered in tar. Most apartments had a can of paint thinner or some other solvent on the front porch and a rag to remove the tar and keep it off the landlord's cheap carpets.

Curiosity got the best of us after several weeks of watching the mysterious drilling ship, which worked with lights blazing throughout the night. So one warm spring day, one of my roommates and I decided to paddle our surfboards out to investigate. Being geology students, we were quite familiar with topographic maps and compasses and were confident in our keen ability to locate ourselves precisely on maps. These skills that enabled you to know where you were standing at any particular moment were fundamental requirements when doing geologic mapping in the field. With our combined talents, we took a few compass bearings of the drill ship from known street intersections in Isla Vista and triangulated to discover the vessel was only about a half mile offshore. We thought, piece of cake, this will be easy.

Fig. 13.1. The *Cuss I*, which was drilling off the coast of Isla Vista when Gary first paddled out to observe offshore drilling in 1964. *photo courtesy Nedcon Maritime*

So we paddled out, full of enthusiasm and exuberance about the adventure ahead. Our first discovery, several hundred yards offshore, was that we were completely surrounded by oil bubbling to the surface. Before long we noticed that the sea surface was nearly completely covered with an iridescent film of oil. As we continued to paddle, our arms soon became dipsticks and had turned almost completely black. Water washed over our boards as well so our boards, chests, and legs were soon covered with oil. Despite some mild discomfort, we were committed and both agreed to continue on our journey. The half mile seemed long, very long in fact, and the ten minutes we expected turned into over an hour.

As we finally approached the drill ship, we noticed that it was much larger and much higher above the water than we had imagined from the beach (Figure 13.1). The swells offshore were much larger than at the shoreline, raising us up and down 10 or 12 feet as each crest passed. We yelled up to several of the crew on deck, who seemed to be as curious about what we were doing out there as we were about the ship. We must have been quite a sight: oil-covered humans on surfboards, bobbing on the water. The response to our question—"How far offshore *are* you?"—was "It's federal water, so we are just past the 3-mile limit." We looked at each other with a mix of confusion and embarrassment. "Wow, how could we have been so far off in our half-mile estimate?"

Although they didn't invite us aboard, the crew took pity on us and threw down some cans of Coke, wishing us luck in our oily return paddle. By this time we were stuck to our boards, and my recollection is that it was a long, sticky, and uncomfortable paddle back to the beach. Emerging from the water an hour later, we aroused a certain amount of unwanted attention from the other students lounging on the beach with our rather extensive covering of tar.

It took some time to remove all the accumulated oil from our bodies and boards, but we then dug out our topographic map to see where we had gone astray. Turns out—and we never admitted this to any of our geology professors—we had taken a compass bearing from two different street intersections to the ship and used simple triangulation. Easy enough. But we realized we had used the wrong street on the map. We swore to secrecy, and our monumental miscalculation never left the confines of our apartment. Keep in mind that this was years before satellite navigation on surfboards and handheld GPS systems.

Oil spill in the Santa Barbara Channel

Five years later, on January 28, 1969, Union Oil's Platform A blew out while drilling in the Santa Barbara Channel 20 miles to the east and 6 miles offshore, releasing an estimated 5,000 barrels of crude oil over the next 11 days. The oil spread out from Goleta to Ventura and stretched from the shoreline all the way offshore to the Channel Islands. At the time, this was the largest oil spill in U.S. waters, although since 1969 at least 44 oil spills over 10,000 barrels (420,000 gallons) each have polluted U.S. waters, including the largest and most recent, the 2010 *Deepwater Horizon* explosion and blowout in the Gulf of Mexico. That spill killed 11 crew members and released more than 4.9 million barrels.

If you have to spill some oil in the ocean, there is no good place. But the shoreline of Santa Barbara is probably one of the worst places. People there are especially protective of their coastline and its rich and sensitive habitat, which up until that time was still relatively pristine. The oil spread by wind, tides, and currents over 800 square miles of

Fig. 13.2. The Santa Barbara oil spill in 1969 was one of the first large spills to impact the shoreline, and cleanup techniques were primitive. *photo courtesy Bob Duncan, 1969*

ocean, blackened 35 miles of shoreline (Figure 13.2), and had a highly visible impact on wildlife. In addition to many marine mammals, fish, and other creatures, it is estimated that almost 3,700 marine birds died from oil exposure. Although many dedicated rescuers did all they could to clean and rehabilitate these traumatized birds, success rates for cleaned and released seabirds are usually not very high.

This blowout and its widespread impact was the unfortunate result of a cost- and time-saving measure on Platform A. Very shallow steel casing was used to line the drill hole, despite the fact that the platform was in an area of well-known faults, where oil was under high pressure, and where natural seepage occurred almost directly beneath a vulnerable ecosystem.

Oil was first described seeping to the ocean surface in the Santa Barbara Channel in 1792, 172 years before our memorable surfboard paddle out. George Vancouver, who was Captain James Cook's navigator as he explored the West Coast of the Americas, recorded in his journal and logbook:

> The surface of the sea, which was perfectly smooth and tranquil, was covered with a thick, slimy substance . . . the light breeze, which came principally from the shore, brought with it a strong smell of tar,

or some such resinous substance. The next morning the sea had the appearance of dissolved tar floating on its surface, which covered the sea in all directions within the limits of our view.

In 1999, 207 years later, an article in the prestigious *Journal of Geophysical Research* entitled "The World's Most Spectacular Marine Hydrocarbon Seeps (Coal Oil Point, Santa Barbara Channel, California)" stated rather emphatically that:

> Literature reviews of marine hydrocarbon seepage usually conclude that the area along the northern Santa Barbara Channel is one of the most prolific hydrocarbon seepage areas in the world.

A novel approach to provide some measure of the quantity of the oil seepage in the area was used in recent years. Underwater tents were anchored on the seafloor over some of the larger seeps to capture some of the escaping oil. At the time, an estimated 4,200 gallons of oil were seeping into the waters of the channel every day, or about 100 barrels of crude oil.

Oil had been leaking out of the seafloor for thousands of years before we paddled through in the twentieth century and before Captain Cook sailed across the oily waters of the channel in 1792. In addition to the geologic evidence, we know that for thousands of years the Native Americans who lived and fished along this coast used the tar along the shoreline to waterproof their canoes.

How petroleum is formed

So where is all of this oil coming from and why is it bubbling out of the seafloor, covering the sea surface, and coating the beaches of the Santa Barbara Channel? As gasoline prices edged above $4 a gallon a few years ago, costing each of us who drive $50 or $60 or more to fill up the tank, the question of where this stuff is coming from started to get more relevant. Most people know that gasoline is refined from oil, which gets pumped from the ground. But why is it in the ground to begin with, and why is oil found only in certain places—like the Santa Barbara Channel, Wilmington and Huntington Beach, Texas and Oklahoma, and the Middle East—and not under your backyard?

The formation of petroleum is usually a product of the coastal ocean. Trillions of diatoms and other marine plankton sacrificed their microscopic bodies to power our SUVs, as well as our global fleets of millions of trucks, buses, planes, ships, and power plants.

Massive blooms of plankton occur in the offshore surface waters when conditions are just right. We can observe this at times, when one particular type of plankton is so abundant that it turns the waters a reddish color, often called a red tide. It actually has nothing to do with the tide and may be green or brown, or have no apparent color at all.

On some spring or summer nights, whether on the beach or at sea, you might have noticed a startling and beautiful glow when the waves break or in a ship's bow wave, as if nature was shining an iridescent green spotlight into the foam. This phenomenon is often incorrectly called phosphorescence but is actually bioluminescence, like what fireflies produce, and can be created by several different types of plankton.

Plankton blooms occur along much of the California coast in late spring, and often into summer and fall, when wind moves surface waters offshore and cooler, nutrient-rich bottom water rises to the surface in a process known as upwelling. The plankton respond like crazy. These little guys don't live long, however. Life is quite short for your average diatom. They go through bloom and bust cycles, sinking to the seafloor when nutrients are exhausted or when the silica in the water (which makes up their skeletons) is used up.

Small planktonic animals such as krill and crab larvae, and small fish, such as sardines and anchovies, consume lots of these microscopic plants, but massive numbers also sink and become part of the accumulating pile of mud on the seafloor. This accumulation is the foundation for the creation of oil. Their ultimate transformation into petroleum, however, involves several steps over a long period of time—long like millions of years.

First, monumental amounts of seafloor organic matter from the plankton must be covered by sediment or surrounded by stagnant, oxygen-poor bottom water before the organic matter can decompose. Next, burial and subsidence beneath additional mud creates a seafloor pressure cooker, where high pressure and elevated temperatures slowly cook the preserved organic matter and convert it into petroleum, a complex mixture of oil and gas. Fortunately for us, this extraordinarily slow process of hydrocarbon production and preservation has been going on for a very long time. Diatoms first appeared in the Cretaceous, right after Jurassic Park, perhaps 100 million years ago, and have been with us ever since.

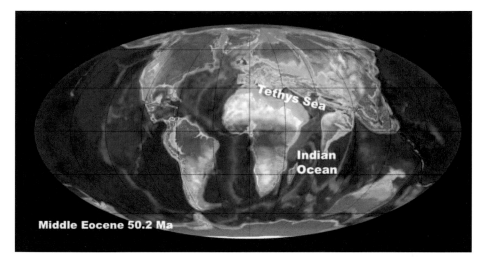

Fig. 13.3. The ancient Tethys Sea was the site of the petroleum formation that now lies buried beneath the nations of the Middle East. This image depicts the sea as it was being compressed 50.2 million years ago. *courtesy Wikipedia Commons*

The formation of large reservoirs of petroleum has taken place at different locations around the planet throughout the past 300 million years or so, perhaps longer. But only in certain oceanic areas did it all come together geologically, and those are the places that today hold the world's largest oil deposits. Curiously, five of the seven countries with the largest reserves of oil on the earth are all in the Persian Gulf: Saudi Arabia, Iran, Iraq, Kuwait, and the United Arab Emirates.

Even though our California coast, especially off Southern California, had that perfect combination of natural factors to cook up lots of petroleum, it's fair to ask why so much oil formed in the Middle East. To answer that, we need to go back about 150 to 200 million years when the distribution of continents and oceans was quite different than it is today. At that time, most of the continents appear to have been bunched together into one mega-landmass known as Pangea. The Atlantic Ocean hadn't yet opened up between continents, so North America was still very much connected to Europe, and South America was joined to Africa. Looking at a map of the east coast of South America and the west coast of Africa reveals the outline of their ancient jigsaw puzzle connection.

The area stretching eastward from this mega-continent, at about the present location of the eastern Mediterranean, was a vast sea known as the Tethys, named after the Greek sea goddess Tethys. This warm body of water straddled the equator and was extremely fertile. Plankton-like diatoms bloomed in profusion, and for eons the dead bodies of these tiny creatures sank to the seafloor and collected there (Figure 13.3). With little oxygen in the overlying water, the organic matter wasn't oxidized or broken down, so it accumulated to great thicknesses. The increased pressure and temperatures at depth from burial and subsidence over millions of years gradually converted the remains of those sacrificial plankton to petroleum.

About 200 million years ago, give or take a few million, as the tectonic plates began to break up and the continents started to shift, Africa and India pulled away from South America, Australia, and Antarctica and began slowly migrating to the north. As these huge plates traveled slowly north toward Asia, they began to compress the Tethys Sea, squeezing and folding the thick layers of sediments with their rich deposits of oil on the floor of this ancient ocean. The waters of the sea gradually drained to the east and west, and the compressed and folded oil-rich sediments became the mountains and deserts of Saudi Arabia, Kuwait, Iraq, and Iran.

Oil becomes an industry

In 1908, just a little over a century ago, a British company had been searching for oil in Persia (now Iran) for some time but still had nothing to show for it. After seven long years, it was ordered to drill one final well, to a depth of 1,600 feet, and then stop. This had been a huge gamble, in part because automobiles were still in their infancy so their fuel demand was relatively trivial. Only later, with the broader use of automobiles and the realization that anything that had run on coal, whether ships, power plants, or factories, could be run on oil, did the picture rapidly begin to change.

At 4 a.m. on May 26, 1908, the British company's last drilling attempt reached a depth of 1,180 feet below the desert sand and struck oil, creating a gusher that shot 75 feet into the air. The British investors reorganized their holdings in 1908 as the Anglo-Persian Oil Company. In 1935 this morphed into the Anglo-Iranian Oil Company, then to British Petroleum in 1954, and finally to BP in 2000. The Middle East was soon awash with drilling rigs and oil companies. So an accident of plate tectonics made billionaires out of the Saudis

Fig. 13.4. The La Brea Tar Pits in 1910 with oil rigs in the background. *Creative Commons Attribution-ShareAlike License*

and some others and dramatically altered the world's economics and history for a century.

California's own share of petroleum deposits, while of high quality, is nowhere near the size of those in the Middle East. Oil and gas fields are concentrated primarily in the Central Valley and along the south coast stretching from near Santa Maria, through Santa Barbara and Ventura, and to Wilmington and Huntington Beach. And they all formed under coastal ocean conditions of high plankton productivity, from burial by mud and sand, and by preservation on the seafloor, followed by pressure-cooker conditions of elevated temperatures and pressure.

Twenty-three years before Captain Cook's oil-stained voyage through the Santa Barbara Channel in 1792, the 1769 Portolá expedition noticed the "geysers of tar issuing from the ground like springs." The native people all along the Southern California coast were able to travel along the coast and as far offshore as the Channel Islands because thousands of years ago they had discovered the value of using the seeps of local tar or pitch to waterproof their canoes.

The largest and best known of these deposits was encountered by Portolá and his crew and is known today as the La Brea Tar Pits (*brea* is Spanish for "pitch")(Figure 13.4). It sits on some prime real estate on Wilshire Boulevard in the Hancock Park area of west Los Angeles. This extraordinary site has preserved the unsuspecting remains of a number of curious and now-extinct early California mammals, including mammoths, saber-toothed tigers, short-faced bears, dire wolves, and ground sloths. They all got trapped in the sticky liquid tar, or were caught trying to eat some other poor beast that had gotten stuck earlier.

California oil boom

In 1865, just a few years after the discovery of oil in Pennsylvania, the earliest oil well in California appears to have been sunk in what were then the dry barrens of the great Central Valley. While that single well did provide for the modest needs of San Francisco at the time, the big California oil strike was yet to come.

According to a local Southern California legend, two mostly unsuccessful gold and silver miners, Edward Doheny and Charles Canfield, noticed a cart near the present downtown area of Los Angeles with its wheels covered with tar. After they inquired where the cart had been, the driver pointed off to an area near the present Dodger Stadium. So in 1892, Doheny and Canfield, first using picks and shovels and then a system of repeatedly dropping a sharpened eucalyptus trunk at depth, sank a shaft to a depth of about 460 feet—where they hit oil.

In the next several years they obtained leases and dug about 300 additional wells. Doheny became a very wealthy man and even made a run for the Democratic vice presidential nomination in 1920. He was also embroiled in the infamous Teapot Dome Scandal, which proved to be a huge disgrace and embarrassment for Warren G. Harding, the president at the time. Oil, the product of quadrillions of preserved diatoms and other plankton from the fertile coastal waters of ancient California, was at the center of the scandal.

The oil boom changed Southern California forever. As production from the oil wells in downtown Los Angeles was beginning to slow, three new major oil fields would be discovered closer to the shoreline: in Huntington Beach in 1920 (Figure 13.5); in Santa Fe Springs in

Fig. 13.5. Oil rigs on the coast at Huntington Beach in the 1930s.
courtesy the Orange County Archives

1921; and the largest of them all, Signal Hill or Long Beach, which followed quickly thereafter. Wildcatters were drilling everywhere trying to find more oil.

While drilling on Signal Hill didn't initially look promising, tenacity and perseverance prevailed and Union Oil ultimately struck black gold at a depth of over half a mile. The gusher started a stampede for the purchase and lease of building lots as the area had recently been subdivided for homes. Within ten months of the original discovery, over 100 wells had been sunk and were producing 14,000 barrels a day. By modern standards, this isn't a lot of oil, but in 1923, it was a gold mine. Expansion continued and Signal Hill became California's largest oil field. Owing in large part to the oil from this field, California soon became the United States' largest oil-producing state. In 1923, 25 percent of the world's entire production of crude oil came from California.

As soon as news of the Signal Hill oil field discovery hit the wires, not unlike the discovery of gold by James Marshall at Sutter's Mill near Sacramento in 1848 (although the news no doubt traveled a bit more slowly in 1848), people began to flock to California to get a piece of the action. Many were probably also motivated by the prospect of better weather in sunny Southern California than wherever they were living at the time. Between 1900 and 1930, the state's population nearly quadrupled, from 1.5 million to 5.7 million.

My great-grandfather, his three sons, and their families were all living in the Pacific Northwest in 1921. Life was good. My great grandfather was what I understood to be a successful attorney and adept businessman. He, along with his sons (the oldest being my grandfather), had managed to acquire, build, or become owners of or partners in a modest business empire on Washington State's Olympic Peninsula. This empire included salmon canneries, a telephone and power company, a hotel, a hot springs resort, an automobile dealership, and an oil-loading dock.

It apparently didn't take long until great-granddad heard about the oil boom in Southern California. In yet another business adventure, he had an offer to partner with a friend who had developed a meter that would accurately measure the flow of a fluid. While we routinely use gasoline pumps to fill our tanks at our local service station without thinking much about it, pumping and metering that gasoline actually was a new challenge back in the early days of distribution. As the automobile and oil and gas became more and more important, great-granddad C.J., as he was known, believed that a liquid meter might be something worth investing in. The entire extended family decided that this was too big an opportunity to pass up, so they liquidated their Pacific Northwest investments and in 1923 joined the latest migration to the California coast and moved to the Los Angeles area.

My great-grandfather and his partner started the American Liquid Meter Company in 1924. The company didn't work out to be the financial success they had hoped for, as there was a lot of competition. The Great Depression hit soon thereafter, which didn't help matters. But the discovery of oil in the Signal Hill area brought my family from the Pacific Northwest to Southern California, where I was born 20 years later.

A hundred miles northwest of Signal Hill, in the beach community of Summerland, between Ventura and Santa Barbara, the natural oil and asphalt seeps also attracted economic interests and enterprising prospectors. The earliest-known oil well in that area was drilled in 1886, before Doheny and Canfield used their sharpened eucalyptus log to reach the oil beneath Los Angeles. The shoreline location and shallow depth of the petroleum deposits were proof enough to

Fig. 13.6. Oil drilling from piers along the coast of Summerland (1901–03). *photo courtesy Summerland Historical Society*

encourage more exploratory drilling. By 1895, the hunt for the black gold was in full swing as wooden drilling derricks were erected along the bluffs and beaches of the previously small spiritualist community of Summerland (Figure 13.6).

Offshore oil drilling

As had occurred in Los Angeles, the small lots that had recently gone on the market for home sites in Summerland for $25 each prior to the oil discovery rapidly escalated in price to as much as $7,500 apiece as the search for petroleum escalated. The oil that could be seen on the ocean surface, along with the shoreline location of the early wells, led a few inventive entrepreneurs to try something that had never been done before anywhere else in the world. In 1886, they built the first piers extending out from the beach in order to tap the oil they believed existed beneath the shallow seafloor. Before long, aspiring oilmen saw millions to be made, and rapidly constructed multiple piers, one with 19 individual derricks for drilling into the offshore oil-bearing rocks.

In an early indicator of things to come with California's coastal policy concerns, especially over oil drilling and other commercial development, this boom also proved controversial. Oil entrepreneurs of many stripes began exploring up and down the coast, expanding their search for petroleum. As new derricks got closer to Santa Barbara, some local vigilantes, led by a newspaper publisher, took matters into their own hands and proceeded to tear down a rig that had been built literally in their backyard on Miramar Beach.

This petroleum reservoir wasn't large enough to sustain long-term extraction, however, and within 20 years, oil recovery had all but ceased. Piers and derricks were abandoned and the flimsier ones were destroyed by storm waves, although it was years before they were all eventually removed.

Not to be upstaged by the tiny town of Summerland and its piers incrementally extending the arm of the oil industry seaward, an oil field was discovered offshore from Seal Beach. That discovery, in turn, led to the construction of the first artificial island for drilling and production equipment in 1954.

Two years later, and 50 years after the shoreline wells in Summerland had shut down, oil was discovered in the same geologic formation, a mile offshore where water was about 100 feet deep. The first offshore drilling and production platform in California, named Hazel for some unknown reason, was towed to the site on a barge in 1958 and then anchored to the seafloor where drilling began in the Summerland Offshore Oil Field. Two years later, Hazel was followed by her sister platform, Hilda, and then to round out what became known as the 4-H Platforms, Hope and then Heidi were installed in 1965, all in state waters. Together, the platforms with their combined 131 individual wells were to extract a total of 62 million barrels of oil and 131 billion cubic feet of natural gas before being removed during the spring and summer of 1996. At the United States' current rate of oil consumption, about 19.4 million barrels a day (in 2015), all the petroleum that was pumped out by the 4-H sisters over their 34-year production lifetime would last just three days. This was a small oil field by today's standards and consumption rate. But small is relative, and the environmental concerns raised by such a field are multiplied by

While some environmental concerns have led to greater constraints on offshore drilling, none have been sufficient to end it.

its location in sensitive ocean habitat and being adjacent to some of the most spectacular of the world's shorelines.

While some of these concerns have led to greater constraints on offshore drilling, none have been sufficient to end it. As of 2016, California's offshore region between Point Arguello on the north and Huntington Beach on the south was home to an alphabet soup of nine active drilling and production platforms in state and municipal

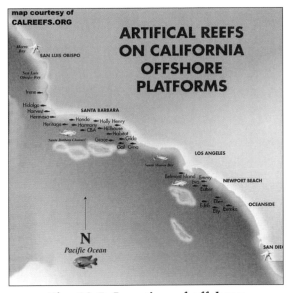

Fig. 13.7. Location of offshore oil platforms along the Southern California coast.
image courtesy CALREEFS.ORG

waters, and 23 active platforms in federal waters. The alliterative platforms off Seal Beach and Huntington Beach include Eva, Emmy, Edith, Elly, Ellen, and Eureka. The Ventura coastline to the west is graced with Gina, Gail, Gilda, and, you guessed it, Grace. And Santa Barbara got more H-platforms, including Heritage, Harmony, Hondo, Habitat, Hillhouse, Henry, Hogan, and Houchin. Around Point Conception, we encounter Hermosa, Harvest, and Hidalgo; and then farther north, there is lonely Irene (Figure 13.7). If there is some official petroleum platform naming board, something like what we use for hurricanes, the rules are not clear.

We have a massive appetite for oil in this country, and about 41 percent of our oil in 2016, roughly 8 million barrels a day, was imported. Imports have dropped over the last decade as domestic production has increased by drilling into deeper water offshore in the Gulf of Mexico, by going to greater depths on land, and also by using controversial methods such as hydrofracturing (sometimes referred to as fracking) to recover oil from rocks that don't give it up easily. Most of that oil is refined into gasoline. In 2015, California's 33.5 million vehicles consumed an average of 41 million gallons of gasoline every day, or 28,700 gallons a minute. If we were to put California's daily gasoline consumption in 1-gallon cans, and lay them down along our coastline, they would extend up and down the 1,100-mile length of our shoreline almost seven times. No matter how you look at it, that's a lot of gasoline.

"Remember—Without phytoplankton there would be no life in the sea!" was a sign posted on a doorway in the oceanography building at Oregon State University when I was in graduate school. I walked by this door often, and this rather ominous message repeatedly got my attention to the point where I thought about it for years afterward. It was actually the door to the phytoplankton lab, where graduate students peered down microscopes for hours on end trying to identify and study tiny floating marine plants like diatoms. It didn't take a mind like a steel trap to realize that the sign was, without a doubt, completely true. Almost all life on the planet, whether in the ocean or on land, is possible only through the wonders of photosynthesis, the ability of plants to take sunlight, carbon dioxide, and water, stimulated by a few nutrients, and make food and oxygen. We animals simply wouldn't be here without plants: we all depend on the simple process of photosynthesis, and one-half of all the oxygen we breathe is produced by those microscopic floating plants in the ocean during photosynthesis.

Oil is a rather amazing natural resource, owing its origin to those tiny little plants that flourish in our coastal waters and that sacrifice themselves for our convenience. California has long been a habitat for petroleum formation, having always had an ocean along our edge. Petroleum played a major role in California's development and economy. It has been a convenient source of energy. In 2015, oil and natural gas provided about 57 percent of all of our global energy. It took millions of years for petroleum to form, but we are consuming it at an astronomically rapid rate. The planet's human beings are now (2016) using about 96 million barrels of oil every day, and our appetite is increasing to the tune of roughly 1 million more barrels a day every year. This rate of consumption is clearly not sustainable because what exists now is all we will ever have. It is not a renewable resource in our lifetime or a thousand lifetimes. The sooner we act on this knowledge, the better.

I think what impressed me about the coast when I first saw it was how natural it was, and rugged, even though it was right there next to the 8 million people of the Bay Area. It wasn't just a recreational space, but it was a natural space.

I've never really lost the curiosity and sense of wonder for how the shoreline environment makes me feel. California's coast is very diverse and almost any place you go you can find these amazing places of exploration where you learn so much, like discovering things in all the nooks and crannies of the tidepools of the surf zone. I've really appreciated that even more with my daughter, whenever we get a chance we go out and poke around on the shoreline. It's just great to find new things and also teach her about those.

The coast makes me feel connected, sort of having a sense of how the whole fits together. Maybe it's because it is that place where land and water meet—there's just such a sense of natural dynamics and interrelationships along the shoreline. That's also part of what's so distressing about what's going on now to our environment, how we have fundamentally altered it in some way. We are having such an effect, at such a scale, that we are raising the specter of changes that can't be undone—climate change, mass extinction, those sorts of things.

Often people don't have the time or luxury, or unfortunately, the inclination, to think about the longer-run implications of some of our actions; we can get caught up in shortsighted economic and political thinking. But given its importance to all kinds of life on our planet, I think it's really important that we keep the protection of our coast front and center, in California and around the globe.

—Former executive director, California Coastal Commission

14

PROTECTING THE COAST

The California Coastal Commission and Other Experiments

Californians zealously guard the edge with the available tools, even in the face of efforts to weaken protections, including the current attempts to roll back environmental safeguards at the federal level.

The Coastal Commission

In 1911, the furthest thing from Hiram Johnson's mind was protecting the state's coast. The quirky California governor was concerned with the notorious corruption and bribery of the "robber barons," mainly the giant railroads like Southern Pacific and the stifling grip they held on California's legislators, judges, and businesses. Having been recently elected on a platform that promised relief from the corruption of the industrialists, bankers, and railroad interests, he probably never even dreamed that the initiative process he was trying to sell to voters would be invoked by the people 60 years later to establish the most ambitious experiment in coastal preservation and environmental management in modern history.

He simply wanted to modernize California's legislative and constitutional processes so that the people would be empowered to take back their government from corrupt forces. The most attractive option seemed able to bypass the self-interested Legislature and have the means to draft and directly enact laws or constitutional amendments, and to reject laws, as could be done in a handful of other states that had initiative and referendum processes.

This power of direct lawmaking by the citizenry was not part of the legislative process originally set out in California's first constitution when it was crafted in a conference at Colton Hall in coastal Monterey, nearly a year before California was recognized as a state. The city of Monterey had been the capital of the former Mexican territory, ceded to the United States in an 1848 agreement that ended the Mexican-American War.

The people of California adopted the new constitution in a popular vote. But the now-independent territory had trouble obtaining approval for statehood in Washington, DC. Approval was slow largely because California's initial constitution banned slavery, and Congress was fiercely debating whether to admit any additional non-slavery states lest they upset the balance between slavery and non-slavery states. But, always on the cutting edge, Californians just plowed ahead and created a provisional government, with representatives and senators, which operated as if California were a state for ten months before it was finally admitted to the Union as the thirty-first state.

The power of direct lawmaking was still not among the amendments adopted at a special 1872 state constitutional convention held to make revisions to the original framework of government. Instead, it took years of legislative paralysis during the late 1800s, and the economic downturns of the period, to sharpen the need for alternate means to combat powerful corporate interests and lobbying, pervasive bribery, and excessive campaign contributions and financing. Do these concerns sound vaguely familiar?

Governor Johnson succeeded in his campaign in 1911. Voters agreed to add this powerful tool to the state constitution, and thus was born the controversial initiative process. During the few decades after this tool became available, many significant citizen-led initiatives were drafted and passed into law that indeed helped to combat the pressing problems of the time. In fact, the people of California have resorted to the initiative process more than 350 times in the years since its inception— and slightly more than a third of these initiatives have been passed into law. Over time, however, the process has become more and more

Fig. 14.1. Long Beach Harbor. *photo courtesy Bruce Perry,*
California State University, Long Beach

separated from its "democratic" roots and has increasingly been used to
further the very commercial and corporate concerns that originally gave
rise to the need for a "people's" legislative tool in the first place.

It wasn't until 1972 that the people finally took into their
own hands the management of the California coast by passing a
citizen-sponsored initiative known as the California Coastal Zone
Conservation Act. The problems of developing, managing, and
creating access to the coastline had become increasingly clear, and
the California State Legislature had tried, and largely failed, to pass
bills that would fortify coastal protection and planning (Figure
14.1). Concerns over coastal development and the lack of protective
legislative action reached a tipping point with the combined effects of
the 1968 construction of a nuclear power plant at Diablo Canyon, the
catastrophic oil spill off the coast of Santa Barbara in 1969, and the
explosive growth in residential building along the coast. So proponents
gathered signatures and Proposition 20 made it onto the ballot in 1972.

The official ballot pamphlet argument in favor of the proposed
initiative said it all:

> Our coast has been plundered by haphazard development and land
> speculators. Beaches formerly open for camping, swimming, fishing and
> picnicking are closed to the public. Campgrounds along the coast are so

overcrowded that thousands of Californians are turned away. Fish are poisoned by sewage and industrial waste dumped into the ocean. Duck and other wildlife habitats are buried under streets and vacation homes for the wealthy. Ocean vistas are walled off behind unsightly high-rise apartments, office buildings, and billboards. Land speculators bank their profits, post their "no trespassing" signs and leave the small property owner with the burden of increased taxes to pay for streets, sewers, police and fire protection. The coast continues to shrink.

The cause of the problem was described as bluntly as could be:

Massive construction projects are often approved solely to benefit corporate landowners. We need a coastal plan, but responsibility is fragmented among 45 cities, 15 counties and dozens of government agencies without the resources to evaluate and prevent developments whose destructive effects may overlap all boundaries . . .

The proposed solution?

YOUR YES VOTE WILL: (1) Give the people direct participation in planning. No important decisions will be made until commissions hold public hearings and the citizen is heard . . .

The passage of this historic initiative and follow-up legislation a few years later (the California Coastal Act of 1976) to further implement it created the California Coastal Commission, which has now been in place for more than 40 years. The concept of controlling development of the people's coast to keep it safe, healthy, and accessible seems a simple one. However, its execution has been anything but.

The concept at the outset was to have an independent, quasi-judicial state agency. Coastal Commission staff was to work with coastal cities and counties to develop plans, known as Local Coastal Programs, or LCPs, which would contain the ground rules for future development and protection of coastal resources in all of the state's coastal cities and counties. Once the ground rules were approved by the commission, the authority to grant or deny permits for coastal development proposals was to be handed over to the local governments for decisions consistent with the adopted LCPs.

If the objectives and the role of the Coastal Commission sound straightforward, you'd be surprised at how much mischief has been imposed by those challenging this framework, from all angles and interests. Nearly every element of the commission's mission has been disputed, fought over, and litigated—some all the way to the United States Supreme Court—and several challenging areas are still in dispute even after more than 40 years of operation. The details of the LCPs, validity of the permit restrictions, authority over private property, the geographic limits of the jurisdiction, the nature of what activities can be described as "development." You name it and it has been, or is being, challenged.

Many local governments do have certified LCPs, but many others chose not to take that route and chose to simply allow the Coastal Commission to be the arbitrating body over local coastal development proposals. Even when local governments with certified LCPs have approved projects, Coastal commissioners still have the authority to appeal a decision. This lack of finality causes many to ask what the LCPs really accomplished for those cities or counties that undertook the time, trouble, and effort to complete them. They're still not completely in the driver's seat in terms of the use of the coast.

From one perspective, it is quite remarkable that an agency, forged out of a grassroots initiative process in 1972, was carefully enough crafted to survive essentially in one piece for so long a period. Times change, politics change, and priorities change. The coast and coastal issues ebb and flow. The commissioners change. The California Coastal Commission has certainly gone through many challenges, but it still remains more or less in its original form.

To be clear, despite its detractors—especially those who have felt that their property rights were being taken away—the Coastal Act undeniably spared the coast of California from the type of massive coastal development found on the coasts of New Jersey or Florida.

The Coastal Act undeniably spared California from the massive coastal development found on the coasts of New Jersey or Florida.

Without doubt, there are those segments of California's coast that no one is particularly proud of, but we do have many miles of coast in its near "natural" state, preserved and protected for generations to come.

These two dramatically different coasts, the developed and the relatively undeveloped or near natural, tend to be split between Southern California and the central and northern portions of the state.

Fig. 14.2. Balboa Peninsula. *photo courtesy Bruce Perry, California State University, Long Beach*

From Santa Barbara to San Diego, nearly the entire coastline has been developed or is intensively used (Figure 14.2). Although state parks, some military bases, and a few undeveloped patches are scattered here and there along these 250 miles of Southern California shoreline, this stretch of coast has felt the heavy impact of a lot of people and a lot of developers and commerce for well over a century.

Topographically, Southern California had a lot of flat, buildable land. However, climate above almost all else, both historically and today, makes it a desirable place to live or visit. There is a lot of sunshine, a mild winter, and a general lack of rain—even though this has required some major, hotly contested plumbing projects to provide water to the millions of residents. Much of the intensive development took place in a growth-is-good era, when there was no California Coastal Commission and no widespread sense of limits to our resource bounty or environmental capacity. We know more today than we ever have about the consequences of unbridled growth and its effects on ecosystems and the quality of our lives, as well as on the lives of native wildlife.

The central and northern parts of the state's coast have been proposed for development of all sorts, but the combination of topography, access, and climate have made this more challenging than the southern coast. Although major development or larger projects have been approved, like the sprawling Ritz-Carlton resort in Half Moon Bay (approval of which was based on preexisting rights), many others have been turned down or rejected because of their environmental impacts and projected loss of habitat, wildlife, valuable agricultural land, or public access. Once a parcel of coastal land is converted from farmland to condominiums, hotels, homes, mobile home parks, or a shopping center, we will never get that piece of coast back in or near its natural state, at least not in our lifetimes. It's lost to us, our children, and their children. It has been said that every conservation victory is temporary, but every loss is permanent.

> Once a parcel of coastal land is converted from farmland to hotels, homes, or a shopping center, we will never get that piece of coast back in or near its natural state.

We have the Coastal Commission to thank for many of the protective decisions, in part because of Peter Douglas, the pioneering executive director who led the commission for 25 years. He had a deeply held commitment to the goals of the Coastal Act, a law that was written with a very clear purpose. Peter Douglas once said that "the coast is never saved, it is always being saved." We should thank the majority of commissioners who frequently looked past local, short-term interests to vote for what they believed was in the best long-term interests of all Californians. We should also thank the vocal and active environmental community that attended every meeting and spoke up against almost every proposal or sought to rein in uncontrolled growth.

However, priorities are a bit different today than in the mid-1970s when the original Coastal Act was written and passed into law. It's fair to say that the headline issues at that time were dominated by the need to ensure environmental and resource protection, shoreline access, and recreational opportunities. These were issues the average citizen understood and felt were being threatened, and with good reason. As the state's political climate and leadership have changed over the years, so has the composition of the twelve-member commission, simply because they're all political appointees. These appointments are evenly apportioned between the governor, the speaker of the Assembly, and the Senate Rules Committee. So over the 40-plus years of the commission's existence, the leanings and decisions of the commissioners have fluctuated between being more development friendly and more environmentally proactive.

The ordinary fluctuation is compounded today by a new agenda being promoted at the federal level to roll back environmental laws, rules, and regulations. This will challenge state and local governments, entities such as the Coastal Commission, and concerned citizens to remain vigilant and active to assure the protections we already have in place are not eliminated.

Despite any challenges, the formal mission of the commission (which is an independent, quasi-judicial state agency) remains: "protecting and enhancing California's coast and ocean for present and future generations. It does so through careful planning and regulation of environmentally-sustainable development, rigorous use of science, strong public participation, education, and effective intergovernmental coordination."

This is quite a lofty goal, however, and subject to multiple interpretations.

Dissatisfaction with the commission's decisions by one group of property rights activists in 2003 led to a lawsuit and subsequent decision by a District Court of Appeal, which deemed that the method of appointing commissioners was unconstitutional. That's not exactly what a state agency wants to hear nearly 30 years and thousands of decisions after it was created. Some have accused the commission of agency creep, getting involved in issues and making decisions that were never contemplated or included in the Coastal Act, issues such as whether or not Sea World can breed orcas in captivity. Or the color of road signs or the types of bicycle racks to be installed as part of a development project. Did the Coastal Act grant this authority to the commission staff to impose these detailed conditions on proposed projects?

As new issues arise that weren't contemplated at the commission's inception, staff often develops new rules or requirements that weren't part of the original legislation or regulations. This evolution is normal for agencies whose existence spans long periods and as circumstances change from the challenges that prompted that initial creation. New rules and regulations are typically legally and publicly reviewed and, if approved and adopted by the commission, may become standard practice of the commissioners. Sometimes these are appropriately adopted within the framework of the commission's legal authority, but at other times some new restrictions have been challenged as "underground regulations" exceeding the scope of its authority or otherwise inappropriate.

One former commissioner has written quite candidly at length about what he learned during his six and a half years on the Coastal Commission regarding some of the many proposals he and his colleagues received and an approach frequently used by large developers. In his view, for those developers, it's all about garnering support from some community group willing to attend commission meetings and speak to the benefits of the proposed development. Six of the appointed commissioners (one-half) must be from local government (either city councils or boards of supervisors), so there is a built-in institutional sensitivity to local residents' views on the part of at least one-half of the commission. Those six commissioners who represent local governments have to stand for reelection to their local offices every few years. This former Coastal commissioner discovered after a short time on the commission that developers apparently love new soccer fields, new parks, new schools, and homes for the disabled, and they generously offer support for these and other improvements to the local community as part of a package—"approve this project and I'll throw in these benefits."

In many of these cases, the developers' goal is to divert the scrutiny away from the specific details of their coastal zone development, and all of the potential violations of or conflicts with the Coastal Act, and get all eyes focused on the unrelated benefits being proposed. This mutual back-scratching seems more transparent than backroom, behind-closed-doors lobbying, which is much harder to see. But it can be even more dangerous, because on the surface a public benefit appears to be achieved when in fact the public benefit will in most cases be at the expense of coastal protection. The trade-off is almost never a net benefit to the public and certainly never to the coast.

To add to the commission's challenges, several examples of language included in the Coastal Act may have seemed quite clear at the time they were enacted but have become increasingly problematic

Fig. 14.3. Protecting development or harbors with armor such as seawalls or rock revetments has become more common: 10 percent of California's entire 1,100-mile shoreline now has some type of protection.

in the intervening years. One of the best examples is the wording regarding when it may be appropriate to approve armoring the shoreline to protect existing development from erosion by waves (Figure 14.3). The essence of this section of the Coastal Act states that protection structures "shall be permitted to . . . protect existing structures . . . in danger from erosion . . . " The intent here was simple: to allow those property owners whose existing homes were threatened by coastal erosion a legal means to protect them, but to discourage future construction in hazardous areas where armor would be required for long-term survival. Recalling that this language was written in the mid-1970s, it seems that a reasonable person would read "existing" to mean existing when the Coastal Act was passed. Seems pretty clear, end of story, right?

Not so fast. Property owners and attorneys for those owners whose homes were built ten, twenty, or thirty years after the legislation was passed but are now threatened by coastal erosion have argued that they have an "existing" structure that is in danger from erosion. Because the structure exists now even though it didn't exist at the time the Coastal Act was passed, they assert a right under the act to protect their home in ways that otherwise would not be acceptable under the act. So apparently the word "existing" isn't that clear after all.

A further complication is the interpretation of the phrase "in danger from erosion." One could argue that any structure within 100 feet of the ocean is in danger of erosion (eventually) and therefore deserving of a permit for a seawall or rock revetment. This wording has never been changed, but it's an example of lack of clarity, which the commission sought to remedy by requiring an added level of proof of erosion danger in order to qualify. The proof had to be that the "primary structure" on the property (a home but not a patio, deck, gazebo, or other structure) must be within one or two storm cycles of being damaged. Is that an easy decision to make with climate changing, with King tides, El Niño events, and larger waves on the horizon? It's not so easy to predict the future of coastal erosion or when an oceanfront home may fall victim to the waves. This lack of clarity in the language poses challenges to administration of the Coastal Act.

Part of the tug-of-war between various interests that is constantly playing out boiled over and became very public in early 2016. At its February public meeting, the commission took up an explosive agenda item that had nothing to do with any specific coastal development proposal—directly. It was a decision involving its leadership, a public hearing on the commission's highly controversial proposal to discharge its executive director of five years. The Coastal Commission had never previously fired an executive director (in this case he also had fourteen years with the agency before becoming executive director), and there was no public information about any specific issue or concern that might warrant such unprecedented action.

Widespread publicity ahead of the meeting cast the story as a battle between development interests and environmental protectionists, some even calling it an apparent "coup" by developers to rid the commission of an executive director who upheld the Coastal Act but whom they didn't like. The potential of a firing that might reflect pro-development bias on the part of the commission sounded alarm bells, and stories about this brewing fight appeared in papers from as far away as the venerable *New York Times*, across the continent on another edge. Suddenly, California's coastal protection was everyone's business, and in this high-stakes drama several

Fig. 14.4. At the February 2016 California Coastal Commission meeting deciding on the question of executive director Charles Lester's possible discharge, speakers throughout the entire day expressed support for him and the work undertaken during his tenure.

papers ran opinion pieces about the possibility of a commission being captured by development interests, urging commissioners to back away from firing their executive director, based on all that was publicly known.

The hearing itself turned out to be a massive public outpouring of concern and support for protection of the California coast, the work of the agency, and the executive director. If there was any doubt that people cared passionately about the state of the coast in 2016, it was definitively erased. Hundreds of people spoke to the commission, more than 20,000 citizens sent written support for the executive director, 35 former commissioners signed a letter, and countless nonprofit organizations (representing more than 3 million members), development interests (like the Pebble Beach Company), and even government representatives testified. Through it all, there was unanimous expression of concern for the possible damage to the mission of coastal protection in the event the commission took the controversial action (Figure 14.4 and Figure 14.5).

Fig. 14.5. Former Coastal Commission executive director Charles Lester (far left) addresses the commissioners (right) at the public meeting before the commission's decision on his status.

In the end, despite the massive public input against such an action, the twelve-member commission voted 7 to 5 to discharge its executive director. While the commission offered no specific or compelling reasons for the firing in the public hearing, the signal to those who came out to communicate their concern was deeply troubling, and public confidence in the commission's ability to carry out its mandate was shaken. If there was a silver lining to this agency's latest, highly controversial moment in a more than 40-year life, it was the mobilization of members of the public to reaffirm their commitment to the underlying principles of the Coastal Act decades after the people of the state of California demanded that a powerful mechanism to protect the coast be established.

Whether the change in leadership to a new executive director can reestablish public confidence in the California Coastal Commission remains to be seen, and its future actions on coastal projects, developments, access, and planning will be the ultimate test. One thing is for certain: a lot of people will be watching. And hopefully participating.

Fig. 14.6. Gill and trammel nets were indiscriminate, catching and killing all members of the sea otter family, including not only adults but moms and pups as well.

Managing the edge of California is a tricky business, as it turns out, and is not for the fainthearted. But Californians keep trying. The Coastal Commission continues in its challenging, dynamic role, trying to evolve to respond to the pressures of both politics and the changing environment. But the Coastal Commission is just one example of many ongoing efforts to create and maintain a framework of policies that will help sustain the coast for future generations, part of a regulatory patchwork.

Californians have used the potent initiative tool to exercise their prerogatives on other occasions as well.

Deadly nets

In 1990, responding to a crisis affecting sea otters and other marine life being accidentally caught up and killed in gill and trammel nets, especially in shallow halibut fisheries, California citizens circulated and gathered signatures for Proposition 132, the Marine Resources Protection Act. Gill nets, which also came to be known as "Walls of Death," are mesh nets joined together in giant walls, suspended vertically in the water. The nets operate by entangling the fish. The openings in the netting are just large enough for the targeted-size fish to get its head through, but not its body. The fish become trapped by their own gills as they try to back out of the net. The monofilament mesh from which these nets are constructed is nearly invisible as they are spread out underwater over wide areas.

The National Marine Fisheries Service estimated that between 1973 and 1983 an average of about 100 sea otters per year were killed by having been trapped and drowned in these types of nets, even though the nets were targeting fish and even though killing sea otters was prohibited. These traps were also indiscriminate; they caught all members of the sea otter family, including moms and pups (Figure 14.6). Relative to the total population of sea otters (today just over 3,000), this added mortality was substantial. But the problem reached far beyond the sea otters. In just one year, 1986–87, more than 6,500 harbor seals, sea lions, and harbor porpoises were also trapped and killed, based on California Fish and Wildlife records. And in the next year, drowning in the gill nets killed more than 4,000 sea lions alone.

One of the reasons people looked to the initiative process for a solution—permanently banning the nets up and down the coast in nearshore ocean waters—was the failure of the California State Legislature to act with sufficient aggressiveness to address this coastal problem. In the case of the people's passage of the Coastal Zone Conservation Act two decades earlier, the Legislature had failed to pass any effective coastal protection despite a half-dozen earlier attempts. In the case of the netting concern, the Legislature had done only slightly better, taking one small step in enacting a ban just a few years before the initiative. That ban was limited to central and Northern California, however, thus leaving the huge Southern California fisheries free to use what had been termed the "relentless killing machines." Because even that limited ban was something that could have been further weakened by the Department of Fish and Wildlife without legislative review, opponents of the practice wanted to make the ban apply to the entire coast and have it etched permanently into the California state constitution.

The 100 otters killed per year before the ban dropped to zero in the first three years of the ban.

Despite a fiercely fought battle between environmentalists teamed with recreational fishermen on the one hand and commercial fishing interests on the other, this initiative amending the constitution passed with a clear majority, approximately 56 percent to 44 percent. These conservation efforts added a new section "X-B" to the state constitution permanently banning the use of gill and trammel nets in the nearshore waters along the entire coast.

The impact on the otters was almost immediate. The 100 or so otters killed per year before the ban was enacted dropped to zero in the first three years of the ban and remained at less than a half dozen per year throughout the remainder of the 1990s. It doesn't take a marine mammal expert to know that for a species such as the sea otter, included as threatened under the Endangered Species Act, a reduction in the number killed from 100 per year to fewer than six is a dramatic improvement.

A two-edged sword?

Ironically, the initiative and referendum process has sometimes been hijacked and produced ballot measures that are not generated (or necessarily supported) by the people in whom this power was intended to be vested. Increasing numbers of ballot measures have been sponsored by large business interests willing to invest the money required to qualify an initiative for the ballot and promote it with massive media advertising.

In 2016, for example, plastic-bag producers funded a referendum to overturn California's cutting-edge law (passed by the State Legislature) that bans single-use plastic bags in order to protect the ocean and marine wildlife. For a large corporate business group to use this process to counter successful citizen-led legislative efforts such as the bag ban seems to run counter to the original purpose. In some ways the initiative and referendum process has come full circle: originally created in the early 1900s to counter the sometimes overly powerful influence of large corporations on public policy all the way to being effectively used by those very interests to establish public policy (or to try to). Fortunately, despite the millions of dollars spent on advertising by the plastic bag industry, the voters rejected the 2016 referendum that would have overturned the plastic bag ban. The ban was upheld.

Californians zealously guard the edge with the available tools, even in the face of efforts to weaken protections, including the current attempts to roll back environmental safeguards at the federal level. More often than not, Californians have effectively used the initiative and referendum process in the environmental arena to serve some very specific—and much-needed—purposes. In the case of the change in fishing technique, there was a narrow but visible result. By contrast, the Coastal Commission has far more wide-reaching goals and long-term impact and will only really be judged through history, even despite its most recent controversy. The test will be in what we can see, what we don't see, and how the health of the shoreline and the nearshore ocean waters survive the decades of pressure from a growing population, a changing economic landscape, and the environmental changes that continually challenge us.

Tricky business indeed.

I saw the California coast for the first time in 1984, and I was very impressed. It was mesmerizing—a combination of serenity and power. I visited a beach in Southern California, and it was very different from the beaches I had known on the gulf coast. It was much cleaner—the sand was white and fine. It was beautiful. From Southern California, I drove north on Highway 1 to San Francisco, so I saw a lot of the California coast on that trip. And it was spectacular and very diverse.

The California coast was very appealing and memorable, but I didn't envision at the time that it would be as important a part of my life as it has become. I look out on it every day, and it has become important for me to see it every day. It's part of my life now. I love the beauty.

Getting married on the beach was, I think, my most memorable moment involving the coast. But there have been other significant life events/passages. Good friends and other family members have also been married along the California coast. The ocean is such a great backdrop for a meaningful life event like a wedding. The coast is so enduring.

It's critical to protect the coast and to educate others who are less aware to protect the coast for this generation and for future generations. It is such an important resource, not just for food, but as a place for contemplation, for recreation, for memories. It really is the edge of a very different universe. There's even an element of fear, but I enjoy being near the water. If the coast weren't here, life would be very different for me. The absence would be notable. I would be sad and there would be an emptiness.

—Coastal fan, age 50

15

The Coastal Records Project

and the People's Coast

Photographing the coast from the air is inherently dangerous, especially in isolated, lonely places like the Lost Coast area in northern California where there are no beaches to land on in an emergency.

The Coastal Records Project

When it comes to protecting the coast, policymaking and enforcement are just two key factors. The participation of individuals in monitoring, study and research, and education also makes a vital difference. Residents from all walks of life have joined in this effort in both large and small ways. Take Kenneth and Gabrielle Adelman, for example.

Kenneth and Gabrielle live along the central coast of California and have always been interested in coastal preservation. They also like ice cream bars, air shows, and electric cars. Both were experienced small-plane pilots when they went to an aerobatic plane show in Torrance in 1993. Gabrielle was tempted by an Aloha ice cream bar that came with a chance at winning a helicopter ride. She won the ride, took the flight, and fell in love with helicopters.

It didn't take long before lessons, licensing, and later the purchase of a helicopter fell into place for these new aficionados (Figure 15.1). They were soon asked to take aerial photographs of several local spots along the San Simeon coast of San Luis Obispo County that were the subject of controversial commercial development proposals.

Fig. 15.1. Gabrielle and Kenneth Adelman, pilot and photographer for the Coastal Records Project. *photo courtesy Kenneth and Gabrielle Adelman, California Coastal Records Project, www.CaliforniaCoastline.org*

The Hearst Corporation planned, among other things, a destination golf course, a resort, and a strip mall. Local citizen antidevelopment activists described the area as:

> Occupied by Chumash and Salinian Indians for more than fifty centuries, this magnificent Central Coast landmark is the last surviving unspoiled coastal point with a harbor between Los Angeles and San Francisco. Rich in Native American artifacts, burial sites, rare sand dunes, and threatened or endangered plants and animals, San Simeon Point is truly a living museum of natural history.

Although they could describe it in rich and evocative terms, activists lacked good photographs of the area. The Adelmans agreed to take the pictures, and their photos were later widely distributed in postcard-size color reproductions as part of the organizing efforts. These simple aerial images proved to be amazingly effective in raising awareness and staving off the proposed development.

This started Kenneth and Gabrielle thinking: "What if we photographed the *entire* coast as a baseline that could help in documenting future coastal land use and change, whether human caused or natural?"

Since this was the 1990s, before the widespread use of digital photography we have come to expect today, they took a few short flights to determine how much would be involved in film, processing, indexing, filing, and retrieving the images they would capture from a thorough survey of all 1,100 miles of California's coast. They estimated about 10,000 photographs would be necessary. At the time, they concluded that doing this through conventional photography would be prohibitively expensive.

But technology soon changed this daunting prospect. Kenneth and Gabrielle decided to photograph the coast using modern digital cameras with large capacity and high-resolution lenses and sensors. At their own expense, they took off in their helicopter and, over the period from March to November 2002, managed to cover the entire California coastline from the Oregon border to Mexico (with the exception of Vandenberg Air Force Base just north of Point Conception on the central coast, where overflights are banned).

They faced the usual types of aviation challenges, such as weather and visibility limitations and frequent small-airport takeoff and landing routes where clear communication and coordination are critical. They also faced novel challenges from the demands of rapidly shooting and keeping track of thousands of photographs for hours on end—from an open helicopter door! Kenneth shot the pictures, which had to be handheld to lessen the flight motion; Gabrielle flew the helicopter along a tricky but steady path, making sure Kenneth captured all stretches of the coastline in an orderly fashion. They also had to devise a system to track the location of each and every picture to be able to piece the giant state coastal jigsaw puzzle back together again once they were back home.

They uploaded these first digital images onto a website they set up (www.californiacoastline.org), and it became an instant hit. Perhaps the one piece of publicity that put the website on the map more than any other was a lawsuit filed by a Hollywood celebrity who wasn't happy with her home in Malibu being included in the aerial photographs. She claimed her privacy was being invaded, even though scores of aerial photographs from other sources already included her house; but these new pictures were high resolution and included considerable detail. The Hollywood celebrity lost the lawsuit, as detailed on the website, but the surrounding publicity led many to

Fig. 15.2. The Lost Coast of Northern California. *photo courtesy Kenneth and Gabrielle Adelman, California Coastal Records Project, www.CaliforniaCoastline.org*

initially discover this valuable set of digital photographs of nearly the entire coast of California.

The Adelmans were not only skilled pilots, but by training and experience were also very technology savvy. They thought carefully about the best equipment and processes for shooting and managing the images before embarking on that first project. Through additional flights in subsequent years, they have progressively updated and modified their technology. They now refly this 1,100-mile coastal route every other year or so and can shoot an image every three seconds, also capturing the longitude, latitude, and altitude of the helicopter into each photo file.

Since their initial flight, they have also upgraded to a helicopter (Robinson R44 Clipper II) that has "pop-out" floats that can be deployed in an emergency, allowing the possibility of a safe water landing. Both Kenneth and Gabrielle are fearless pioneers when it comes to advancing new approaches to saving the coast, but they have also lost friends in air crashes and understand the dangers of this hazardous work. Especially in isolated, lonely places like the Lost Coast area in Northern California, there are no beaches to land on in an emergency (Figure 15.2).

This innovative aerial photographic project rests on the shoulders of a history of aerial picture taking that began nearly 90 years ago. As part of early efforts to plan an ocean shore highway along the central California coast from San Francisco to Monterey Bay, one of the earliest (if not the very first) aerial photography missions was flown along the West Coast in 1928. The flight extended from San Francisco into central Monterey Bay and produced a remarkable set of vertical stereo aerial photographs at a scale of 1:12,000. These invaluable and historic photos were lost and forgotten about for decades until their discovery by chance.

In 1983, one of my UCSC graduate students was searching for topographic maps in a local county surveyor's office and came across the 1928 Santa Cruz County coastal photographs in an old filing cabinet. The significance of a systematic aerial photo flight taken in 1928 is even greater knowing that it was very early in the history of aviation. Charles Lindbergh had flown across the entire Atlantic only two years earlier.

Within a few years of the historic 1928 flight to survey part of the Northern California coast, aerial photographs began to be taken regularly by a number of state and federal agencies, such that vertical stereo aerials now exist for the entire California coast. A little over a half century later, while I was meeting with George Armstrong, a coastal engineer working at the time for a little-known state agency known as the California Department of Boating and Waterways, I noticed several very high stacks of 35 mm carousel slide reels in his office. They were stacked all the way to the ceiling. When I asked him about the carousels, he explained that he had flown and photographed the entire California coast twice from offshore, and the carousels were filled with the slides he had taken. His collection included 5,833 color slides taken in 1972 and an additional 8,000 slides from 1979, but very few people but George knew of their existence.

When George retired some years later, I asked if the map and photo library at the University of California, Santa Cruz, could become the permanent repository for his slides, as I feared his collection would probably end up, unidentified, in some state warehouse and be permanently forgotten or discarded. A few months later, a number of large cardboard boxes filled with nearly 14,000 valuable 35 mm color slides were delivered to my office.

With Kenneth and Gabrielle's help, these images were painstakingly scanned and uploaded to the website, joining the Adelman's initial aerial survey. The 1928 aerial photos were also added. As the collection grew, and the photo locations were identified in the online user database, other sources of coastal aerial photographs came forward and were added to the growing collection from the California Coastal Commission and the Coastal Conservancy.

Nearly 110,000 images are now publicly accessible at californiacoastline.org. Anyone with access to the Internet can bring up high-resolution, color, oblique images of any location on the entire coast of California (with the initial exception of Vandenberg Air Force Base). You can fly the length of the California coast from your home or office armchair, clicking on the overlapping images and see the details, whether looking for geology, coastal processes, beaches and cliffs, coastal protection, or development, without ever having to charter an airplane or leave your computer screen. You can see any location and go back in time to see previous shots of the same spot, in some cases now going back to the 1920s.

Nearly 110,000 images of the coast are now publicly accessible at www. CaliforniaCoastline.org.

There is a very high value in having a permanent record of the coastline that can be easily observed, downloaded, and then used for a wide variety of land use and development, conservation, research, or educational purposes. This is especially true now, as human migration to coastal regions in the United States and globally continues; coastal urbanization with shoreline and infrastructure development expands; and tsunamis, hurricanes, ENSO[1] events with elevated sea levels and storm waves, King tides, and rising sea levels affect these areas.

The accessible database is also an extremely useful resource that serves as a model for any coastal state or nation. With new drone technology and photographic capabilities, such an effort may become more common, at least on a local level.

Such is photography in the twenty-first century.

The approach taken by Kenneth and Gabrielle and others involved in that effort has moved photography to new levels in support of

---

1. El Niño Southern Oscillation

coastal conservation. But photography has always played a key role in conservation, worldwide. The early examples set by *National Geographic* and, on the ocean front, Jacques Cousteau and others, provide lessons in how people are moved by images of nature. Once moved, people are inclined to care about what they see. That, in turn, leads to the possibility of action to protect against threats of any sort.

Photography expands the caring audience. Not everyone can get to the ocean, visit a beach, see a whale spout, or observe a sea otter eating lunch. Nor can anyone but a handful of divers and researchers directly see what lies beneath the surface of the ocean.

Photography expands the number of people who can experience the coast, and it also expands what we can see. Through the advent of extraordinary technology, we can now see things that can't even be viewed with the naked eye, whether they be too distant, too small, too hidden, too dark, too remote, or too ethereal. We can capture and slow events down to speeds at which they can be watched and understood where they would otherwise be invisible or incomprehensible if observed in real time. With photography and sophisticated data management and analysis, we can capture and identify patterns that are otherwise impossible to fathom.

Without the visibility brought about by rich imagery, fewer people would be exposed to fewer things, and our coast and wildlife would ultimately be worse off. Valuable research would be hamstrung. Vital new information and understandings about the coast would be fewer and further between. Caring would be more limited.

Yet there is another more personal dimension to one of the most striking developments in photography in the last 20 years. Because of the ubiquity of smart-phone cameras today, images taken of the coast and coastal wildlife have multiplied exponentially. Every one of those images can serve as the basis not just for a personal memory but for a memory shared with others, spreading the images and awareness of the coast farther and wider, reaching more people. This new technology will help grow the interested and caring audience just as surely as *National Geographic* expanded the audience of those concerned about the wildlife, habitats, and cultures that it showcases, or as Jacques Cousteau expanded the pool of those who care about the oceans.

What better ambassadors for coastal conservation and protection than humpback whales, dolphins, or sea otters seen in photographs? Or the rich imagery of underwater canyons and kelp forests?

Photography is in rapid transition, and we will see what changes emerge in the years ahead. What new approaches will arise in this era of those disruptive drones, of advances in image recognition, instantaneous geolocation and wireless uploading, data aggregation algorithms, and whatever else is on the horizon?

The people's coast

Every Wednesday at 7:30 a.m., Buddy Nethercutt grabs his coffee and jacket and heads out the door to his car. It takes about 20 minutes to get to his destination, and another 20 minutes of walking along a path that he has come to know well through his routine of nearly four years. It is usually chilly, foggy, and damp until the sun breaks through later in the morning—if it does at all.

He takes up his position at the edge of Elkhorn Slough near the center of Monterey Bay and waits for the time (Figure 15.3). In six other carefully designated spots around the slough, six other volunteers take up their positions and wait patiently. The sun is

Fig. 15.3. Some of the many ponds and fingers of Elkhorn Slough, which did not open directly to the ocean until the Army Corps of Engineers cut a channel in 1947.

Fig. 15.4. A large raft of southern sea otters appear in Elkhorn Slough, where the species is being monitored and counted.

barely up, but its light is trapped behind that layer of fog. They have binoculars. They have warm jackets and caps. And they have two-way radios set to talk to each other.

Buddy readies himself by looking intently around the water in front of him. He's especially got his eye out for sea otters. He checks his watch. At exactly 8:30 a.m., he scans his designated area of the slough to see if any otters have appeared. He's lucky again today: several of these furry little creatures are cruising the waters in his zone. He begins his count. One, two, three . . . twelve. He double-checks to avoid duplicate counting, since they bob up and down and sometimes when two are close together, they may look like one, or even a tangle of three. One may dive and come back up 20 or 30 feet away, which can fool him into thinking it's a different animal. It takes experience and knowledge of their behavior to get an accurate count. The running joke is that sometimes it might be easier to count paws and flippers and divide by four (Figure 15.4).

On the half hour, he logs his count. He identifies and records the total number of otters he sees, as well as breaking it down further by category: adults, large pups, and small pups. He also records the types of activities they are engaged in: foraging, traveling, patrolling, grooming, or resting.

He records his tallies every half hour for several hours on a data sheet he will turn in to the project's coordinator, who is also in the field that day. They will radio in to each other before the end of the morning so all the volunteers can share their totals with one another. They report from places with exotic names like Hummingbird Island, Seal Island, Yampah Island, Avila, and Kirby Park. There are also a few slightly less exotic locations such as the "harbor" and the "state wildlife platform."

Today, at 8:30 a.m., a total of 112 otters have been counted in Elkhorn Slough. All the information captured this day will be entered into a growing database consisting of the observations of this dedicated group. Buddy sounds a common theme for the group when he says he "feels really good to be doing something so important, to feel like I'm making a real difference in the world."

They share the responsibility for the hard, long-term fieldwork that goes into gathering vital information on the sea otter population and its location within the slough. This data can, in turn, be used by researchers who will probe, prod, and press it into service, drawing conclusions on questions about sea otter health and survival, the health of the estuarine waters, and the impact of humans on both. It will lead to new questions.

Their particular project was launched through the Elkhorn Slough National Estuarine Research Reserve with its Elkhorn Slough Foundation and the Monterey Bay Aquarium's widely respected Sea Otter Research and Conservation (SORAC) program. SORAC has also monitored other aspects of the sea otter population using GPS and other tracking devices, combined with good old-fashioned observations from the shoreline, conducted by both staff and volunteers. Today, many trained volunteers participate in a wide variety of ways to capture facts needed to help further vital research.

Citizen science is helping expand the reach of traditional science and research by adding to limited human resources and funding. More eyes and ears on the ground, and in the sea. Gathering data in the field is an important way to leverage resources. Not only does participation yield valuable data, it also deepens individuals' involvement in—and commitment to—stewardship.

Coordinated data gathering by making observations in a planned framework is an important aspect of citizen involvement. So are activities like monitoring the shoreline, tending to beaches and wetlands, and educating the public. There are hundreds of examples, and Monterey Bay seems to be an epicenter for volunteers and docents. They devote thousands of hours of their time at multiple sites and facilities around the bay's 38-mile shoreline. Whether younger or older, male or female, experienced or newcomers, they are all dedicated to preserving the coast and the ocean. They work through state parks, aquariums, nature, or discovery centers, educational organizations, and nonprofit ocean conservation groups.

Citizen science is helping expand the reach of traditional science and research by adding to limited human resources and funding.

This robust level of activity may be based on a combination of factors: the existence of the Monterey Bay National Marine Sanctuary as well as the bay itself and all of the natural resources it supports. It also reflects the grave threats that the bay faces. It has seen more than its fair share of development. It has been exploited for its natural resources for centuries. It has seen the upside but also the downside of massive tourism from throughout the world as well as nearby, especially since it's within an hour's travel for the millions of annual visitors from the inland valleys and the area's nearby international airports.

We are all indebted to these many individuals and the multiple roles they perform in education, preservation, and stewardship because they leverage and expand the typically modest staff that these facilities or centers can afford to maintain from their own limited budgets. These volunteers are relied on to make a difference, whether it's at the Monterey Bay Aquarium, the Seymour Marine Discovery Center, or the Sanctuary Exploration Center; or at any of the coastal state parks around the bay, such as Wilder Ranch, Natural Bridges, or Seacliff; or at the many coastal nonprofit organizations, such as Save Our Shores, O'Neill Sea Odyssey, Surfrider, or Friends of the Sea Otter, to name a few.

Fig. 15.5. This complete, 87-foot-longblue whale skeleton outside the Seymour Marine Discovery Center in Santa Cruz comes from a dead whale discovered in 1979 near Pescadero, 35 miles north of Santa Cruz.

For the Seymour Marine Discovery Center of UC Santa Cruz' Long Marine Laboratory, over 200 trained docents form the necessary complement to the small staff, providing about 25,000 hours of service each year that gives 70,000 visitors a memorable and informative experience (Figure 15.5). Indeed, these docents make the entire education program possible. They also develop a deep sense of satisfaction and reward for the roles they fill and the programs they staff.

In the same way, the multiplying effect of the thousands of committed volunteers helps make it all work throughout California for other valuable advocacy organizations from Crescent City to San Diego. We cannot overstate the contribution of well-functioning nonprofits such as aquariums, along with governmental organizations and coastal state parks, as well as research, educational, and legal groups, in taking action and spreading a message of awareness.

I recall how important volunteering was to me in deepening my understanding of the California shoreline. Several years ago, I became a docent at Seacliff State Beach, which is one of those long, sandy shoreline beaches in Northern California with its very own pier and the iconic concrete ship (Figure 15.6, Figure 15.7, Figure 15.8). I was

Fig. 15.6. This pier was constructed at Seacliff Beach to allow access to the SS *Palo Alto,* a concrete ship turned into a tourist attraction that opened in June 1930 but closed less than two years later due to the economic pressures of the Great Depression, despite the ship's popular success. Today, Seacliff State Beach is one of the state's most visited parks.

just one of the more than 75 volunteers who regularly work in that park. Volunteers staff the visitor center and interpret local nature to the public. They tend to the aquarium display, keep the native garden growing, and provide hundreds of programs for schoolchildren each year. For many of the children, it is their first coastal access, their first exposure to the beach and the ocean, to 3-million-year-old marine fossils, and to the dynamic forces of nature in action.

Like so many other volunteers before me, I was able to follow a path that built on my own interests, and I soon began to offer a natural and cultural history walk that also forced me to go ever further into studying and understanding the workings and history of the coast. Every organization builds on people's unique interests, commitment, and involvement, making the experience of the edge, and the research and education by and about the edge, richer for all to enjoy.

Fig. 15.7 and 15.8. Although the ship suffered its first major crack from storms in 1936, high winds and huge waves took their toll in late January 2017.

It would be a grave mistake to think that volunteer efforts should or could replace the role of funded organizations or paid staff. The fortunate fact that there are thousands of dedicated volunteers cannot be used as an excuse, as it sometimes is, to reduce support and funding for vital services that protect our shoreline, help us better understand it, and expand its accessibility, all while preserving it for generations to come. By leveraging resources with volunteers and working closely with those individuals and institutions with vital expertise, we can ensure that there continues to be an informed, active, and engaged community looking out for the best of our coast.

A vivid example of this partnership was the people's concerted push over time, following the wake-up call of the 1969 Santa Barbara Channel oil spill, that led to California's then-congressman Leon Panetta's sponsorship of a bill to create the Monterey Bay National Marine Sanctuary in 1992. At that time, it was the nation's largest marine sanctuary. Once it was created, a stretch of nearly 300 miles of the California coast from near Point Reyes to the north and Cambria to the south was placed permanently off-limits to oil drilling and protected against other potentially damaging uses. The sanctuary's boundaries extend an average of 30 miles offshore, and studies have shown that this wide zone of ocean waters and all the life living within it are healthier as a result.

The sanctuary has not been a panacea, however, as the challenges of managing continuing development along the shoreline and the specter of large and damaging impacts of climate change, among other threats, continue to loom despite the sanctuary's protection. These ongoing issues are evidence of the complexity of "managing" the ocean, with its vast array of interfaces with human activity and its inherent connectedness to many aspects of our existence.

The successful creation of the sanctuary was built on the foundation of active volunteers and those committed to protecting the coast. Both the sanctuary and the subsequently expanded string of Marine Protected Areas along our coast have also given rise to groups of stewards that have formed to support each of the protected areas. Their cooperation and support are great examples of a virtuous cycle, how commitment generates heightened involvement by more knowledgeable individuals with perspectives on coastal issues. Such involvement translates into improved policy, in part through selecting and educating politicians whose views capture the values of coastal preservation and accessibility. In part, it also leads to greater participation in public hearings or administrative proceedings held by those agencies charged with developing key rules and regulations, and with implementing and enforcing them. And it leads to better education of the public on coastal issues.

Stewardship of the people's coast requires just that, lots of active, dedicated, and engaged people. When we consider the wonders of the California edge today, we hope that 50 years from now people will look on us as good stewards of the coast and the ocean, and all that depends on it.

I've been living for 13 years on the edge. I think I really enjoy the ocean most when it's in composition with something else, like Highway 1, where it's very rocky and you get these really high cliffs or rocky shores. That composition of rocks, sand and water and sky.

My favorite spot is not very far from here, at Bean Hollow. Where you get an otherworldly landscape right next to the ocean that I think is one of the most magical places I've ever been. When you're there you don't feel like you could be anywhere else. It's a singular experience with that abundance and beauty that I haven't seen even in other parts of the world.

If we neglect or fail to conserve the ocean, I think it will survive and still be there in the future—but the real question is probably: will all of the species in the ocean survive? If anything, I think that Californians, I've noticed, have such pride in the ocean and the coast, that I'm pretty optimistic in that area. Regardless of politics and what comes into play, I expect that the people of California will protect their ocean and their coast. The people of the state will do their best to preserve it. I think that's the one thing that I'm pretty confident in. And that's an important value; it is definitely something that keeps me in California.

We have a physical connection to water, and water is vital to us for health, for survival even. And the oceans are capturing the vast majority of our carbon emissions and keeping the world healthy. I don't think life would exist without the ocean, so I think that's a big enough reason to preserve it, don't you?
—Former Ohio resident, age 55

A FINAL WORD

It's taken hundreds of years and countless human decisions affecting our coast to land us where we are today, pointed toward failure but positioned for success. We have overdeveloped and overfished, exploited, poked, and prodded this great natural wonder to its limits, maybe beyond. And on top of everything else, climate change, sea-level rise, and other seemingly insurmountable challenges test our capacity and political will to make the fundamental changes we need to survive.

There are plenty of indications that we are in deep trouble. Our weaknesses have been exposed. The mechanisms we have put in place to help save us from ourselves are being challenged now as they never have been. Decades of successful efforts to build protections for our environment are today being rolled back. Political pressure plays a big part. But it is also economic pressure, related to the race-to-the-bottom of a global marketplace that places a premium on cutting costs and growing GDP without full regard to the environmental or social costs. It's not really a new story.

Along our coast, oil production and the fight over hydraulic fracturing are emblematic of this tension. The economics of electricity generation, water and gas supplies, and a host of other infrastructure issues, as well as fisheries management and shoreline ownership, continue to test our ability to preserve this edge for future generations. The pressure of population growth on coastal land development, expansion of beach cottages to mega-mansions, and coastal armoring persists despite development and growth control tools such as the California Coastal Commission. Sometimes we legislate one step forward, two steps back.

One of the biggest challenges we now face is how to act decisively to reduce the impact of our industrial society on the twin problems of global warming and sea-level rise. Science outliers, those who would disregard scientific consensus (often for political reasons), have made it more difficult than it already was to take effective action on a problem of such enormous magnitude. Education, dedication, and the sustained action and vigilance of many community groups and the media will be required.

It is not by coincidence we have written here about environmental science, law, politics, nature, history, and personal adventure. We believe that it will take a little of each of these to forge the future, looking to leave a legacy of success.

It is simple but true: we must make our voices heard when it comes to tipping the balance, making the economic and political calculus work out to favor coastal preservation and sustainability. This can be accomplished with education and advocacy, with innovation and advances in technologies, with new approaches to infrastructure and commercial activity, and by impressing upon our colleagues, our friends, our neighbors, and our policymakers the value of working together to maintain a healthy, long-term future for our coast—and all that depends on it.

Gazing out over the natural beauty and vast richness of the undeveloped portions of the California coast, we are still inspired. We can see that the tasks ahead will take vision and leadership. We know it will also take a commitment of time, energy, money, and other resources like never before to recover and build a sustainable future. But as a community, as a people, we have begun to make the decisions we need to make, and take the actions we need to take, to achieve this goal.

We believe we are at a turning point in our history. It is not just our legacy that is at stake—it is the People's Coast.

Santa Cruz, March 1, 2017

Acknowledgments

This book would not have been possible, nor would it have a useful purpose, if not for the many people who have worked tirelessly over the years protecting California's coast and all the life it supports. We're thankful that these stewards made such impressive efforts and that they continue to do so today. *The Edge* would have been a different set of tales with a very different attitude were it not for their inspiring accomplishments.

When it comes to the production of this book, we are grateful for the help and support of more people than we could reasonably list here. But we especially would like to thank several whose contributions were above and beyond: Thanks to Madelyn Choi, Deepika Shrestha-Ross, and Barbara Steinhardt-Carter. We'd like to thank the good folks at Craven Street Books, whose ever-optimistic and professional approach made transforming this book from concept into reality fun. We also appreciate the openness of more than a dozen individuals who were willing to answer our questions out on the shoreline so we could anonymously include their comments at the end of each chapter. We are indebted to the coastal photographers who have taken the time and have the talent to capture the essence and beauty of California's coast, and were generous enough to share their images for this book. And finally, since the story only began because we were each fortunately placed and raised on the edge by our respective parents, we are grateful to David and Janith Steinhardt and Dean and Barbara Griggs.

We hope you have enjoyed reading *The Edge*!

Please stay in touch with us, and share your comments and thoughts, by visiting **www.OurCaliforniaCoast.com**. There you'll find information on news and upcoming events, and can send us a message. We'd love to hear from you!

—Kim and Gary

INDEX

ABOUT KIM STEINHARDT

KIM STEINHARDT delivers popular lectures and photographic programs exploring the universe of sea otters and coastal conservation for aquariums and marine centers, universities, state parks, and other audiences. He has been recognized for his award-winning marine wildlife photography and is currently working with National Geographic Books on publication of a collection of his sea otter images and coastal storytelling. He has also served as an advisor regarding sea otters for the NatGeo Kids Explore My World series and, for the last five years, has written a newsletter column about marine wildlife and the ocean. As a longtime conservationist drawing on his former service as a California state administrative law judge, litigator, and public interest advocate, he helps translate ocean conservation concerns to the public to build support for citizen action and legislative policymaking.

About Gary Griggs

GARY GRIGGS has written or coauthored ten books about
the coast and coastal issues both in California and globally. As
a Distinguished Professor of Earth and Planetary Sciences at the
University of California at Santa Cruz, he is known for his expertise in
oceanography and coastal geology. He is a frequent contact for news
media on questions of climate change, sea-level rise, coastal erosion,
and other related issues. He has written a popular biweekly newspaper
column, "Our Ocean Backyard," for nine years and is in high demand
for talks throughout California. He serves as the director of the
Institute of Marine Sciences at the University of California at Santa
Cruz, which includes the Long Marine Laboratory and the Seymour
Marine Discovery Center, a popular educational destination for tens of
thousands of visitors each year.

Explore California with more great Craven Street Books

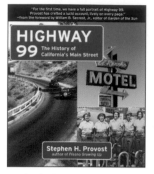

$18.95

Highway 99

The History of California's Main Street

by Stephen H. Provost

Highway 99 turns back the clock to the days when U.S. Highway 99 was the Main Street binding California's cities together, with plenty of classic road trip fun along the way. Illustrated throughout with historic photographs, **Highway 99** documents the communities, personalities, historical events, hotels, restaurants, and roadside attractions that defined the great highway and a lost era of classic Americana.

$16.95

Walking San Francisco's 49 Mile Scenic Drive

Explore the Famous Sites, Neighborhoods, and Vistas in 17 Enchanting Walks

by Kristine Poggioli and Carolyn Eidson

Walking San Francisco's 49 Mile Scenic Drive takes you the length of the famous 49 Mile Drive in 17 bite-size walks, complete with turn-by-turn instructions, maps, and historical facts—a perfect guidebook for today's urban enthusiast who values walkable neighborhoods, hyperlocal culture, and the pleasure of walking.

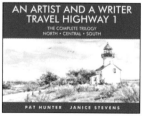

Volume 1: North
$21.95

Volume 2: Central
$26.95

Volume 3: South
$26.95

An Artist and a Writer Travel Highway 1: North • Central • South

by Pat Hunter and Janice Stevens

This unique literary and artistic trilogy takes the reader on a journey along the entire length of California's fabled State Highway 1, from Leggett in far northern California to the Mexican border. Lavishly illustrated with hundreds of original full-color Pat Hunter illustrations, **An Artist and a Writer Travel Highway 1** is a thinking person's travel guide to the history, culture, and architecture of the California coast—plus the best in lodging, dining, and more!

Available from bookstores, online bookstores, and CravenStreetBooks.com, or by calling toll-free 1-800-345-4447.